Wake Up and Smell the Coffee -

Northern New England Edition

Laura Zahn

Down to Earth Publications
St. Paul, Minnesota

Other books by Laura Zahn:

WAKE UP & SMELL THE COFFEE - Lake States Edition
WAKE UP & SMELL THE COFFEE - Pacific Northwest Edition
WAKE UP & SMELL THE COFFEE - Southwest Edition
Chocolate for Breakfast and Tea
Innkeepers' Best Muffins
Innkeepers' Best Low-Fat Breakfasts
Bringing Baby Home: An Owner's Manual for First-Time Parents

To Helene Anderson

who has always believed in
good books,
good food,
and good friends,
and is one!

Published by **Down to Earth Publications, Inc.**
1032 West Montana Avenue
St. Paul, Minnesota 55117
651-488-2205
(note area code change from 612 on 7/12/98)

ISBN 0-939301-13-X

Library of Congress Cataloging in Publication Data

Zahn, Laura C., 1957-
    Wake Up and Smell the Coffee - Northern New England Edition.

    Includes index.

1. Breakfasts 2. Cookery 3. Bed and Breakfast Accommodations - New England - Directories

TX 733.Z3

Dewey System - Ideas and Recipes for Breakfast and Brunch - 641.52

Cover Photo courtesy of the Inn at Maplewood Farm, Hillsborough, New Hampshire
    Photo by Tom Bagley, Styling by Gail Greco

Cover Design by Helene Anderson, Stillwater, Minnesota

Maps by Andrea Rud, Osceola, Wisconsin

Chapter Illustrations by Lynn Fellman, Golden Valley, Minnesota

Printed in the USA

Many thanks to
Helene Anderson, Andrea Rud, Kristina Ford, Ann Burckhardt and Kathy O'Neill

Special thanks to Don Johnson and Susan Sinclair, Bar Harbor, Maine,
Jody Schmoll and Dennis Hayden, Camden, Maine, and
Laura Simoes, Hillsborough, New Hampshire,
for helping this book come to be!

Special thanks to the innkeepers
for sharing their best recipes and artwork,
for their cooking hints and ideas,
for their contacts and willingness to "spread the word"
and for their enthusiasm and encouragement.

I also thank them for the privilege
of being the "middleperson" in communicating their favorite recipes --
and a little about themselves --
to many hungry cooks and readers.

Introduction

Maine, Vermont and New Hampshire. If you don't think "B&Bs and country inns" right away, you probably thought "maple syrup" or "fall colors." Maybe "farms, woods, waters." Or "Ben & Jerry's."

But Bed & Breakfasts probably would have made your Top 10 List of Things We Think About When We Think About New England. B&Bs -- now tremendously popular all over the U.S. -- got their start in this country in New England. Then, credit (or blame) Bob Newhart for bringing a Vermont inn, no matter how fictional, to the living rooms of millions of people all over the world. Bob never did much work at his inn, and waited in the dining room for someone else to serve him. But he was right about at least one aspect of innkeeping: Lots of folks want to chuck the corporate life and open an inn in New England.

What I found when I researched this book is that lots of folks have. This is my fifth Wake Up & Smell the Coffee (the original Upper Midwest Edition is out-of-print) and the first time I've gotten to write about inns in this region. It's always so interesting to me to find out who the innkeepers are, how and why they got into innkeeping, and how they choose the inn and location they did.

Some got fed up with the high-pressure corporate life, "cashed out" and moved to New England and bought an inn. Others opened their own home as a B&B after deciding they were compatible with the innkeeping lifestyle. Some spent years looking for just the right property to come up for sale in just the right town. At least one literally got lost and stumbled upon a building that was for sale and decided to buy it and open an inn. Another couple came for a first-time visit, went home and sold the house and returned as innkeepers. Some "retired" into innkeeping, opening perhaps just a few guestrooms in a quiet village where they wanted to settle. Others buy grand properties in resort communities and work hard to see their investment expand into a booming year 'round business.

In this book, you'll find summer cottages in the woods turned into year 'round lodging establishments, expansive Victorian-era homes, a couple farmhouses, at least one of which is on a working farm, B&Bs built from the ground up to have all the amenities sophisticated inngoers expect, historic stagecoach inns still serving weary travelers, impressive summer estates of the formerly-rich and famous, and just plain nice old homes-turned-inns when the kids grew up and moved out.

Their differences, and the different backgrounds of the innkeepers, are, after all, what make them so very appealing. But despite their differences, travelers should find one constant in their B&B adventures: hospitality. And the innkeepers in this book know that food is an important part of it.

Luckily, these innkeepers agreed to share their most favorite recipes. They know that food is more than fuel for our bodies, that it can simply say, "welcome," or that it can nourish the very soul. (And those who have gotten off that faced-paced treadmill are now greeting guests still on it, knowing their guests need "nourishment" and relaxation, at least temporarily.)

Whether sea coast, mountains, forest or farmlands, this is beautiful country. There's a reason so many people visit here (and don't wait for color "season" to find out why!). There's also a reason lots of them came as visitors and never left. If you can, make plans for a B&B vacation soon. If you can't visit soon, at least you can bring the pleasures of a B&B breakfast (don't forget that pure maple syrup!) to your own breakfast table. Whether you are dreaming about your own inn, your next getaway or just a new recipe to add to your file of favorites, I hope your expectations will be met -- and surpassed -- on these pages! Happy trails and bon appetit! - LZ

Things You Should Know

▣ Before beginning to cook or bake, please read the entire recipe to find out how hot to preheat the oven, what size pan(s) to grease, or how many hours or days ahead of time the recipe must be started. Warning: we have one "pretend" recipe in here (it's supposed to be funny!), so read it all first!

▣ We tried to include only inns with guestrooms and kitchens in the same building -- small places enough so guests literally can wake up and smell the coffee.

▣ "From-scratch" recipes were solicited. Recipes which were submitted but contained a number of pre-packaged ingredients, or which were tested and turned out really awful, were rejected.

▣ Innkeepers had the opportunity to double-check and re-test their recipes before printing, so not all recipes were tested by the author. While "tester's comments" appear on many recipes, some recipes were tested but no comment was made simply because none was necessary. Testing was done in a non-commercial home kitchen.

▣ Recipes have been listed in chapters according to the way in which innkeepers serve them. For instance, you will find some fruit dishes in chapters other than "Fruit," breads in "Holiday Fare," and fruit crisps, cakes and coffeecakes in "Dessert for Breakfast." The longer table of contents, therefore, also serves as an index so you can double-check other chapters at a glance. An index to major ingredients is in the back.

▣ Most innkeepers encouraged experimentation with their recipes, such as substituting or adding ingredients for personal preferences or health reasons.

▣ Cooks are urged to make sure any dishes using egg yolks or egg whites are heated to at least 160 degrees Fahrenheit, which is necessary to kill salmonella virus that may be present in raw eggs, or to use pasteurized eggs, now available in many grocery stores.

▣ Baking and cooking temperatures are listed in degrees Fahrenheit. Remember to preheat the oven to the temperature listed in the recipe before baking. Ovens and cookware varies, so watch carefully.

▣ We said "butter" rather than "grease" a cookie sheet or pan, since greasing is a filthy job that you do to your car, not something you'd do at a fine B&B inn. But do not use butter to do this to your baking pans; use shortening or non-stick cooking spray, which don't burn as easily as butter.

▣ Assume that white (granulated) sugar is called for in these recipes when the ingredient listed is "sugar." Powdered (confectioner's) or brown sugar are listed as such. Unbleached flour is listed simply as "flour;" hardly any innkeeper is using all-purpose white (bleached) flour these days.

▣ Brown sugar is "packed" into the measuring cup, not loose.

▣ Rolled oats means uncooked oatmeal. Cocoa means dry cocoa powder, not the liquid beverage.

▣ For yeast breads or for preserves and recipes which involve canning, read the package instructions on yeast or pectin thoroughly. We suggest you also consult an all-purpose cookbook with detailed instructions for these processes. (We can't possibly go into all the detail they do.)

▣ Use insulated cookie sheets and baking pans whenever possible - they're worth the investment.

Contents by Chapter

Contents

Breads

Preserves, Butters, Syrups & Sauces

Fruit

Entrées

Eggs:

French Toast:

Pancakes:

Waffles:

Other Entrees:

Holiday Fare

Dessert for Breakfast

Other Favorites

MAINE

1. **Bar Harbor**
    - Black Friar Inn
    - The Maples Inn
    - Mira Monte Inn
2. **Bath**
    - Fairhaven Inn
    - The Galen C. Moses House
    - Packard House
3. **Belfast** - The Jeweled Turret Inn
4. **Blue Hill** - The Blue Hill Inn
5. **Brunswick**
    - Bethel Point B&B
    - Brunswick B&B
6. **Camden**
    - Abigail's B&B by the Sea
    - Blue Harbor House
    - Captain Swift Inn
    - The Elms B&B
    - Maine Stay Inn
    - Swan House B&B
    - The Victorian by the Sea
7. **Caribou** - The Old Iron Inn B&B
8. **Dennysville** - Lincoln House Country Inn
9. **Freeport (Durham)** - The Bagley House

10. **Fryeburg** - Admiral Peary House B&B
11. **Kennebunkport**
    - Bufflehead Cove Inn
    - The Inn on South Street
    - Maine Stay Inn & Cottages
12. **Naples** - Lamb's Mill Inn
13. **Newcastle** - The Newcastle Inn
14. **Phippsburg** - Small Point B&B
15. **Portland** - Andrews Lodging B&B
16. **Rockland** - Lakeshore Inn
17. **Sorrento** - Bass Cove Farm B&B
18. **Southwest Harbor** - The Inn at Southwest

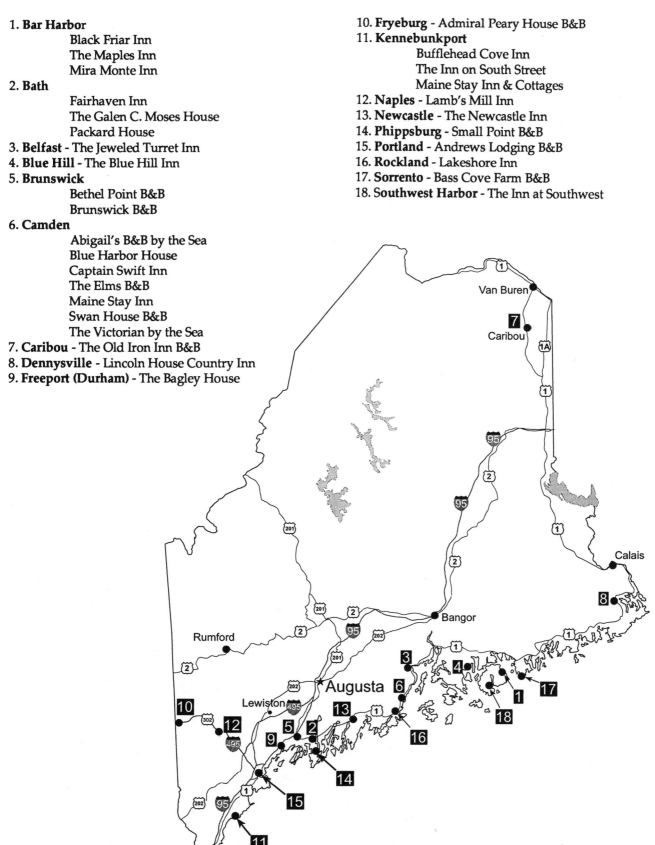

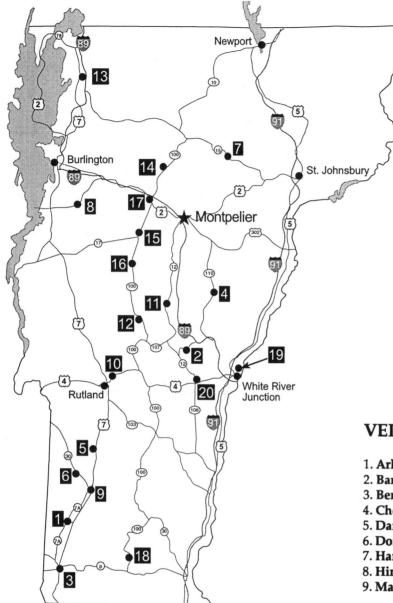

VERMONT

1. **Arlington** - Hill Farm Inn
2. **Barnard** - The Maple Leaf Inn
3. **Bennington** - Molly Stark Inn
4. **Chelsea** - Shire Inn
5. **Danby** - The Quail's Nest B&B
6. **Dorset** - Cornucopia of Dorset
7. **Hardwick** - Somerset House B&B
8. **Hinesburg** - By the Old Mill Stream
9. **Manchester Area**
      The Battenkill Inn
      The Inn at Manchester
      The Inn at Ormsby Hill
      Manchester Highlands Inn
10. **Mendon** - Red Clover Inn
11. **Randolph** - Placidia Farm B&B
12. **Rochester** - Liberty Hill Farm
13. **St. Albans** - Old Mill River Place
14. **Stowe** - Brass Lantern Inn
15. **Waitsfield** - The Inn at the Round Barn Farm
16. **Warren** - The Sugartree, A Country Inn
17. **Waterbury**
      Grünberg Haus B&B
      Thatcher Brook Inn
18. **West Dover** - Deerhill Inn
19. **Wilder** - Stonecrest Farm B&B
20. **Woodstock** - Ardmore Inn

NEW HAMPSHIRE

1. **Bradford**
    The Candlelite Inn
    Rosewood Country Inn
2. **Center Harbor** - Watch Hill B&B
3. **Charlestown** - MapleHedge B&B Inn
4. **Colebrook** - Rooms With a View B&B
5. **Durham** - University Guest House
6. **Fitzwilliam** - Hannah Davis House
7. **Glen** - The Bernerhof Inn
8. **Greenfield** - The Greenfield Inn B&B
9. **Hart's Location** - The Notchland Inn
10. **Hillsborough** - The Inn at Maplewood Farm
11. **Holderness** - The Inn on Golden Pond
12. **Hopkinton** - The Country Porch B&B
13. **Jackson**
    Ellis River House
    The Village House
14. **Jaffrey** - The Benjamin Prescott Inn
15. **Jefferson** - Applebrook B&B
16. **Madison** - Maple Grove House
17. **Milford**
    The Ram in the Thicket
    Zahn's Alpine Guesthouse
18. **North Conway**
    The Buttonwood Inn
    Nereledge Inn
19. **Peterborough** - Apple Gate B&B
20. **Plymouth** - The Crab Apple Inn B&B
21. **Sugar Hill** - Foxglove, A Country Inn
22. **Tamworth**
    The Tamworth Inn
    The Whispering Pines B&B
23. **Temple** - Birchwood Inn
24. **Weare** - The Weare-House B&B

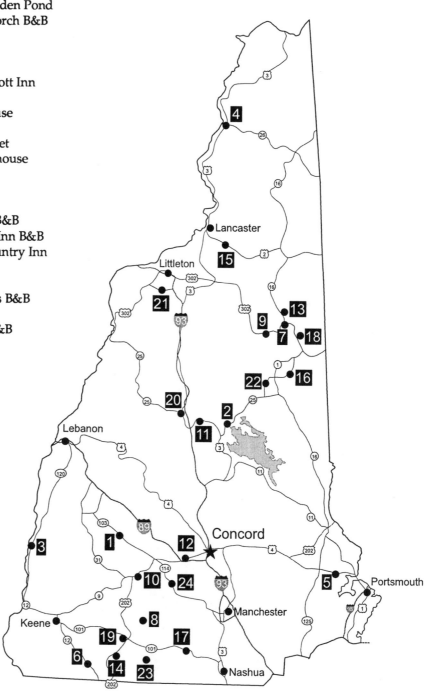

Beverages

A Proper Cup of Tea

Ingredients:

Teakettle of freshly drawn water
Good English tea leaves from China or India "or even teabags as the English use"

Also:

Tea cozy (cloth covering which keeps the teapot warm)
Tea strainer
Milk, optional
Sugar, optional
Lemon slices, optional

🍵 Place kettle of water on stove to boil.

🍵 After water boils, warm the teapot by placing a bit of the hot water in it and swishing it around. If time permits, let water warm the teapot for 5 minutes.

🍵 In teapot, place one teaspoon of tea leaves per person plus "one for the pot."

🍵 Pour enough boiling water into the teapot to accommodate number of tea drinkers.

🍵 Put the lid on and allow tea to steep under a tea cozy for 3 to 4 minutes.

🍵 Using a tea strainer, pour tea into cups (with the milk poured in first, if desired). Pass the sugar and plate of lemon slices.

Makes 1 to 6 servings

from **Somerset House B&B**
24 Highland Avenue
P.O. Box 1098
Hardwick, VT 05843
802-472-5484
800-838-8074

"We all try to make the best coffee for our guests, but so often the tea served is just a lonely tea bag perched on a plate besides a container of barely warm water," said Innkeeper Ruth Gaillard. "A really inviting cup of tea, served the way I learned to do it growing up in England and Wales, is what our increasing number of British guests are happy and relieved to find when they arrive here."

Ruth's breakfasts are served in the B&B's dining room. The meal may include freshly-made dishes using free range eggs and organically-grown fruit, vegetables and herbs, whenever possible, she notes. Ingredients come from their organic garden or from local suppliers.

Ruth and her husband, David, call the work on their 1894 home "sympathetic renovation." Located on a quiet street lined with maple trees, the B&B has four guestrooms. Guests can enjoy the piano in the sitting room, or rock in the rockers on the porch. Hardwick is a village of 2,500, "with friendly people and a lovely small-town atmosphere," Ruth explained. It is "off the beaten track in the Northeast Kingdom, the most rural and unspoiled corner of Vermont."

🏠 *Another Somerset House recipe:*
Breakfast Burritos, page 106

Banana Froth

Ingredients:

1 banana, preferably a little over-ripe
1-1/2 cups orange or cranberry juice
2 large ice cubes

Also:

Mint sprigs

- In a blender, process banana, juice and ice cubes on high setting until smooth and frothy.
- Pour the beverage into tall, stemmed six-ounce glasses and garnish with mint. Serve immediately.

Makes 3 servings

from **MapleHedge B&B Inn**
355 Main Street
P.O. Box 638
Charlestown, NH 03603
603-826-5237
1-800-9-MAPLE-9

"When my family was growing up, there always seemed to be a banana left in the fruit bowl too long," confessed Innkeeper Joan DeBrine. "There didn't seem to be much to do with just one, so I disguised it in this wholesome drink." She notes the color of the drink, either orange or pink, depending on the juice used, is particularly attractive in a fancy glass.

Joan entered innkeeping after a "first" career as homemaker and mother. "Innkeeping had always been a dream of mine and a big part of the dream had been doing it in New England," she said. "While our younger son was in college in Plymouth, New Hampshire, I discovered the state. It seemed perfect for a retirement plan -- no state income tax, no sales tax -- plus, with all its lakes and mountains and rivers, it seemed to be the playground for the rest of New England." Never one to rush into anything, she narrowed her search to five towns, then waited two-and-a-half years to find the right property. It came on the market in Charlestown, an historic town on the Connecticut River.

She and husband Dick bought this 18th century home and began another two-and-a-half years of renovation that involved everything from adding bedrooms and bathrooms to redecorating. Still, Joan notes, it is never "finished," nor is there ever a dull moment. "I continually am upgrading with furniture -- a piece will come up at an auction I can't resist." The DeBrines' B&B has five guestrooms and is open April through December.

Charlestown boasts one of the largest National Historic Districts in New Hampshire. The district has 63 structures, including 10 buildings pre-dating 1880, and seven different architectural styles are represented. Joan notes the undeveloped river here adds to the peacefulness of the surroundings.

Other MapleHedge recipes:
Cheese Cream-Filled Baked Pears, page 96
Grandma's Fruit Bread, page 158

Hot Cocoa Mix

Ingredients:

    1-1/3 cups non-fat dry milk powder
    1/4 cup Dutch-process cocoa
    1/2 cup sugar

Also:

    Cinnamon
    Peppermint sticks
    Marshmallows

- Combine dry milk powder, cocoa and sugar. Place in an attractive container.
- To make a cup of cocoa, place 4 to 6 heaping teaspoons of the mix into a mug.
- Add hot water, desired extras, and stir.

Makes 6 to 8 servings

from **The Weare-House B&B**
76 Quaker Street
Weare, NH 03281
603-529-2660

"This simple cocoa recipe is a hit in the afternoon or for breakfast," said Innkeeper Ellen Goldsberry. She keeps hot water available all day so guests can help themselves to as much as they like after a day of skiing or while relaxing by the fire. "Many guests find it a nice alternative to morning coffee," she notes, "and, of course, kids love it!" Children who visit the Weare-House, as well as adults, also love to visit the huge barn, where they discover two miniature Sicilian donkeys, horses and laying hens -- the source of fresh eggs.

Ellen and Curt, her spouse, bought this large house and turned it into a B&B in 1993. They previously resided in Sudbury, Mass., west of Boston. Both grew up in a suburb of Columbus, Ohio, and were high school sweethearts. They were married in 1985 and they have two young sons, Nathan and Jacob.

Their decision to pursue innkeeping as a career and lifestyle led them to Weare, where they found this farmhouse, built in 1819, within walking distance of town. With its original wide pine floors, hand-hewn beams and low windows that overlook the surrounding pastures and hills, they decided it would be a perfect country B&B. After six months of renovations, they opened their B&B.

The four guestrooms are furnished with antiques. The living room is a popular place for guests to relax and read or chat by the fireplace. Children enjoy the toys and games available, as well as meeting Nathan and Jacob and the family's two dogs, which are friendly canines of mixed-Labrador descent.

Other Weare-House recipes:
Applesauce Muffins, page 45
Low-Fat Granola, page 194

Minted Watermelon Refresher

Ingredients:

1/2 of a large, ripe watermelon, seeds and rind removed, then cubed
3/4 cup fresh mint leaves, washed
1/2 cup frozen orange juice concentrate
Juice of 1 lime

Also:

Ice cubes
Lime slices or mint leaves

🖙 In a blender, combine part of the watermelon, mint, orange juice concentrate and lime juice. Process until liquid, and repeat until all watermelon is used. Stir all ingredients together after processing.

🖙 Cover and refrigerate overnight to blend flavors.

🖙 When ready to serve, crush ice cubes and add to drink. Stir well.

🖙 Serve in large goblets, garnished with lime slices or mint leaves.

Makes about 10 servings

from **The Inn on South Street**
5 South Street
P.O. Box 478A
Kennebunkport, ME 04046
207-967-5151
800-963-5151

"We serve this drink with breakfast on hot summer days. It is also very refreshing in the afternoon or evening," notes Innkeeper Eva Downs.

Breakfasting guests might enjoy this eye-opener along with homemade breads and jams, fresh fruit and one of Eva's main entrees, such as Herbed Cheese Soufflé, using herbs from her gardens. Guests gather in the second floor country kitchen where they enjoy breakfast with plenty of coffee, conversation, and a view of the river and ocean. The breakfast table is always set with blue and white Canton china, some of the many items that now decorate the inn, collected during travels of Eva and Jack, her husband.

Jack specializes in early American trade with China as a professor emeritus of American History at the University of New England in Biddeford. Eva formerly had careers as an occupational therapist and child care administrator. Jack and Eva bought this house in 1963 and raised three children here. Twenty years later, they turned the home into a four-guestroom inn. The home was built between 1806 and 1823. In 1901, it was moved from around the corner because it blocked the view of the river from the nearby Captain Lord Mansion. It's a short walk to restaurants, shops and the ocean.

🏠 *Other Inn on South Street recipes:*
Zucchini Apple Coffeecake, page 41
Herbed Cheese Soufflé, page 113

Notchland "Muddled" Cider

Ingredients:

1/2 gallon apple cider
1 cup cranberry juice
1/4 cup maple syrup
3 cinnamon sticks
1/2 teaspoon orange zest (may substitute several orange slices)
1/4 teaspoon nutmeg
6 to 8 whole cloves

🥄 In a large non-reactive stock pot or saucepan, stir together apple cider, cranberry juice and maple syrup. Then stir in cinnamon sticks, orange zest, nutmeg and cloves.

🥄 Heat slowly and simmer for 30 minutes.

🥄 Strain out the "muddled flavorings" (cinnamon sticks, orange peel and cloves) and set aside. Serve hot.

🥄 Reserve flavorings and refrigerate together with any leftover liquid.

Makes 8 to 10 servings

from **The Notchland Inn**
Route 302
Hart's Location, NH 03812
603-374-6131
800-866-6131

"'Muddled' Cider grew out of serving treats following fall and winter afternoon carriage and sleigh rides," said Innkeeper Les Schoof. "Mixing and adding the various flavors over time evolved into an interesting drink which is great on cold winter mornings, too," he said.

The Notchland sleigh and carriage were ably pulled by Dolly, the Belgian draft horse, now retired and residing on some of the 100 acres making up the inn's property. Dolly's animal friends include Mork and Mindy, the miniature horses; D.C. and Sid, the llamas; and Coco, the Bernese Mountain dog.

Guests who want to recreate or relax never have to leave the property. In addition to visiting Dolly, mountain biking, cross-country skiing, snowshoeing and soaking in the gazebo's wood-fired hot tub are available for guests. The inn's 8,000 feet of Saco River frontage afford plenty of fishing and swimming opportunities, and a number of hiking trails begin at or near the inn.

Les and Ed Butler found this 1862 granite mansion after a three-year search for the perfect property. The secluded White Mountain buildings had been operating as an inn since the 1920s. Today Les and Ed offer guests seven rooms and five suites as well as a renowned five-course dinner.

🏠 *Other Notchland Inn recipes:*
Favorite Popovers, page 51
Boiled Fruit Cake, page 154
Cranberry Bread Pudding, page 181

Rhubarb Tea

Ingredients:

4 cups rhubarb, diced
4 cups water
Grated rind of 1 lemon or orange
3/4 to 1 cup sugar

● In a saucepan, place rhubarb in water and simmer until rhubarb is very tender, about 20 to 25 minutes. Strain and discard pulp.

● Add grated lemon or orange rind and sugar to taste to rhubarb juice. Stir until sugar is dissolved.

● Serve hot or chill and serve over ice.

Tester's Comments: Those who think that the "pie plant" is sour or bitter should taste this tea! Iced, it's much like pink lemonade, with a very pretty pink color.

Makes about 4 cups

from **Mira Monte Inn**
69 Mt. Desert Street
Bar Harbor, ME 04609
207-288-4263
800-553-5109

"This is good served hot on a rainy spring afternoon by the fire in the parlor. Or serve it with ice on the terrace on those lovely June days," said Innkeeper Marian Burns, who grows her own rhubarb in the inn's gardens. She also makes rhubarb into a sauce ("made like applesauce only with more sugar to taste") and offers it to top pancakes or oatmeal. "I find that many Americans have never heard of it or have never tasted it. It's a great conversation starter and a great way to find who of your guests is the more adventurous!"

Many of Marian's guests are quite adventurous, coming to Bar Harbor to sail, whale watch, hike, cross-country ski, rock-climb, beach-comb, or otherwise explore Acadia National Park, a five-minute drive away. The inn is within walking distance of Bar Harbor's shops and restaurants.

Marian's inn was built in 1864 as a summer "cottage" for one of the wealthy families (and their servants) that summered in Bar Harbor. In 1890 it was named by its Philadelphia owners; the name means "behold the mountains." Marian, a Bar Harbor native who raised her children in town, always wanted one of the summer homes with gorgeous gardens. Now hers, Mira Monte Inn has 12 guestrooms in the main house and three suites in a separate building on the two-acre property, with gardens that bloom from May to November. Guests may enjoy the wrap-around porch, the garden terraces, the library and the parlor, and they are treated to refreshments such as this each afternoon.

🏠*Another Mira Monte recipe:*
Blueberry Sour Cream Coffeecake, page 32

Strawberry Orange Juice

Ingredients:

3/4 cup sliced fresh strawberries
4-1/3 cups orange juice (or approximately 12 oranges)

Apricot Orange Variation:
1 8-ounce can apricots, in place of strawberries

☛ Place strawberries and orange juice in a blender and purée.
☛ Strain mixture and chill. Then serve "in your most interesting glasses or tall flutes. Add fresh fruit and tie a colorful ribbon on the stem."
☛ For the Apricot Orange variation, drain the apricots before blending.

Makes 5 cups

from **Abigail's B&B by the Sea**
8 High Street
Camden, ME 04843
207-236-2501
800-292-2501

Innkeepers Donna and Ed Misner often serve this juice to guests who meet in the sunny dining room for breakfast. Breakfast might include fruits, souffles, quiche, French toast, or waffles, plus scones, muffins or coffeecakes. Or the Misners will bring breakfast on a tray to guestrooms for breakfast in bed.

Abigail's is a Greek Revival-style home listed on the National Register of Historic Places. The home was built in 1847 for a member of the U.S. House of Representatives, E.K. Smart. His good friend, Jefferson Davis, was a frequent overnight guest.

Today, guests come to Camden for the sailing, special events, shopping and outdoor adventures. The harbor and town, with quaint shops, galleries and restaurants, are within walking distance of Abigail's.

Donna and Ed opened this home as a B&B in 1990. They came to Camden looking for another restoration project, since they enjoy working on historic homes. They previously owned Abigail Adams B&B in Cape May, New Jersey. Their "new" Camden inn also was named in honor of Mrs. Adams.

Prior to innkeeping, Donna had been a retail clothing store owner, and Ed was a commercial airline pilot for 26 years. They enjoy traveling and the winter months might find them in London or other exotic locales.

🏠*Another Abigail's recipe:*
"High Hat" Irish Soda Bread, page 159

Summer Cantaloupe Cooler

Ingredients:

1 cup diced cantaloupe
1/2 cup plain or vanilla yogurt
2 teaspoons honey
1 teaspoon lemon juice
1/2 teaspoon grated lemon peel

Also:

Mint leaves and thin lemon slices

- In a blender, place cantaloupe, yogurt, honey, lemon juice and lemon peel.
- Cover and purée until smooth.
- Pour into chilled glasses and garnish with mint leaves and lemon slices.

Makes 2 servings

from **The Bernerhof Inn**
Route 302
P.O. Box 240
Glen, NH 03838
603-383-9132
800-548-8007

This is a quick-yet-delicious morning beverage that Chef Mark Prince created to go along with breakfast he serves to guests. In the summer, guests are usually heading out to theme park attractions, outlet shopping or a wide variety of outdoor recreation in the Mt. Washington Valley, including rock climbing, hiking, mountain biking, trout fishing or canoeing the Saco River.

Innkeepers Ted and Sharon Wroblewski have owned this inn since 1977 and raised their four children here. Ted first saw the place when he and Sharon had only one child, Brooke, 3 months, and were living in New York. He suggested Sharon come and look at it, and soon it was theirs.

Originally built in the late 1800s and named "Pleasant Valley Hall," the inn has always served White Mountain travelers heading through the Crawford Notch. Several owners over the years involved several name changes, including Glenwood on the Saco, named after the inn's large Glenwood stove. A family with Swiss roots named it the Bernerhof, meaning the House of Bern, a region in Switzerland, and featuring fine Swiss cuisine in the restaurant.

European and continental dishes are still highly-acclaimed in the 80-seat restaurant. Sharon and Ted have added the Black Bear Pub and have remodeled the inn at least twice during their ownership. During the spring, summer and fall, many guests come to take small, hands-on courses at A Taste of the Mountains cooking school, taught to home cooks by respected chefs.

Other Bernerhof recipes:
Cider Molasses Doughnuts, page 68
Eggs Bernerhof, page 109

Sunshine Punch

Ingredients:

1 watermelon
1 12-ounce can frozen fruit punch concentrate, partially thawed
1 12-ounce can frozen cranberry juice concentrate, partially thawed
Ginger ale
Oranges, thinly sliced
Lemons, thinly sliced
Mint sprigs
Ice

🐾 Cut open watermelon and remove all fruit, seeds included (if you split the rind in half lengthwise, it can be used for a fruit bowl). Save the large, seed-free section in the middle to mix with other fruit or eat as is. Place the rest of the fruit, with seeds, in a colander set in a large bowl.

🐾 Using a potato masher, squash fruit. When as much juice as possible has been extracted, discard mashed pulp and seeds. Place juice in covered container and refrigerate.

🐾 Just before serving, mix together watermelon juice and the slushy fruit punch and cranberry juice concentrates. Add ginger ale to taste.

🐾 Add orange slices, lemon slices, mint and ice and serve.

Tester's Comments: A great way to use up the "seedy" fruit -- and it makes enough to serve a crowd!

Makes 18 8-ounce servings

from **The Old Iron Inn B&B**
155 High Street
Caribou, ME 04736
207-492-IRON (4766)

"I first served this punch at a meeting of the Caribou Historical Society," said Innkeeper Kate McCartney. "The punch was a big success" and members enjoyed it after hearing Kate and Kevin, her spouse, speak on their collection of antique irons, after which they named the inn. The house is decorated throughout with the irons and other antiques. Their collection includes hundreds of irons in use during the last 200 years. Kevin began collecting 20 years ago, and can explain unusual ones, such as soapstone and charcoal irons.

Kevin, a paleontologist who teaches geology at the University of Maine at Presque Isle, and Kate, who is getting her masters in English literature, decided to open a B&B for many reasons. There are very few B&Bs in Caribou or Aroostook County, which covers nearly one-third of northernmost Maine. Kate had stayed in European B&Bs and thought she and Kevin would enjoy sharing their home with guests from all over. Their B&B has four guestrooms and guests are treated to a full breakfast, usually with homemade muffins.

🏠 *Other Old Iron Inn recipes:*
Chocolate Cheesecake Muffins, page 49
Green One-Eyed Jacks, page 112

This is Such Good Punch

Ingredients:

    1 12-ounce can frozen orange juice concentrate, thawed
    1 12-ounce can frozen lemonade concentrate, thawed
    1 12-ounce can frozen pineapple juice concentrate, thawed
    3 quarts water, ice cold
    3 large, ripe bananas

Also:

    Orange, lemon and banana slices
    Additional orange juice
    Mint sprig

- In a large bowl, mix all thawed fruit juice concentrates and cold water.
- Place bananas and two cups of juice mixture in a blender. Purée until smooth.
- Add banana mixture to punch and stir thoroughly. Cover and refrigerate until use.
- To create a frozen fruit ring, place slices of orange, lemon and banana in a ring mold, fill with additional orange juice, and freeze.
- Pour punch into a punch bowl. Garnish with frozen fruit ring and a mint sprig in the middle.

Makes 4 quarts, about 30 servings

from **The Country Porch B&B**
281 Moran Road
Hopkinton, NH 03229
603-746-6391

"This is such good punch," is the constant comment of Wendy Solomon's guests at showers or open houses, when she is most likely to serve it. It is also called "Golden Banana Punch," named after its appealing coloring.

Wendy and Tom Solomon became innkeepers in 1994 when they opened their three-guestroom inn. Their home is a reproduction of an 18-century colonial, complete with wide pine floors, a Rumford fireplace in the Keeping Room, and a wrap-around porch. It is the porch to which guests are often drawn to settle into a rocker and enjoy the view of the meadow and lawn.

Those who can rouse themselves from the rockers can explore the 15 acres, including a hike to the marsh or a climb to the barn's cupola to view the mountains. A swimming pool, horsehoes and badminton are available for guests, or they can enjoy the nine-hole golf course down the road. The B&B is a short drive from Concord and is located near sugar bushes, you-pick berry farms, apple orchards, skiing and the Shaker Village in Canterbury.

⌂ Other Country Porch B&B recipes:
Buttery Orange Pecan Scones, page 48
Light and Fluffy Pancakes, page 136

Coffeecakes

Blueberry Sour Cream Coffeecake

Ingredients:

1/2 cup butter or margarine
1 cup sugar
2 eggs
1 cup sour cream
1 teaspoon vanilla extract
2 cups flour
1/2 teaspoon baking soda
1-1/2 teaspoons baking powder
1/2 teaspoon salt
1 teaspoon nutmeg

Filling:
Juice of 1 lemon
Peel of 1 lemon
1 tablespoon cornstarch
3 cups Maine wild blueberries, fresh or
frozen dry-pack

Topping:
1/4 cup butter or margarine
1 teaspoon cinnamon
1/2 cup chopped walnuts
1/2 cup flour
1/2 cup sugar

✍ With an electric mixer, cream together butter, sugar, eggs, sour cream and vanilla.

✍ In a separate bowl, sift together flour, baking soda, baking powder, salt and nutmeg.

✍ Beat flour mixture into egg mixture. Spread half of batter into a butterered 9 x 13-inch pan.

✍ For Filling: Squeeze the juice of one lemon into a bowl. Add lemon peel and cornstarch and stir to dissolve. Add blueberries and mix gently to coat them with the cornstarch mixture.

✍ Pour filling over batter in pan. "Dollop" the remaining batter in six or eight equal portions on top of the filling. Then spread it to sides and to cover berries as much as possible.

✍ For Topping: With fork or a pastry cutter, cut together butter, cinnamon, walnuts, flour and sugar. Sprinkle topping evenly over batter.

✍ Bake in a preheated oven at 350 degrees for 35 minutes. Remove and let cool a bit; cut into squares and serve while still warm.

Makes 24 servings

from **Mira Monte Inn**
69 Mt. Desert Street
Bar Harbor, ME 04609
207-288-4263
800-553-5109

Innkeeper Marian Burns loves the flavor of wild Maine blueberries, so this appears often on her breakfast buffet, which she and her staff serve to guests in the 15 guestrooms and suites each day from 8 to 10 a.m. Guests fortify themselves for a day at Acadia National Park or in Bar Harbor shops.

Marian's inn is one of the many grand Bar Harbor residences built as summer homes for wealthy families. Built in 1864, the home now has 12 guestrooms in the main house and three more in a separate building. Marian is a Bar Harbor native who acquired this two-acre property to host B&B guests.

🏠*Another Mira Monte recipe:*
Rhubarb Tea, page 25

Brown Sugar Coffeecake

Ingredients:

   2 cups flour
   1/2 teaspoon salt
   1/2 teaspoon baking powder
   1/2 cup vegetable shortening
   1 cup sour milk (7/8 cup milk and 1 to 2 tablespoons vinegar stirred together)
   1 egg, beaten
   1 teaspoon baking soda
   2 cups light brown sugar, packed

🍂 In a large bowl, mix together flour, salt and baking powder.

🍂 With a pastry cutter or fork, cut in shortening until crumbly. Remove 1/2 cup of crumbly mixture to be used for topping and set aside.

🍂 In a separate bowl, whisk together milk, egg and baking soda. Then stir in brown sugar. (Batter will be lumpy, which is OK, unless you are using an electric mixer.)

🍂 Stir in remaining flour mixture. Pour batter into a buttered 8 x 8 or 8-1/2 x 11-inch pan and sprinkle top with reserved mixture.

🍂 Bake in a preheated oven at 350 degrees for at least 40 minutes, or until toothpick inserted in center comes out clean.

Tester's Comments: This smells wonderful while baking. (I preferred using the larger pan for 10 to 12 servings.)

Makes 6 to 8 servings

from **The Blue Hill Inn**
P.O. Box 403
Route 177, Union Street
Blue Hill, ME 04614
207-374-2844
Fax 207-374-2829

"This recipe was my great-grandmother's. She ran a boarding home in Pennsylvania Dutch country," said Mary Hartley, innkeeper. "The texture is similar to shoofly pie, and, if covered tightly, this stays moist for several days." It is one of the several homemade breads Mary serves at breakfast.

Mary isn't the only one whose history includes some hospitality genes. The Blue Hill Inn itself has been the village inn since 1840, a mere decade after it was built by blacksmith Varnum Stevens. Stevens traded the inn to his brother-in-law, a sea captain, and the "women folk" and their descendents operated the inn until the 1930s. Several innkeepers later, Mary and Don bought the inn in 1987. They changed professions to live and work in Maine, where they appreciate the outdoors and "caring, independent" Mainers. The inn, which has 11 guestrooms and also offers dinner, is one of 76 buildings in Blue Hill designated as a National Register Historic District.

🏠*Another Blue Hill Inn recipe:*
Almond French Toast, page 119

Chocolate Chip Sour Cream Coffeecake

Ingredients:

    1/2 cup butter or margarine
    1 cup sugar
    2 eggs
    1 cup sour cream (not low-fat)
    2 tablespoons milk
    2 cups flour
    1 teaspoon baking soda
    1 teaspoon baking powder
    1 6-ounce package semisweet chocolate chips or miniature chips

Filling/Topping:
    1/2 cup sugar
    2 teaspoons cinnamon

Also:

    Powdered sugar

🥄 With an electric mixer, cream together butter or margarine and sugar.

🥄 Beat in eggs until the mixture is light and fluffy.

🥄 In separate bowl, combine the sour cream and milk. Set aside.

🥄 In another large bowl, sift together flour, baking soda and baking powder.

🥄 Beat in the flour mixture, then sour cream mixture, alternately into the batter until well blended.

🥄 Fold in chocolate chips by hand.

🥄 For Filling/Topping: In a small bowl, mix together cinnamon and sugar.

🥄 Spoon half of batter into a buttered and floured Bundt or tube baking pan. Sprinkle half of the cinnamon and sugar mixture over the batter. Then repeat with remaining batter and Filling/Topping.

🥄 Bake in a preheated oven at 350 degrees for 40 to 45 minutes or until a toothpick inserted in center comes out clean. Remove from oven, cool, remove from pan and dust top with powdered sugar.

Tester's Comments: Very rich and delicious (almost, but not quite, sinful for breakfast!). I liked mini-chips best.

Makes 16 servings (well, that depends..fewer for chocoholics!)

from **The Buttonwood Inn**
Mt. Surprise Road
P.O. Box 1817
North Conway, NH 03860
603-356-2625
800-258-2625

    "I found this recipe in a file folder when we first moved into The Buttonwood Inn," said Claudia Needham. "When I read descriptions of some of our breakfast items in guidebooks we were listed in, this coffeecake was referenced more than once!" It's a hit with guests, especially children, she notes, yet it's easy to make. Claudia and Peter Needham bought this inn in 1993, 10 years after it first opened. Originally constructed in 1820 as a four-room Cape-style farm house, today it has 10 guestrooms, including family suites, in a secluded, woodsy location.

🏠*Other Buttonwood Inn recipes:*
Overnight Cranberry Scones, page 55
Peanut Crunch Cookies, page 201

French Almond Coffeecake

Ingredients:

2 cups flour
1 cup plus 2 tablespoons cold water
1 cup butter or margarine
1 teaspoon almond extract
3 large eggs

Frosting:
3 tablespoons margarine, melted
2 tablespoons milk, hot
1/2 teaspoon almond extract
1 cup powdered sugar

Also:

2 tablespoons sliced almonds

🍂 In a medium bowl, beat together 1 cup flour, 2 tablespoons cold water and 1/2 cup of the butter or margarine. Divide mixture in half.

🍂 Roll each half between palms to form an 8-inch log. Roll in waxed paper and refrigerate overnight.

🍂 The next morning, place remaining 1/2 cup butter and 1 cup water in a saucepan. Bring to a boil. Stir in almond extract.

🍂 Remove from stove and stir in remaining 1 cup flour until smooth.

🍂 Add eggs, one at a time, stirring after each addition until smooth. Set aside and let cool.

🍂 Remove chilled dough from refrigerator and flatten each portion onto an unbuttered cookie sheet, forming each log into a 3 x 12-inch strip.

🍂 Divide the cooled egg mixture equally down the center of each strip.

🍂 Bake in a preheated oven at 350 degrees for 60 minutes or until puffed and golden brown.

🍂 For Frosting: Melt margarine in hot milk. Mix in almond extract and powdered sugar. Stir until smooth.

🍂 Frost cakes while still warm and sprinkle almonds on top of frosting. Serve immediately. "This recipe is best when baked right before serving; it does not keep well overnight."

Makes 2 cakes or 10 servings

from **Swan House B&B**
49 Mountain Street
Camden, ME 04843
207-236-8275
800-207-8275

"This recipe is one of the most requested by our guests," said Innkeeper Lyn Kohl, who serves it as part of a popular breakfast buffet. "We deal with some pretty hefty appetites since we are situated right at the foot of beautiful Mt. Battie, and a shortcut through the forest in our 'backyard' meets up with a hiking trail that leads to the top of the mountain." Some guests get up early to hike, and one hiker "told me that the aroma of the baked goods coming from the Inn actually wafted up the mountain as they descended from their hike. Needless to say, their appetites were ravenous!" The Victorian B&B was built in 1870 by the Swan Family. Lyn and Ken, her husband, purchased the B&B in 1993 and offer six guestrooms in the main house and the Cygnet Annex.

🏠Another Swan House recipe:
Cheesecake Squares, page 180

Mom's Chocolate Chip Sour Cream Coffeecake

Ingredients:

1/2 cup butter, softened
1 cup sugar
2 eggs
1-1/4 cups sour cream
1 teaspoon vanilla extract
2 cups flour
1 teaspoon baking powder
1 teaspoon baking soda
1/2 teaspoon salt

Filling:
3/4 cup brown sugar, packed
1/4 cup sugar
2 tablespoons flour
1 tablespoon cinnamon
1 tablespoon butter, softened
1 6-ounce package semisweet chocolate chips or miniature chips
3/4 cup chopped walnuts, optional

- With an electric mixer, cream together butter and sugar. Beat in eggs, sour cream and vanilla.
- In a separate bowl or on a sheet of waxed paper, sift together flour, baking powder and baking soda.
- Slowly fold flour mixture into batter (do not over-mix). Batter will be thick.
- For Filling: In a separate bowl, stir together brown sugar, sugar, flour, cinnamon and butter with a pastry cutter or fork. Then stir in chocolate chips and optional walnuts.
- Pour one-third of batter into a well-buttered tube or Bundt pan. Sprinkle one-third of filling on top.
- Repeat layering batter and filling two more times, ending up with the filling on top as a topping.
- Bake in a preheated oven at 350 degrees for 50 to 60 minutes or until a toothpick inserted in center comes out clean. Remove from oven and cool on a wire rack before removing cake to a serving plate.

Tester's Comments: Mmmm. The combination of cinnamon, sugar and chocolate is wonderful (with or without the nuts). I preferred using miniature chips. This went fast at a potluck.

Makes 10 to 16 servings

from **The Newcastle Inn**
River Road
Newcastle, ME 04553
207-563-5685
800-832-8669

"This is an old family recipe passed down from generation to generation," said Howard Levitan, who, with his wife, Rebecca, bought this popular inn in 1995. Howard and Rebecca left careers in law and corporate marketing, respectively, to settle in Newcastle, a lovely mid-coast town that's off the beaten tourist path, yet a short drive to popular attractions and activities. Just beyond the inn's lupine garden is the Damariscotta River, and guests are invited to enjoy the lawn and gardens as well as the inn's public rooms.

The Newcastle Inn has been serving the public since the early 1900s. Today, the Levitans and their chef offer a hearty breakfast to all guests staying in the 15 guestrooms, as well as an optional five-course dinner, served by candlelight on linen-covered tables situated by the fireplace. "Our goal is to present taste-tantilizing food, made from the finest ingedients, in an informal, relaxed country inn setting," Howard said.

Overnight Crunch Coffeecake

Ingredients:

2 cups flour
1 teaspoon baking powder
1 teaspoon baking soda
1 teaspoon cinnamon
1/4 teaspoon salt
2/3 cup margarine or butter, softened
1 cup sugar
1/2 cup brown sugar, packed
2 eggs
1 cup buttermilk

Topping:
1/2 cup brown sugar, packed
1/2 cup walnuts, chopped
1/2 teaspoon cinnamon
1/4 teaspoon nutmeg

- Sift together flour, baking powder, baking soda, cinnamon and salt.
- With an electric mixer, cream together margarine, sugar and brown sugar until light and fluffy.
- Add eggs, one at a time, to batter, beating well after each addition.
- Add flour mixture alternately with buttermilk to margarine mixture, beating well after each addition.
- Spread batter in a buttered and floured 9 x 13-inch pan.
- For Topping: Stir together brown sugar, walnuts, cinnamon and nutmeg. Sprinkle over batter.
- Cover and refrigerate overnight.
- In the morning, remove cake from refrigerator while oven preheats to 350 degrees. Remove cover and bake for 35 to 40 minutes or until a toothpick inserted in the middle comes out clean.

Tester's Comments: The topping may not appear to be enough, but, sure enough, it spreads out while baking and the melted brown sugar makes a nice "crunch." Delicious warm from the oven!

Makes 12 to 16 servings

from **Brunswick B&B**
165 Park Row
Brunswick, ME 04011
207-729-4914
800-299-4914

Mercie and Steve Normand's breakfast is served between 8 and 9 a.m. in their B&B's twin parlors. "The triple-hung windows let in the morning light and look out over the town green," Mercie said. "In the summer, our guests watch the activity at the twice-weekly Farmer's Market. And in the winter, they enjoy watching the ice skaters on the man-made pond." The in-town location of this 1849 Greek Revival home played a large part in the Normands' purchase of the operating B&B. Steve, an architect, was looking for an in-town location for his practice. "We had often thought we might run a B&B when we retired, but now seemed to be the time," Mercie said. Mercie works part-time as an occupational therapist. Bowdoin College is just down the street. The Normand's inn has eight guestrooms.

⌂ Another Brunswick B&B recipe:
Spicy Apple Pancakes with Cider Sauce, page 140

Raspberry Cream Cheese Coffeecake

Ingredients:

1/2 cup butter, softened
1-1/4 cups sugar
2 eggs
2 cups flour
1 tablespoon baking powder
1 teaspoon salt
3/4 cup milk
1/4 cup water
2 cups raspberries, fresh or frozen "dry pack"
1 8-ounce package cream cheese, cut into small cubes

Topping:
1/4 cup sugar
1/4 cup flour
2 tablespoons butter
1 teaspoon grated lemon peel

🐝 With an electric mixer, cream together butter and sugar. Then beat in eggs one at a time.

🐝 In a separate bowl, stir together flour, baking powder and salt.

🐝 Stir together milk and water in a measuring cup.

🐝 Add flour and milk mixtures to butter mixture alternately, scraping the side of the bowl after each addition.

🐝 Fold in raspberries by hand. Turn batter into a buttered 9 x 13-inch pan.

🐝 For Topping: With a pastry cutter or fork, blend sugar, flour, butter and lemon peel. Sprinkle over coffeecake batter.

🐝 Bake in a preheated oven at 375 degrees for 40 minutes or until a toothpick inserted in the center comes out clean. Remove from the oven and let set a few minutes before serving.

Tester's Comments: This raspberry coffeecake would be good anyhow, but a little bite of cream cheese makes it great!

Makes 12 to 16 servings

from **The Village House**
P.O. Box 359
Route 16A
Jackson, NH 03846
800-972-8343
Fax 603-383-6464

Innkeeper Robin Crocker's recipes are "creative home cooking," she says, either passed down from generation-to-generation or "thoroughly tested by all of the most discriminating family members" (translation: picky eaters) before being served to guests. Breakfast at the inn is served on the wrap-around porch in the summer or the sun room in the winter.

Built in 1860, the inn has been serving guests from the heart of the village of Jackson for more than a century. Robin bought the operating inn in 1986. "Over the last four years, we've renovated almost everything," closing a floor at a time to do so. The barn has been converted into five guestrooms and family suites with kitchenettes. Ten more guestrooms are in the main inn. Guests can enjoy the outdoor hot tub year 'round. Jackson's famous 167 kilometers of x-c ski trails leave from the doorstep.

🏠*Another Village House recipe:*
Blueberry Peach Cobbler, page 176

Raspberry Streusel Coffeecake

Ingredients:

1-1/2 cups flour
1/2 cup sugar
2 teaspoons baking powder
1 egg
1/2 cup butter, melted
1/2 cup milk
1 cup raspberries, fresh or frozen "dry pack"

Streusel Topping:
1/4 cup flour
1/4 cup brown sugar, packed
2 tablespoons butter, melted
1/4 cup coarsely chopped pecans

- In a large bowl, stir together flour, sugar and baking powder.
- In a separate bowl, whisk together the egg, butter and milk.
- Stir the egg mixture into the flour mixture just until blended.
- Spoon half the mixture into a buttered 9-inch square pan. Top with berries.
- Spoon remaining batter on top, spreading gently to cover most of the berries.
- For Streusel Topping: With a pastry cutter or fork, cut together flour, brown sugar, butter and pecans. Sprinkle over top of batter.
- Bake in a preheated oven at 375 degrees for 30 minutes.

Tester's Comments: Easy to whip up on a weekend morning. A simple, basic recipe that should be in everyone's repertoire. Blueberries can be substituted with equally delicious results.

Makes 9 servings

from **Maple Grove House**
Maple Grove Road
P.O. Box 340
Madison, NH 03849
603-367-8208

Innkeeper Celia Pray's breakfasts, served from 7 to 9:30 a.m. each morning, were a long time in the making: she draws upon years of cooking experience aboard charter boats based in the Caribbean. A Brit who grew up in Barbados and Jamaica, she and her family have happily settled on dry land and found innkeeping and life in Madison to their liking.

Celia and her husband, Donald, found this former guest house on 216 acres standing vacant with "only a two-holer out back." The couple arrived with their children, Whitney and Andrew, the week before Christmas, 1994, and lived with constant renovation until the B&B opened in July 1995.

The Prays offer four guestrooms plus a two-room suite for families or small groups. Guests are welcome to explore the hiking or cross-country ski trails, brooks and beaver ponds on the acreage. Those who prefer to relax can enjoy the White Mountain views from two piazzas or read in the library. The outlet stores and restaurants in North Conway are just a few minutes' drive.

Another Maple Grove House recipe:
Scottish Shortbread, page 203

Wild Blueberry Streusel Coffeecake

Ingredients:

2 cups wild Maine blueberries, fresh
2 tablespoons fresh lemon juice
2 cups flour
1/2 cup sugar
1 tablespoon baking powder
1/2 teaspoon salt
2 egg whites, beaten
1 cup skim milk
1 teaspoon vanilla extract
1/2 cup melted butter or margarine

Streusel Topping:
3/4 cup sugar
1/2 cup flour
1/2 teaspoon cinnamon
1/4 cup melted butter or margarine

🖝 Sprinkle washed and picked-over blueberries with lemon juice and set aside.

🖝 In a large bowl, stir together flour, sugar, baking powder and salt.

🖝 Beat egg whites, milk, vanilla and butter into flour mixture. Mix well.

🖝 Coat a 9 x 13-inch pan with non-stick cooking spray and dust with flour. Pour batter into pan, spread to edges, and sprinkle with blueberries.

🖝 For Streusel Topping: In a medium bowl, mix together sugar, flour, cinnamon and butter or margarine with a fork or pastry cutter. Sprinkle topping over blueberries.

🖝 Bake in a preheated oven at 375 degrees for about 30 minutes or until a toothpick inserted in the center of the cake (don't skewer a berry!) comes out clean.

Makes 12 to 18 servings

from **Lamb's Mill Inn**
RR #1, Box 676
Lamb's Mill Road
Naples, ME 04055
207-693-6253

Innkeeper Laurel Tinkham adapted this recipe from an apple cake, making it lower in fat and "wonderful and appealing because of the Maine blueberries!" During the past decade that Lamb's Mill Inn has been open, many guests have returned, in part because of the breakfasts, Laurel believes. "We make our own bread, muffins and entrees from traditional homemade ingredients -- no prepackaged anything," she said. "Many of guests comment on how large breakfast is. However, many empty plates return to the kitchen!"

Laurel and her partner, Sandy Long, opened this six-guestroom inn on the site of the old Lamb brother's grain mill. It's in Naples, a picturesque village situated between Long Lake and Sebago Lake. As their name suggests, "ewe hike, ewe bike, ewe ski, ewe Zzzz." Guests can walk to the village, enjoy many activities on the lakes, go antiquing, play golf and tennis, canoe the Saco River or take a day trip to North Conway, New Hampshire. Wintertime offers both alpine and cross-country skiing. Laurel and Sandy, who both have careers in mental health and education, enjoy meeting new guests, cooking and tending the two large gardens, from which many of the meals come.

Zucchini Apple Coffeecake

Ingredients:

3 cups flour
1 cup sugar
1 teaspoon baking powder
1-1/2 teaspoons baking soda
2 teaspoons cinnamon
1/2 teaspoon salt
1/4 teaspoon nutmeg
1/2 teaspoon cloves
3 eggs
3/4 cup vegetable oil
1/4 cup molasses
2 cups zucchini, grated
2 teaspoons vanilla extract
1 cup tart apple, chopped
1 cup nuts, chopped
2/3 cup raisins

Streusel Topping:
1/4 cup butter or margarine
1/2 cup sugar
1/3 cup flour
1/2 teaspoon cinnamon
1/4 teaspoon nutmeg

🍂 In a large bowl, sift together flour, sugar, baking powder, baking soda, cinnamon, salt, nutmeg and cloves. Set aside.

🍂 In a second large bowl, mix together eggs, oil, molasses, zucchini and vanilla.

🍂 Stir flour mixture into egg mixture.

🍂 Mix in apple, nuts and raisins.

🍂 Spread mixture into a well-buttered 9 x 13-inch baking dish.

🍂 For Streusel Topping: With a fork or pastry cutter, mix together butter, sugar, flour, cinnamon and nutmeg. Sprinkle streusel over cake.

🍂 Bake in a preheated oven at 350 degrees for 45 minutes, or until a toothpick inserted in the center comes out clean.

Makes up to 24 servings

from **The Inn on South Street**
5 South Street
P.O. Box 478A
Kennebunkport, ME 04046
207-967-5151
800-963-5151

Fresh-baked pastries such as this are always on the breakfast table at Eva and Jack Downs' inn, located in Kennebunkport's historic district. The Downses turned this former sea captain's home into an inn after raising their family here. Located in the town's historic district, the B&B offers four guestrooms and plenty of hospitality. Widely traveled themselves, Eva and Jack enjoy hosting guests from all over the world.

🏠 *Other Inn on South Street recipes:*
Minted Watermelon Refresher, page 23
Herbed Cheese Soufflé, page 113

Muffins, Scones
& Popovers

Almond and Dried Cherry Muffins

Ingredients:

3/4 cup low-fat yogurt
1/2 cup skim (or low-fat) buttermilk
1/2 cup dried sour cherries
1/8 teaspoon cinnamon
Pinch of ground ginger
1/2 teaspoon vanilla extract
1/4 cup butter, cut into bits
1-1/2 cups flour
1/2 cup dark maple syrup
2 teaspoons baking powder
1/4 teaspoon salt
1 egg, lightly beaten
1/3 cup slivered almonds

- In small saucepan, whisk together yogurt, buttermilk, cherries, cinnamon and ginger. Gently simmer for 2 to 3 minutes.
- Remove pan from heat. Stir in the vanilla and butter until melted. Let cool. Stir in maple syrup.
- Meanwhile, in a large bowl, whisk together flour, baking powder and salt.
- Whisk the egg and almonds into the cherry mixture.
- Pour cherry batter over the flour mixture, stirring until ingredients are just combined.
- Spoon batter into 12 buttered muffin cups.
- Bake in a preheated oven at 350 degrees for 15 to 20 minutes, or until muffins are golden and springy.
- Remove pans from oven, let cool for 5 minutes and turn out onto cooling rack.

Makes 12 muffins

from **Molly Stark Inn**
1067 Main Street
Bennington, VT 05201
802-442-9631
800-356-3076

Innkeeper Reed Fendler often makes these as part of his breakfasts, served in the sun room recently added onto this 1890 Queen Anne Victorian. "I used to cook for family and friends, so now it feels as though my family is expanding and I just have to be more creative and cook more frequently," he said. He bought this operating inn in 1988 to work for himself. "I am not a typical 9-to-5er and I own only one suit!" He was smitten with the inn, located on Main Street just a mile from the center of town and four miles from the Appalachian Trail and the entrance to the Green Mountain National Forest trail system. A year later, he was smitten with a guest, Cammi, who is now his wife. Cammi is working on a master's degree in psychology and helps run the inn.

Other Molly Stark Inn recipes:
Smoked Salmon Quesadilla, page 148
Granola Trail Mix Cookies, page 193

Applesauce Muffins

Ingredients:
2 cups unbleached flour
1 teaspoon cinnamon
2 teaspoons baking powder
1/2 cup sugar
1 egg
1/2 cup low-fat milk
2/3 cup applesauce
1/2 teaspoon vanilla extract

Also:
Diced apples, shredded carrots or chopped nuts
1 tablespoon sugar
1/2 teaspoon cinnamon

- In a large bowl, mix flour, cinnamon, baking powder and sugar. Set aside.
- In a second large bowl, beat egg. Whisk in milk, applesauce and vanilla, mixing well.
- Stir the flour mixture into the applesauce mixture, stirring only to moisten all ingredients. Add optional apples, carrots or nuts.
- Coat muffin tins with non-stick cooking spray. Fill cups at least 3/4-full with batter.
- In a small bowl, combine 1 tablespoon sugar and 1/2 teaspoon cinnamon. Sprinkle on top of muffins.
- Bake in a preheated oven at 350 degrees for 20 minutes.

Tester's Comments: I didn't have apples, so I diced a fresh, ripe pear, added some raisins and substituted ginger for the cinnamon in the muffins (left cinnamon on the top). Especially moist for low-fat!

Makes 11 or 12 muffins

from **The Weare-House B&B**
76 Quaker Street
Weare, NH 03281
603-529-2660

"I adapted this recipe from one my son's preschool teacher used with her class," said Innkeeper Ellen Goldsberry. "It has all of the requirements I look for -- easy, healthy and tastes great." It's also very versatile, and cooks can add shredded carrots, raisins, diced apples, nuts or anything else they have on hand that might sound good.

Ellen, Curt and their son Nathan settled in Weare in 1993, opening the four-guestroom inn six months later. A sceond son, Jacob, was born in 1997. Their 1819 farmhouse is a 20-minute drive from either Concord or Manchester, in the heart of antiquing country. Guests are welcome to bring their children, who enjoy the hens, horses and miniature donkeys residing on the 12 acres.

Other Weare-House recipes:
Hot Cocoa Mix, page 22
Low-Fat Granola, page 194

Apricot Scones

Ingredients:

3 cups flour
1 tablespoon baking powder
1 cup butter or margarine
1/4 cup sugar
3 eggs
1 teaspoon vanilla extract
2/3 cup plain yogurt

Filling:
4 ounces dried apricots
1/4 cup warm water
2 tablespoons honey

🍂 For Filling: In a food processor, place apricots, water and honey. Finely chop and mix until a thick purée consistency. Set aside.

🍂 For Dough: In a medium bowl, mix together flour and baking powder.

🍂 With an electric mixer, beat butter until creamy. Add sugar, eggs and vanilla. Beat until mixture is fluffy.

🍂 Add flour mixture to egg mixture and beat until well blended. Scrape sides of bowl.

🍂 Add yogurt and mix until well blended.

🍂 Fold apricot purée into the batter with a rubber spatula just until purée is swirled through.

🍂 Using an ice cream scooper, scoop dough onto an ungreased cookie sheet, placing the mounds about 2 inches apart.

🍂 To bake immediately, bake in a preheated oven at 350 degrees for 15 minutes or until golden brown.

🍂 To make ahead, loosely cover with plastic wrap and freeze overnight. When the individual scones are hard, remove to a freezer bag or airtight container and freeze for up to 6 weeks. When ready to bake, place frozen scones on a cookie sheet and bake in a preheated oven at 350 degrees for 25 minutes.

🍂 Cool uncovered on a wire rack. Serve warm with butter.

Makes 12 to 14 scones

from **Maine Stay Inn & Cottages**
34 Maine Street
P.O. Box 500-A
Kennebunkport, ME 04046
207-967-2117
800-950-2117

Innkeeper Carol Copeland adapted this scone recipe from several others. "The scones are very light," she said, and she appreciates the make-ahead-and-freeze option. The scones often are on the menu for breakfast, which is served in the dining room or, in the summer, on the wrap-around porch. Guests in the six guestrooms in the main house gather for breakfast, and those in the 11 cottages can choose to have a breakfast basket delivered to their door. The 1860s home has offered lodging since the 1940s. Carol and Lindsay, her husband, bought the inn in 1989 and are raising two daughters here.

🏠*Other Maine Stay Inn & Cottages recipes:*
Pumpkin Ginger Muffins, page 56
Applesauce Spice Pancakes, page 126
Christmas Prelude Gingersnaps, page 156
Mrs. Milld's Oatmeal Cookies, page 199

Buttermilk Oatmeal Muffins

Ingredients:

1 cup old-fashioned or quick-cooking rolled oats
1 cup buttermilk
1/3 cup vegetable shortening or butter, softened
1/2 cup brown sugar, packed
1 egg
1 cup flour
1 teaspoon baking powder
1/2 teaspoon baking soda
1 teaspoon salt

🖛 Mix oats and buttermilk thoroughly and let set for 1 hour.

🖛 With an electric mixer, cream shortening or butter and brown sugar. Beat in egg. Then beat in oats.

🖛 Sift together flour, baking powder, baking soda and salt. Stir into oats mixture by hand, being careful to mix only until all ingredients are moist.

🖛 Fill buttered or paper-lined muffin tins 3/4-full.

🖛 Bake in preheated oven at 400 degrees for 20 to 25 minutes. Remove pans from oven and allow to cool for a few minutes before removing muffins. Serve muffins hot.

Makes 12 muffins

from **Rooms With a View B&B**
Forbes Road
RR1, Box 215
Colebrook, NH 03576
603-237-5106
800-499-5106

Innkeeper Sonja Sheldon might make these muffins in her 3-ton soapstone stove, a Tulikivi, which heats the first floor of this home and bakes the homemade bread with which she makes French toast. Guests can have breakfast anytime they like, up to 10 a.m., since "we like to accommodate them in every way," said Sonja.

Sonja and her husband, Charles, were living in Boston when they came up for some skiing. "We fell in love with the area" and began looking for an old farmhouse to turn into a B&B. Eventually, this 3-acre lot was found, and the views in all directions hooked the Sheldons. "We see Dixville Notch to the east, where the first votes are cast in the presidential primaries, and to the south, the beginning of the White Mountains, to the west, Mt. Monadnock in Vermont just across the Connecticut River, and north is Canada."

They built a seven-guestroom B&B to capture the views from every room and the wrap-around porch. The back porch has a hot tub, and indoors, books, conversation and board games are enjoyed in front of the fireplace.

🏠*Other Rooms With a View recipes:*
Peach Cream Pie, page 186
Mimi's Favorite Cookies, page 197

Buttery Orange Pecan Scones

Ingredients:

4 cups flour
1/2 cup non-fat dry milk powder
1/3 cup sugar
2 tablespoons baking powder
1/2 cup butter
1/2 cup margarine
2 teaspoons grated orange rind
1/2 cup chopped pecans
4 eggs, beaten
1 cup milk

☛ In a large bowl, mix flour, dry milk, sugar and baking powder.

☛ Cut in butter and margarine with a pastry cutter or fork until the mixture resembles coarse crumbs.

☛ Stir in orange rind and pecans.

☛ In a separate bowl, whisk together eggs and milk.

☛ Pour egg mixture into crumbs and stir until all ingredients are moist ("batter" will be stiff).

☛ Using a tablespoon, drop dough in 24 mounds on two buttered cookie sheets. Flatten mounds slightly.

☛ Bake in a preheated oven at 350 degrees for 20 to 25 minutes, until scones are golden brown.

☛ Remove from oven and serve hot with butter, ginger preserves or other favorite preserves, such as orange marmalade.

Makes 24 scones

from **The Country Porch B&B**
281 Moran Road
Hopkinton, NH 03229
603-746-6391

Innkeeper Wendy Solomon created this recipe after receiving a package of scone mix as a gift and finding "it was so good I wanted to make it often, but to purchase the mix as often as I would like was too costly." She keeps the mix of dry ingredients in a covered container in the refrigerator and adds the butter, margarine, orange rind, nuts, eggs and milk when ready to bake. She sometimes varies the recipe by substituting lemon rind and walnuts.

Wendy has had a long career as a registered dietitian, so breakfast guests are in for a treat. Her husband, Tom, whose career has been with Lucent Technologies, enjoys farming as a hobby. Their 15 acres includes woods, meadow, lawn, barn and a swimming pool, all of which guests often enjoy. They also take advantage of the wrap-around porch on this three-guestroom inn, complete with rockers.

🏠 *Other Country Porch B&B recipes:*
This is Such Good Punch, page 29
Light and Fluffy Pancakes, page 136

Chocolate Cheesecake Muffins

Ingredients:

1 cup flour
1/2 cup sugar
2 teaspoons baking powder
1/4 cup cocoa
1/2 cup milk
1 egg
1/4 cup vegetable oil
1 teaspoon almond extract

Filling:
4 ounces (half of an 8-ounce package)
    cream cheese (not low-fat), softened
1/4 cup powdered sugar
2 drops almond extract
1 tablespoon cornstarch

✒ In a large bowl, mix together flour, sugar, baking powder and cocoa. Cover and set aside.

✒ For Filling: With an electric mixer, beat together cream cheese, powdered sugar, almond extract and cornstarch until fluffy. Set aside.

✒ In a separate bowl, whisk together milk, egg, vegetable oil and almond extract. Stir into flour mixture just until all ingredients are combined.

✒ Fill the bottoms of buttered muffin cups with about 2 tablespoons of batter (about 1/3-full).

✒ Dab a teaspoonful of filling in middle of each cup, making sure none touches the sides of the pan.

✒ Cover cream cheese filling with rest of batter. Fill the cups full, until they are level with top of tin.

✒ Bake in a preheated oven at 350 degrees for 20 minutes. "They are done when they smell so good you can't stand it any longer."

Makes 6 muffins

from **The Old Iron Inn B&B**
155 High Street
Caribou, ME 04736
207-492-IRON (4766)

Kate McCartney's breakfasts often include homemade muffins, and these are on the breakfast table if a guest is celebrating a birthday. "They also make decadent desserts — while hot out of the oven, split open and put a scoop of French vanilla ice cream in the middle, and drizzle with chocolate sauce!"

Kate and Kevin, her spouse, opened their four-guestroom B&B in 1992 after moving to Caribou, where Kevin teaches geology at the University of Maine Presque Isle. "We are proud to be a TV-free zone," Kate notes, with plenty of reading material available and "simply too much else to do" in Aroostook County, the largest county east of the Mississippi, where half of the admittedly very few residents speak French. The McCartneys enjoy sharing their home with visitors and business travelers who have come to the "far off the beaten tourist path" to explore remote northern Maine.

🏠 *Other Old Iron Inn recipes:*
Sunshine Punch, page 28
Green One-Eyed Jacks, page 112

Chocolate Mint Scones

Ingredients:

3 cups flour
1/3 cup sugar
1 tablespoon baking powder
1 cup unsalted butter
3 eggs
1/3 cup buttermilk
1/8 teaspoon pure peppermint extract
1/3 to 1/2 cup miniature mint chocolate chips

Also:

Buttermilk
Sugar

- In a large bowl, stir together flour, sugar and baking powder with a pastry blender. Cut in butter.
- In a small bowl, whisk together eggs, buttermilk and peppermint extract.
- Pour egg mixture into flour mixture, stirring until dough begins to clump.
- Stir chips into dough and gently knead about 1 minute to make a semi-stiff dough (do not over-knead).
- Roll dough out onto a floured surface to approximately 1-inch thick and cut out with a 2-1/2-inch round biscuit cutter.
- Place on a buttered cookie sheet. Brush the top of each scone with a little buttermilk and sprinkle with sugar.
- Bake in a preheated oven at 350 degrees for 20 minutes, or until scones are pale golden brown and set.

Makes 12 scones

from **The Jeweled Turret Inn**
40 Pearl Street
Belfast, ME 04915
207-338-2304
800-696-2304

Scones are a specialty of Innkeeper Cathy Heffentrager, who serves breakfast in the formal dining room of this large 1898 home, built for a prominent local attorney and now on the National Register of Historic Places. Cathy and Carl, her husband, named their inn after the grand stairway, housed in a round turret with stained and leaded glass panels and jewel-like details.

The Heffentragers have been innkeepers for more than a decade, moving from their native Anchorage, Alaska. When they were only in their 20s, they chose to become innkeepers in a small coastal town with a keen sense of history. The inn is just two blocks from the historically-intact commercial district, with a wide variety of historically-significant architectural styles.

Other Jeweled Turret Inn recipes:
German Crown Pancakes, page 132
Sourdough Gingerbread Belgian Waffles, page 143

Favorite Popovers

Ingredients:

2 eggs, at room temperature
1 cup milk, at room temperature
1 tablespoon vegetable oil
1 cup flour
1/2 teaspoon salt

🍴 Whisk eggs, milk and vegetable oil. Then whisk in flour and salt.

🍴 Divide batter among the six cups of a well-seasoned or buttered oversized popover pan (or 12 muffin cups). Bake in a preheated oven at 425 degrees for 35 minutes or until deep golden brown. "Do not open the oven while cooking!"

🍴 Remove pan and serve popovers immediately with plenty of butter and jams and jellies.

Makes 6 popovers

from **The Notchland Inn**
Route 302
Hart's Location, NH 03812
603-374-6131
800-866-6131

These popovers really "hit the spot" with Notchland Inn guests, say Innkeepers Les Schoof and Ed Butler. Breakfast is served to inn guests in the dining room overlooking the pond and gazebo. Whether guests are staying in the 12 suites and guestrooms in the main inn or in adjacent buildings constructed by Les and Ed, they may all gather for breakfast here.

The dining room was the tavern at the 18th century Mt. Crawford House, owned and operated by Able Crawford. The main inn was cut from native granite and completed in 1862, built for Samuel Bemis as a getaway "cottage" from Boston. The front parlor was designed by Gustav Stickely, a founder of the Arts & Crafts movement.

Les and Ed began their search for an inn in 1990 after stressful big-city careers (Les had been the general manager of the American Ballet Theatre and Ed was a RN and a nursing home administrator). Three years later and after looking at dozens of properties they found "an inspiring setting (which) framed a unique property with just the right amount of warmth, grace and elegance."

Today, Notchland guests come to enjoy the beauty and recreational opportunities of the surrounding White Mountains or to shop-'til-they-drop in North Conway, a 25-minute drive. The inn is well-known for its five-course dinners and many outdoor "pets," including Coco, the Bernese Mountain dog.

🏠 *Other Notchland Inn recipes:*
Notchland 'Muddled' Cider, page 24
Boiled Fruit Cake, page 154
Cranberry Bread Pudding, page 181

Gaye's Currant Scones

Ingredients:

- 2 cups flour
- 1/4 cup powdered sugar
- 1-1/2 tablespoons baking powder
- 1/4 teaspoon salt
- 1/2 cup unsalted butter, cold
- 1/2 cup currants or any dried fruit, diced (optional)
- Nutmeg to taste (optional)
- 1 cup whipping cream ("heaviest you can find")

Also:

Cinnamon-sugar mixture

- In a large bowl or with a heavy duty electric mixer, mix flour, powdered sugar, baking powder and salt.

- Cut in butter "until the pieces are no larger than the tip of your little finger."

- Stir in currants or other dried fruit and nutmeg.

- Pour in cream and mix until blended.

- Knead gently on a well-floured surface. Roll to about 3/8-inch thick and cut out with a glass or biscuit cutter.

- Place scones on a parchment-lined cookie sheet. Sprinkle tops with cinnamon and sugar.

- Bake in a preheated oven at 375 degrees for 15 to 20 minutes. "If you find that the scones are not rising properly, check your oven temperature. Too hot is better than too cool."

Makes 18 2-inch or 12 3-inch scones

from **Fairhaven Inn**
North Bath Road
Bath, ME 04530
888-443-4391
Fax 207-443-6412

This recipe came from Roland Messiner, the White House pastry chef, under whom Innkeeper Susie Reed studied. Susie and husband Dave owned Sweet Surrender pastry shop in Washington, D.C., and they refined the recipe over the years until the Washington Post declared the scones "best in Washington" in 1993. They are named after Gaye, a baker, who made about 1,000 a week.

Today, Susie and Dave need to bake only enough for the guests in Fairhaven's eight guestrooms. But they are still committed to turning out "the best" from the kitchen. They bought this operating inn in 1995 after having stayed here "about 20 times" while their son attended a nearby school. The 1790 Colonial is nestled on 16 acres overlooking the Kennebec River. Guests find comfort and quiet while being close to Mid-Coast Maine attractions.

Other Fairhaven Inn recipes:
David's Gingerbread, page 69
Vegetable Hash, page 150
Cranberry Bars, page 190

Maine Blueberry Muffins

Ingredients:
  1/2 cup margarine, softened, or vegetable oil
  1 cup sugar
  2 eggs
  1 teaspoon vanilla extract
  1/2 cup milk
  2 cups flour
  2 teaspoons baking powder
  1/2 teaspoon salt
  1/2 teaspooon cinnamon
  2 cup fresh blueberries, wild Maine ones, if possible

Also:
  Sugar

- With an electric mixer, cream margarine and sugar.
- Beat in eggs, vanilla and milk.
- In a separate bowl, sift together flour, baking powder, salt and cinnamon.
- Stir the egg mixture into the flour mixture by hand, until all ingredients are moist.
- Fold in blueberries by hand.
- Fill buttered or paper-lined muffin tins quite full. Sprinkle the top of each with a little sugar.
- Bake in a preheated oven at 375 degrees for 28 minutes or until tops are golden brown.
- Remove pans from oven, cool a few minutes before removing muffins, and serve hot with butter.

Makes 10 or 11 muffins

from **Bethel Point B&B**
RR 5 Bethel Point Road
P.O. Box 2387
Brunswick, ME 04011
207-725-1115
888-238-8262

"We thought it would be appropriate to have a breakfast menu that reflects the specialties of the state," said Innkeeper Betsy Packard, who serves breakfast in the dining room that looks out at the ocean. "Or, on a perfect summer day, we might set up a table by the water so guests can enjoy the sea breeze and morning sun as they look out at seals basking in the sun, the sea gulls circling overhead, and lobster boats busy at work in the bay."

Betsy (and her guests) are openly enamoured of the setting on Casco Bay, especially since Betsy and her spouse, Peter, spent 30 land-locked years in Kansas before "retiring" to their three-guestroom B&B in 1988. Located eight miles from the fishing community of Brunswick, the B&B is set at the water's edge, and is "so quiet you feel as though you are in another world."

Another Bethel Point recipe:
Lobster Omelette, page 115

Miracle Muffins

Ingredients:

1/2 cup golden raisins
1 cup dark raisins
2 cups boiling water
1-3/4 cups flour
1/2 cup butter, cold
1 cup unprocessed wheat bran
1/2 cup rolled oats
4 teaspoons baking powder
1 teaspoon baking soda
1 teaspoon cinnamon
3/4 teaspoon cloves
1/2 teaspoon salt
1-1/2 cups chopped walnuts
2 eggs
1 cup milk, soured with 1 tablespoon vinegar
3/4 cup molasses

Also:

Raw sesame and hulled sunflower seeds

- Plump raisins by pouring boiling water over them and letting soak 5 minutes. Then drain.
- Place flour in a food processor. Add butter and process until mixture is the texture of cornmeal.
- In a large bowl, mix bran, oats, baking powder, baking soda, cinnamon, cloves, salt and flour mixture.
- Stir in drained raisins and walnuts.
- In a separate bowl, beat together eggs, milk and molasses.
- Pour egg mixture into flour mixture and stir only until all ingredients are moist.
- Fill paper-lined muffin tins nearly full. Sprinkle tops of muffins with raw sesame and sunflower seeds.
- Bake in a preheated oven at 375 degrees for 25 to 30 minutes or until a toothpick inserted in the center comes out clean.

Makes 24 muffins

from **The Greenfield Inn B&B**
Routes 136 and 31 North
P.O. Box 400
Greenfield, NH 03047
603-547-6327

Innkeeper Barbara Mangini was given this recipe by a woman who claimed these muffins helped rid her of her doctor and her pills. They are often part of the party-atmosphere breakfast Barbara and her husband, Vic, serve to guests in the 11 guestrooms. The Manginis bought this 1817 mansion after getting lost on a house-hunting trip. They were planning to retire here from Sudbury, Mass., but instead turned this into a B&B in 1986. They cater to couples on weekend getaways and to business people mid-week.

Another Greenfield Inn recipe:
Barb's Cranberry Nut Bread, page 65

Overnight Cranberry Scones

Ingredients:

1/2 cup chopped cranberries (finely chopped in the food processor)
2 tablespoons sugar
1 teaspoon orange zest
1-1/4 cups flour
1-1/4 cups quick-cooking rolled oats
1/4 cup whole wheat flour
3 tablespoons sugar
1 tablespoon baking powder
1/8 teaspoon salt
1/4 cup plus 2 tablespoons skim milk
1/4 cup margarine, melted
1 egg, beaten

Topping:
2 teaspoons sugar
1/4 teaspoon cinnamon

- The night before, mix chopped cranberries, sugar and orange zest. Cover and refrigerate overnight.

- In the morning, in a separate bowl, mix flour, oats, whole wheat flour, sugar, baking powder and salt.

- In a separate bowl, whisk together milk, margarine and egg.

- Pour milk mixture into the flour mixture. Stir with a fork just until all ingredients are moist. (Dough will be stiff and sticky). Stir in cranberry mixture.

- Turn dough out onto a sheet of waxed paper and knead lightly 4 or 5 times. Roll dough into an 8-inch circle. (Make the scones fatter rather than skinnier, so don't go bigger than 8 inches.)

- For Topping: Mix sugar and cinnamon. Sprinkle over dough.

- With a very sharp knife, cut dough into 16 wedges. Place on a buttered cookie sheet.

- Bake in a preheated oven at 375 degrees for 10 minutes or until golden brown. Serve hot with butter.

Makes 16 scones

from **The Buttonwood Inn**
Mt. Surprise Road
P.O. Box 1817
North Conway, NH 03860
603-356-2625
800-258-2625

Innkeeper Peter Needham is in the kitchen making this recipe at least once a week. The scones are part of a full breakfast served to guests in the formal dining room, the same room where a four-course candlelight dinner is available only to guests in January and February. Guests enjoy the 10- guestroom inn for a winter ski getaway, cross-country or downhill, and some of the ski trails leave from the back of the secluded, 17-acre property. In the summer, guests enjoy the award-winning perennial gardens, outdoor pool, or hiking those ski trails. The 1820 inn has been operating since 1983. Peter and Claudia, his wife, began innkeeping in 1993. Their inn is especially popular with families and groups.

Other Buttonwood Inn recipes:
Chocolate Chip Sour Cream Coffeecake, page 34
Peanut Crunch Cookies, page 201

Pumpkin Ginger Muffins

Ingredients:

6 cups flour, sifted
7 teaspoons baking powder
2 teaspoons baking soda
1 teaspoon salt
3 teaspoons ginger
2 teaspoons cinnamon
1/2 teaspoon cloves
1-1/2 cups margarine
1-1/3 cups sugar
1-1/3 cups dark brown sugar, firmly packed
4 eggs
2 cups plus 2 tablespoons canned solid pack pumpkin
2 cups milk
2 cups currants

Topping:
8 teaspoons sugar
1 teaspoon cinnamon

☛ Sift together flour, baking powder, baking soda, salt, ginger, cinnamon and cloves.

☛ With an electric mixer, beat margarine, sugar and brown sugar until fluffy. Beat in eggs and pumpkin.

☛ Add flour mixture alternately with milk to pumpkin mixture, blending after each addition, beginning and ending with flour mixture. Fold in currants by hand.

☛ Line muffin pans with paper liners. Fill tins 3/4 full with batter.

☛ For Topping: Stir together sugar and cinnamon. Sprinkle over tops of muffins.

☛ At this point, you can bake muffins in a preheated oven at 350 degrees for 20 to 30 minutes, or until a toothpick inserted in the center comes out clean. Or you can freeze muffins in the tins, uncovered, until solid. Remove frozen individual muffins from pans with their liners. Store in an airtight container in the freezer until ready to bake. To bake frozen muffins, return muffins and their liners to tins. Bake in a preheated oven at 350 degrees for 30 minutes or until a toothpick inserted in the center comes out clean.

Makes 48 muffins

from **Maine Stay Inn & Cottages**
34 Maine Street
P.O. Box 500-A
Kennebunkport, ME 04046
207-967-2117
800-950-2117

Innkeeper Carol Copeland loves this recipe because she can make four dozen at once, freeze them, then take out however many she needs and bake them fresh. "These muffins are very popular with our guests in the fall," she said. Kennebunkport offers four seasons of activities, and Carol and her husband, Lindsay, try to help guests explore the area. A five-mile biking/hiking path goes right by the Maine Stay Inn, which is located in the town's historic district.

🏠Other Maine Stay Inn & Cottages recipes:
Apricot Scones, page 46
Applesauce Spice Pancakes, page 126
Christmas Prelude Gingersnaps, page 156
Mrs. Milld's Oatmeal Cookies, page 199

Refrigerated Gingerbread Muffins

Ingredients:

1 cup solid vegetable shortening
1 cup sugar
1 cup dark molasses
4 eggs
1 cup buttermilk
4 cups flour
2 teaspoons baking soda
2 teaspoons ginger
1/2 teaspoon allspice
1/2 teaspoon cloves
1/2 teaspoon cinnamon
1 cup chopped walnuts
1 cup raisins

- With an electric mixer, cream shortening and sugar until light and fluffy.

- Stir in molasses. Beat in eggs, one at a time. Then beat in buttermilk.

- In another separate bowl, sift together flour, baking soda, ginger, allspice, cloves and cinnamon. Add to creamed mixture.

- Stir in walnuts and raisins.

- At this point, batter can be refrigerated in a covered container for a few weeks.

- When ready to bake, pour batter into buttered or paper-lined muffin tins 3/4-full.

- Bake in a preheated oven at 350 degrees for 20 to 25 minutes or until a toothpick inserted in the center comes out clean.

Makes about 36 muffins (if you make whole batch of batter)

from **Zahn's Alpine Guesthouse**
Rt. 13 at the Milford Town Line
P.O. Box 75
Milford, NH 03055
603-673-2334
Fax 603-673-8415

Manager Pat Bernston appreciates having this muffin batter in the refrigerator so she can make fresh muffins for however many guests are staying, without starting the muffin batter from scratch each day.

Owners Bud and Anne Zahn (no relation to the author), in their 30 years of importing and leading biking and skiing groups, spent a lot of time in Austria and Northern Italy. They preferred to stay in small, out-of-the-way lodging establishments, where they really got to know their hosts and other guests. In 1991, they opened this accurate replica of an Austrian pension. A hand-built tile oven is located in the Stube (breakfast room), where guests in the eight guestrooms may gather at any time during the day.

Scones for Aspiring Anglophiles

Ingredients:

2 cups flour
1/4 cup sugar
1 tablespoon baking powder
1/2 teaspoon salt
5 tablespoons butter, chilled and cut into pieces
1/2 cup currants or dried cranberries, optional
1 teaspoon grated orange peel or 1/2 teaspoon orange extract, optional
1 egg
1 egg, separated
1/3 cup milk
1/3 cup low-fat yogurt, plain or vanilla

- In a large bowl, mix flour, sugar, baking powder and salt.
- With a pastry cutter or fork, cut in butter until consistency of coarse cornmeal.
- Add optional currant or cranberries and orange peel (or, if using extract, add it with milk). Mix well.
- In a separate bowl, beat together egg, egg yolk, milk and yogurt.
- Stir egg mixture into flour mixture rapidly with a fork until dough pulls away from bowl.
- Turn dough out onto a lightly-floured board and knead gently until smooth.
- Pat dough out to 1-inch thickness and cut into 3-inch rounds using a glass or cookie cutter.
- Place rounds onto an ungreased baking sheet. Brush tops with beaten remaining egg white.
- Sprinkle with sugar and bake in a preheated oven at 400 degrees for 18 to 20 minutes. Serve scones warm or room temperature with butter and honey or jam.

Makes 10 scones

from **The Bagley House**
1290 Royalsborough Road
Durham, ME 04222
207-865-6566
800-765-1772

Innkeeper Susan Backhouse makes scones the authentic way, as she she did in her native Great Britain. She has many easy variations of this recipe and encourages others to experiment with fruits and spices or cheese.

Susan and Suzanne O'Connor, "the two Sues," bought this 1772 Greek Revival/Colonial home in 1993 as a five-guestroom inn. The B&B is located on six quiet country acres, complete with blueberry bushes, just 10 minutes from the outlets and the flagship L.L. Bean store in downtown Freeport. Decorated in antiques, this popular inn has the original pine plank floors and handmade quilts and comforters. Guests often chat with Sue & Sue as they make breakfast in the large kitchen with its fireplace and hand-hewn beams.

Another Bagley House recipe:
Swiss Apple Müesli, page 204

Sweet Corn Muffins

Ingredients:

3/4 cup yellow cornmeal
1 cup flour
3 tablespoons brown sugar, packed
1 tablespoon baking powder
1 egg, slightly beaten
1 cup sour cream
1/3 cup milk
2 tablespoons butter or margarine, melted
1/4 cup finely chopped scallions, optional

- In a large bowl, stir together cornmeal, flour, brown sugar and baking powder.
- In a separate bowl, whisk together egg, sour cream, milk, butter and optional scallions. Mix well.
- Pour egg mixture into cornmeal mixture and stir until just blended. Batter will be thick.
- Fill buttered or paper-lined muffin cups 3/4-full.
- Bake in a preheated oven at 400 degrees for 20 minutes, or until golden brown.
- Remove pans from oven and let sit for a few minutes before removing muffins. Serve hot with butter and honey.

Tester's Comments: These are wonderful with whipped honey butter. Consider adding chopped jalapenos or roasted red peppers for dinner muffins.

Makes 12 muffins

from **Lincoln House Country Inn**
Routes 1 and 86
RR 1, Box 136A
Dennysville, ME 04628
207-726-3953

These muffins might be served with a sausage and egg casserole and home-fried potatoes, said Innkeeper Mary Carol Haggerty. Breakfast is served in the dining room of this 1787 home, built by Judge Theodore Lincoln.

As the first house in Dennysville, the home is listed on the National Register of Historic Places. John James Audubon stayed here in 1832 as a guest of the Lincoln family, and he was so charmed that he named the Lincoln sparrow in their honor. The yellow Colonial inn is situated above the Dennys River on wooded acreage, from which guests can ride bikes or hike.

Mary Carol and Jerry Haggerty began restoration work in 1976. Today they offer six guestrooms, open June through September.

Breads

Almond Poppyseed Bread

Ingredients:

3 cups flour
1-1/2 teaspoons salt
1-1/2 teaspoons baking powder
3 eggs
2-1/4 cups sugar
1-1/2 cups milk
1-1/8 cups vegetable oil
1-1/2 tablespoons poppyseeds
1-1/2 teaspoons almond extract
1-1/2 teaspoons vanilla extract
1-1/2 teaspoons butter flavoring

Glaze:
3/4 cup powdered sugar
1/4 cup orange juice
1/2 teaspoon almond extract
1/2 teaspoon vanilla extract
1/2 teaspoon butter flavoring

- In a large bowl, mix flour, salt and baking powder.

- With an electric mixer, beat together eggs, sugar, milk, oil, poppyseeds, almond and vanilla extracts and butter flavoring.

- Mix in the flour. Then beat on medium or medium-high speed for 2 minutes.

- Pour batter into two buttered 9 x 5-inch bread loaf pans. Bake in a preheated oven at 350 degrees for about 60 minutes or until a toothpick inserted in the center comes out clean.

- Remove pans from oven and cool for no longer than 5 minutes while preparing Glaze: In a small bowl, mix powdered sugar, orange juice, almond and vanilla extracts and butter flavoring until smooth. Pour over bread that's still hot and in the pans.

- Cool bread another 15 minutes before turning bread out onto a wire rack to finish cooling. Then slice and serve.

Makes 2 loaves

from **The Maple Leaf Inn**
Route 12
P.O. Box 273
Barnard, VT 05031
802-234-5342
800-51-MAPLE

"This is a very moist, luscious bread that gets rave reviews from our guests," said Janet Robison. "My husband, Gary, and I like to serve it as a first course for breakfast or as an afternoon treat with a cup of freshly brewed coffee."

Gary and Janet opened their inn on their wedding anniversary in 1994. Like a solid marriage, the inn was built from the ground up, based on their plans. Gary, a talented engineer, designed the inn "to make it look and feel like a turn-of-the-century Victorian farmhouse, incorporating such features as gables, dormers, gingerbread trim, a wrap-around porch with gazebo, tall windows and soaring chimneys." The inn has seven guestrooms and seven fireplaces, each with an antique mantel. Afternoon refreshments are served in the parlor each day.

Another Maple Leaf Inn recipe:
Apple Fritters, page 64

Anadama Bread

Ingredients:

3-1/2 cups water
3/4 cup molasses
1/2 cup margarine
1 cup yellow cornmeal
2 packages (2 tablespoons) active dry yeast
1 tablespoon salt
10 cups (more or less) flour

🥄 In a medium saucepan, heat water, molasses and margarine to boiling. Whisk in cornmeal and cook for 2 minutes, stirring constantly. Set aside for 45 minutes.

🥄 Meanwhile, in a large bowl, stir together yeast, salt and 2 cups of the flour.

🥄 Beat cooled cornmeal mixture into flour mixture and continue beating for 5 minutes.

🥄 Beat in 1-1/2 cups of the flour and beat for another 5 minutes.

🥄 Stir in 5 cups of the flour to form a soft dough. Turn out on a floured board and knead for 5 to 10 minutes, adding more flour, as needed, to keep dough from being too sticky.

🥄 Shape dough into a ball. Place in a buttered bowl and cover with a damp cloth. Set in a warm place and let rise for 90 minutes. Punch dough down and let rest 15 minutes.

🥄 Divide dough in half and roll out to fit in two buttered 9 x 5-inch bread pans. Place in pans and let rise in a warm place for 45 minutes.

🥄 Bake in a preheated oven at 350 degrees for 30 to 35 minutes. Remove from oven and invert pans to remove bread, then place loaves on a wire rack to cool.

Makes 2 loaves

from **Brass Lantern Inn**
717 Maple Street
Stowe, VT 05672
802-252-2229
800-729-2980

This dark bread is a favorite of guests and is always requested for a local fund-raiser donation, said Innkeeper Andy Aldrich. Popular regionally, the name is short for "Anna, damn her, makes good bread," Andy said.

Homemade bread is one of the hallmarks of the service and attention to detail found at this inn. A builder by trade, Andy has enjoyed cooking as a lifelong hobby. When he restored the circa 1800 farmhouse-style inn and opened nine guestrooms in 1988, cooking became an essential part of the business and has earned him several awards. His breakfasts fortify guests for a day on the famous ski slopes of Stowe, snowshoeing, hiking Mt. Mansfield, biking or enjoying other pursuits in and around Stowe. Guests return to enjoy homebaked goodies by the fireplace or on the patio, and to sink into a whirlpool tub. As a plus, most guestrooms have views of Mt. Mansfield.

🏠 *Another Brass Lantern Inn recipe:*
Rhubarb Bread, page 74

Apple Fritters

Ingredients:

  1 cup flour
  1-1/2 teaspoons baking powder
  1/2 teaspoon salt
  2 tablespoons sugar
  1/4 teaspoon cinnamon
  1/2 cup milk
  1-1/2 cups unpeeled apples, cored and diced

Also:

  Vegetable oil
  Vermont maple syrup

- In a large bowl, sift together flour, baking powder, salt, sugar and cinnamon.
- Pour the milk into the flour mixture and stir until the batter is smooth.
- Stir in the diced apples.
- Heat oil in a heavy skillet, electric frying pan or electric deep fryer to 375 degrees.
- Drop batter by tablespoons into hot oil. Turn and fry until fritters are golden brown on both sides.
- Remove fritters and drain on paper towels. Serve hot with warmed maple syrup.

Makes about 16 fritters

from **The Maple Leaf Inn**
Route 12
P.O. Box 273
Barnard, VT 05031
802-234-5342
800-51-MAPLE

"We serve these aromatic apple fritters with warm Vermont maple syrup poured from small crystal pitchers as a first course at our candlelit breakfast," said Innkeeper Janet Robison. Tables for two are set by the dining room fireplace.

Gary and Janet met and married overseas, and when they returned to engineering and teaching jobs, respectively, they traveled throughout the U.S. on vacations, looking for the perfect place to settle someday. After staying in many inns, they decided to try a career as innkeepers, then began a long search for the perfect inn. "We couldn't find one that spoke to our hearts," Janet said, so they designed their own on 16 acres of maple and birch in the village of Barnard, 10 miles north of Woodstock. Their seven guestroom-inn, a faithful reproduction of a three-story Victorian farmhouse tucked under the trees, opened in 1984.

Guests fill their days with antiquing, visiting art galleries, or touring historic sites. The Green Mountains and country lanes invite hiking, bicycling, fishing, skiing, golfing, tennis and horseback riding. Quechee Gorge, the Appalachian Trail and Long Trail are nearby, as are excellent restaurants in Woodstock.

Another Maple Leaf Inn recipe:
Almond Poppyseed Bread, page 62

Barb's Cranberry Nut Bread

Ingredients:

2 cups flour
1 cup sugar
1-1/2 teaspoons baking powder
1 teaspoon salt
1/2 teaspoon baking soda
1/4 cup solid vegetable shortening
1/4 cup fresh-squeezed orange juice
1 egg, well beaten
1 teaspoon grated orange peel
1 cup fresh cranberries, washed and dried
1/2 cup chopped walnuts or pecans

Into a large bowl, sift together flour, sugar, baking powder, salt and baking soda.

With a pastry cutter, cut in shortening.

In a separate bowl, whisk together orange juice, egg and orange peel. Stir mixture into dry ingredients only until all ingredients are moist.

Fold in cranberries and nuts.

Turn batter into a buttered and floured 9 x 5-inch loaf pan.

Bake in a preheated oven at 350 degrees for about 1 hour, or until knife inserted in center comes out clean.

Cool pan on wire rack before removing bread from pan.

Wrap in plastic wrap and store overnight "to develop flavors" before slicing.

Makes 1 loaf

from **The Greenfield Inn B&B**
Routes 136 and 31 North
P.O. Box 400
Greenfield, NH 03047
603-547-6327

Sometimes Innkeeper Barbara Mangini will divide this batter into four mini-loaf pans, and then the baking time is 35 minutes.

Barbara is the cook (often rising at 4:30 a.m. to start breakfast for guests in the 11 guestrooms) and her husband, Vic, is the marketing man behind this inn in a very small town. Barbara had the idea to turn the vacant 1817 mansion into a B&B, and Vic liked the low price and the marketing challenge it posed. Barbara redecorated and furnished the rooms and the inn opened in 1986. They have since counted Bob Hope among their guests.

Situated on three acres in the town center, the inn is a short drive from restaurants in Peterborough or from skiing at Crotched or Temple Mountains.

*Another Greenfield Inn recipe:
Miracle Muffins, page 54*

Barry's Beer Bread

Ingredients:

3 cups flour
1 cup sugar
1 tablespoon baking powder
1 12-ounce bottle of beer, "less 1 sip for the cook," Budweiser® preferred, at room temperature

- In a large bowl, stir together flour, sugar and baking powder.
- Stir in warm beer. Batter will be thin.
- Pour batter into a buttered 9 x 5-inch loaf pan.
- Bake in a preheated oven at 350 degrees for 1 hour.
- Cool pan on wire rack before removing bread from pan. Serve warm.

Makes 1 loaf

from **Ellis River House**
Route 16
P.O. Box 656
Jackson, NH 03846
603-383-9339
800-233-8309

This is one of the homemade breads for which Innkeeper Barry Lubao's breakfasts are famous, and this one is easier than most! Served in the farmhouse dining room, breakfast is offered to guests and includes pancakes, French toast or waffles, omelette of the day, bacon and eggs, breads and fruit.

Guests also have the option of enjoying a romantic dinner by candlelight, and a pub with billiards and darts also is open to guests only. After a day on the famed slopes or cross country trails of the area, hiking or visiting Jackson and North Conway attractions, guests often want to curl up at the inn for an evening of cider, cookies and conversation by the fire.

Barry and Barbara, his spouse, bought this farmhouse in 1985. It had been in the Andrew Harriman family for three generations, and then was owned by a Manhattan stockbroker when the Lubao family bought it. Built in 1893, it is perched on the banks of the Ellis River.

Barry spent 13 years with Sheraton and Barbara had a sales background, so they felt they'd be successful as innkeepers, starting with six guestrooms. In 1993, Barbara and Barry added 14 rooms and an outdoor swimming pool. Cross-country ski trails leave from the property, and the inn's 380-feet of river frontage offer trout fishing and river swimming.

The Lubaos love the White Mountains and suggest guests spend at least three days to explore. They provide directions to hiking, mountain biking, rock and ice climbing, skiing, snowmobiling, theme parks and outlet stores. Jackson's often-photographed covered bridge is a short walk from the inn.

Buttermilk Whole Wheat Bread

Ingredients:

2 cups buttermilk or sour milk
2 tablespoons butter, melted
3 cups whole wheat flour
1 cup brown sugar, lightly packed
1 teaspoon baking powder
1 teaspoon baking soda
1 teaspoon salt

Herb Butter Spread:
1/2 cup unsalted butter
2 tablespoons fresh herbs, chopped
1 tablespoon orange or lemon zest

- In a small bowl, whisk together milk and butter.
- In a large bowl, stir together flour, brown sugar, baking powder, baking soda and salt.
- Make a "well" in the center of the flour mixture and pour in milk mixture. Stir until smooth.
- Generously grease 9 x 5-inch loaf pan. Spread batter evenly in pan.
- Bake on center rack of an oven preheated to 350 degrees for 1 hour or until bread is golden brown (remove loaf from pan and tap it on the side to make sure it sounds hollow, which it does when done).
- For Herb Butter Spread: With an electric mixer, beat the butter, herbs and zest until smooth.
- Serve bread warm with Herb Butter Spread.

Makes 1 loaf

from **Watch Hill B&B**
Old Meredith Road
P.O. Box 1605
Center Harbor, NH 03226
603-253-4334

This is an easy, hearty, non-yeast bread that Innkeeper Barbara Lauterbach makes often. The herb spread makes the bread good for any meal. Breakfast guests here are promised a meal to remember, cooked and served by Barbara, a one-woman dynamo who has been running her own B&B business since 1989. Barbara has a long list of culinary credits, including acting as an occasional instructor at the New England Culinary Institute in Montpelier. She also serves as a spokesperson for the King Arthur Flour Co., the Norwich, Vermont, institution that produces flour about which bread makers across the country rave. She likes to showcase New Hampshire products at the breakfast table, so locally-made sausage and brown eggs might be featured.

Barbara opened this 1772 home, one of the oldest in Center Harbor, as a four-guestroom B&B. It is named after the Watch Hill Kennel in Cincinnati, Ohio, from which her champion bull mastiffs came. She no longer raises canines, but there are a couple of felines who share the B&B. The B&B is a short walk from the Lake Winnipesaukee beach, boat rides, shops and restaurants.

🏠 *Other Watch Hill B&B recipes:*
Spiced Tomato Jam, page 92
Mulled Cider Applesauce, page 102
Savory Christmas Bread, page 163
Firehouse Brownies, page 191

Cider Molasses Doughnuts

Ingredients:

3 eggs
1 cup sugar
1/4 cup molasses
3/4 cup apple cider
4 cups flour
2 teaspoons baking powder
2 teaspoons baking soda
1/4 teaspoon cinnamon
1/2 teaspoon nutmeg
1/2 teaspoon salt
1-1/2 teaspoons ginger
2 quarts vegetable oil

Also:

Powdered sugar

- In a large bowl beat eggs, sugar and molasses well. Stir in cider.
- In a separate bowl, sift together flour, baking powder, baking soda, cinnamon, nutmeg, salt and ginger. Pour egg mixture into flour mixture and stir.
- Roll dough out on a floured board to 1/3-inch thick and cut out with a floured doughnut cutter.
- In a heavy saucepan or electric fry pan, heat oil to 350 to 375 degrees.
- Carefully place doughnuts in oil and fry until bottom is golden brown. Flip and brown other side.
- Remove doughnuts and drain on paper towels.
- Allow doughnuts to cool somewhat and dust generously with powdered sugar.

Tester's Comments: I never even considered making homemade donuts, thinking they're too difficult -- these are not! I needed only about 1/2 quart oil in the non-stick electric frying pan. Instead of using powdered sugar, we preferred to roll hot donuts in a pan with a cinnamon-sugar-nutmeg mixture. Eat them hot!

Makes about 24 doughnuts (without re-rolling dough scraps)

from **The Bernerhof Inn**
Route 302
P.O. Box 240
Glen, NH 03838
603-383-9132
800-548-8007

Chef Mark Prince might serve these doughnuts, hot from the fryer, along with a complete breakfast to fortify guests before hitting the ski slopes, hiking trails or outlet shops. The Bernerhof is a turreted-and-dormered nine-guestroom inn originally built in the late 1800s to house travelers on their way north through Crawford Notch. Today its fine dining and A Taste of the Mountains cooking school are nationally acclaimed. Attitash skiing is just two minutes away.

Other Bernerhof recipes:
Summer Cantaloupe Cooler, page 27
Eggs Bernerhof, page 109

David's Gingerbread

1/2 teaspoon salt
2 teaspoons baking soda
2 teaspoons cinnamon
2 teaspoons ginger
2 teaspoons cloves
1 cup buttermilk

- By hand or with an electric mixer, beat together sugar, oil and molasses.
- Beat in eggs and mix until smooth.
- In a separate bowl, combine flour, salt, baking soda, cinnamon, ginger and cloves. Mix well.
- Add the flour mixture to the molasses mixture, alternating with the buttermilk. Beat until smooth.
- Spray two 9-inch loaf pans with non-stick cooking spray and divide batter between the two pans.
- Bake in a preheated oven at 325 degrees for 55 minutes or until a toothpick inserted in the center comes out clean. "Avoid opening the oven door, which may cause the center to fall."

Makes 2 loaves

from **Fairhaven Inn**
North Bath Road
Bath, ME 04530
888-443-4391
Fax 207-443-6412

Innkeeper David Reed sometimes adds raisins or dried cranberries and serves this when his men's group meets. Co-innkeeper/spouse Susie Reed likes to serve it in the summertime as an accompaniment to chilled fruit soups.

David and Susie know their sweet breads. They are the former owners of Sweet Surrender pastry shop in Washington, D.C. While successful, they were "burned-out workaholics" who needed a major change in their lives. They bought this eight-guestroom inn from Sallie and George Pollard in 1995. The Pollards had hosted them many times while the Reeds' son, Ken, attended school nearby, and Susie loved the inn and its "casual, comforting and inviting" atmosphere. Located in Mid-Coast Maine on 16 acres of meadows, lawns and woods, the Reeds now offer guests the same haven they found here.

🏠 *Other Fairhaven Inn recipes:*
Gaye's Currant Scones, page 52
Vegetable Hash, page 150
Cranberry Bars, page 190

Green Mountain Lemon Bread

Ingredients:

1-1/2 cups flour
1 cup sugar
1 teaspoon baking powder
1/2 teaspoon salt
Grated peel of 1 lemon (about 1 tablespoon)
2 eggs
1/2 cup milk
1/2 cup vegetable oil

Glaze:
1/3 cup sugar
Juice of 1 lemon (2 to 3 tablespoons)

- In a large bowl, stir together flour, sugar, baking powder, salt and lemon peel.
- In a separate bowl, whisk together eggs, milk and oil.
- Pour egg mixture into flour mixture and stir until thoroughly combined.
- Pour batter into a 9 x 5-inch buttered loaf pan.
- Bake in a preheated oven at 325 degrees for approximately 1 hour, or until toothpick inserted in center comes out clean.
- Remove pan from oven. Cool bread in pan for 10 minutes.
- Using a chop stick or ice pick, poke 20 holes all over the top of loaf.
- For Glaze: In a microwave-proof bowl, stir together sugar and lemon juice. Microwave on "high" for 30 seconds, stir, and heat again for a few seconds, if necessary, to make glaze hot.
- Drizzle hot lemon glaze over loaf. Cool completely and slice.

Tester's Comments: This is a very versatile recipe, turning out delicious no matter what. Buttermilk or 2/3 cup yogurt can substitute for the milk. Try adding 1/2 teaspoon lemon extract and 1 to 2 teaspoons poppyseeds.

Makes 1 loaf

from **Grünberg Haus B&B**
RR 2, Box 1595
Route 100 South
Waterbury, VT 05676
802-244-7726
800-800-7760

"Our cake-like bread is a favorite with guests, and they love to feed leftovers to our chickens!" notes Innkeeper Chris Sellers. The flock of fancy chickens, which provides eggs for the inn's entrées, also allows guests to help collect eggs. Co-innkeeper Mark Frohman tended chickens growing up in central Wisconsin, but it wasn't until 1989, when he and Chris bought the Grünberg Haus, that he was able to keep them again. The Tyrolean chalet had fallen into disrepair, and Chris and Mark began the long process of renovation and restoration. Today they have 10 guestrooms in the main inn plus two cottages and a carriage house, all tucked into the wooded hillside near Waterbury.

🏠 *Other Grünberg Haus recipes:*
Glazed Orange Slices, page 99
Lemon Ricotta Pancakes, page 135
Vermont Cheddar Pie, page 151

Miss Fay's Brown Bread

Ingredients:

  1-1/2 cups flour
  1-1/2 cups whole wheat flour
  1 teaspoon baking soda
  1 tablespoon brown sugar
  1 teaspoon salt
  1/2 cup golden raisins
  1/2 cup dark raisins

Also:

  Buttermilk

🥄 In a large mixing bowl, stir together flour, whole wheat flour, baking soda, brown sugar, salt and raisins by hand.

🥄 Add enough buttermilk to moisten, approximately 1/2 cup.

🥄 Place dough in a buttered 9 x 5-inch loaf pan.

🥄 Bake in a preheated oven at 350 degrees for 45 minutes, or until dark brown.

Makes 1 loaf

from **Ardmore Inn**
23 Pleasant Street
Woodstock, VT 05091
802-457-3887
Fax 802-457-9006

Two of the earliest guests at the Ardmore were the Fay sisters from Ireland. Kathleen Fay, a noted Irish baker, entrusted Innkeeper Giorgio Ortiz with this family recipe. Afterall, homemade breads such as this are one of the reasons that guests return and that Giorgio has earned a reputation for his cooking. Guests gather in the "great hall" dining room for a formal breakfast.

Giorgio and Bill Gallagher, a native Vermonter who owns the inn, opened the B&B in October 1994. Located in Woodstock's historic district within walking distance to the shops, restaurants and other attractions makes the inn convenient for travelers who come to relax and enjoy the Currier-and-Ives-like village, often called one of the 10 prettiest towns in the USA.

The inn was built in 1850 as a private home. Many of the original architectural details, such as the carved plaster ceiling medallions and ornate woodwork, remain. The bathrooms were built with Vermont marble.

Guests can enjoy fine dining locally, as well as walking tours, golf, tennis, fishing, or sleigh rides. Killington skiing is just 15 miles away, and Pico, Ascutney, Okemo and Suicide Six are nearby, as well.

🏠*Another Ardmore Inn recipe:*
Balsamic Maple Sauce, page 79

Mother's Easy Banana Bread

Ingredients:

1/4 cup melted butter or vegetable oil
1 egg
3 ripe bananas, mashed
2 cups flour
1 cup sugar
1 teaspoon baking soda
1/4 teaspoon salt
Chopped nuts, optional

- In a large bowl, whisk together butter or oil, egg and mashed bananas.

- Stir in flour, sugar, baking soda, salt and optional nuts.

- Spray a 9 x 5-inch bread loaf pan with non-stick cooking spray and pour in batter.

- Bake in a preheated oven at 350 degrees for about 45 minutes or until a toothpick or knife inserted in the middle comes out clean.

- Remove pan from oven, let cool for 10 minutes before inverting to remove bread. Serve warm, cold or toasted. Wrap and refrigerate leftovers.

Tester's Comments: It is easy and good, too, even using oil instead of butter.

Makes 1 loaf

from **Old Mill River Place**
Route 3, Box 301D
Georgia Shore Road
St. Albans, VT 05478
802-524-7211
Fax 802-524-7211

This is Anna Neville's mother's recipe, and her mother used to prepare it for guests in this 1799 home, where Anna grew up. Anna's family had opened it as a summer tourist retreat in the 1930s. In 1993, Anna and her daughter, Jennifer Bright, opened the home as the Old Mill River Place B&B.

Built as a wedding present for Ethan Allen's niece, only four families have owned the Federal-style home. This is the place to come if you are traveling with children, who will enjoy exploring the nooks and crannies, checking out the brook in back, or taking a hike with Anna down the road and through the woods to see the waterfall on the Mill River.

Three guestrooms have been opened in the large home, and breakfast is cooked on the green Aga cooker, the Swedish woodburning stove that heats much of the house and is the subject of much breakfast table conversation. Both Anna and Jennifer have traveled widely and guests from overseas will feel welcome here. Anna can direct guests to the best Lake Champlain beaches, St. Alban's restaurants, hiking, biking and berry picking, or to the Amtrak station in St. Albans, 10 minutes away. The B&B is a 30-minute drive from Burlington.

Oats 'n Wheat Bread

Ingredients:

1-3/4 cups water
1/2 cup light corn syrup
1/2 cup margarine
2-1/2 cups flour, plus extra to knead in
1 cup rolled oats
2 teaspoons salt
2 tablespoons (2 packages) active dry yeast
2 eggs
2 cups whole wheat flour
1 cup rye flour

Also:

Vegetable shortening

- Place water, corn syrup and margarine in a microwave-safe bowl and heat on high for 3 minutes.

- With a heavy-duty electric mixer using dough hooks, mix 1-1/2 cups of flour, oats, salt and yeast.

- Add warm liquids and eggs. Beat for three minutes.

- Add whole wheat flour and rye flour. Continue beating.

- Gradually add remaining 1 cup white flour and continue adding flour, kneading by hand on a floured board, until dough is not sticky.

- Round dough into a ball. Place in an oiled bowl and turn dough over so the oiled side is on top.

- Cover bowl with plastic wrap. Set in a warm place and let rise until it doubles in size (about 1 hour).

- Punch down dough and remove from bowl.

- Divide the dough into thirds and form three loaves. Place each in a buttered 9 x 5-inch loaf pan.

- Butter top of each loaf with vegetable shortening. Cover with plastic wrap and let rise until loaves reach top of pan.

- Remove plastic wrap and place in cold oven. Turn oven to 375 degrees and bake for 30 minutes.

- Immediately after baking, remove from pans and place on a rack to cool. Butter tops of loaves.

Makes 3 loaves

from **Hill Farm Inn**
RR 2, Box 2015
Arlington, VT 05250
802-375-2269
800-882-2545

Innkeeper Joanne Hardy, who grew up baking bread on a farm in Oregon, still enjoys the process and often makes homemade bread at the inn. In 1983, she and her husband, George, bought this post-and-beam farmhouse, which had been operating as Hill's Farm Inn since 1905. Today they have seven guestrooms in the main inn and serve breakfast and dinner to guests.

⌂ Other Hill Farm Inn recipes:
Strawberry Rhubarb Jam, page 94
Buttermilk Blueberry Pancakes, page 129

Rhubarb Bread

Ingredients:

1-1/2 cups brown sugar, packed
3/4 cup vegetable oil
1 egg or equivalent egg substitute
1 teaspoon vanilla extract
1 cup buttermilk or sour milk
2-1/2 cups flour
1 teaspoon salt
1 teaspoon baking soda
1 teaspoon cinnamon
2-1/2 cups fresh or frozen "dry pack" chopped rhubarb
1/2 cup walnuts or pecans, optional

Glaze:
1/2 cup sugar
1 tablespoon butter, melted

- In a large bowl, whisk together brown sugar, oil and egg or egg substitute, vanilla and milk.
- Stir in flour, salt, baking soda and cinnamon.
- Fold in rhubarb and optional nuts.
- Divide batter between two buttered 9 x 5-inch loaf pans.
- For Glaze: Stir together sugar and melted butter. Spread half on the top of each loaf.
- Bake in a preheated oven at 325 degrees for 60 minutes. Remove from oven and cool before inverting pans to remove bread.

Makes 2 loaves

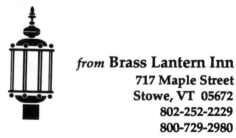

from **Brass Lantern Inn**
717 Maple Street
Stowe, VT 05672
802-252-2229
800-729-2980

Innkeeper Andy Aldrich serves this moist bread as a coffeecake, but notes it could accompany any meal. His guests are treated to breakfast according to their schedule, and it may include fruit-topped waffles or an apple crepe, this or other homemade bread and other dishes featuring Vermont products.

Andy, who grew up on a Vermont dairy farm and was a custom home builder by profession, renovated this 1800s farmhouse himself. He added nine unique guestrooms, put in fireplaces and whirlpool tubs, and decorated with quilts, antiques, stenciled walls and exposed-beam ceilings. The brick farmhouse has views of Mt. Mansfield which guests can enjoy from their guestroom, the dining room or the patio. Andy and his then-teenaged son, Dustin, opened the inn in 1988, and a number of dining and travel awards have followed. Located on Stowe's main street, the inn is a short distance from acclaimed restaurants and skiing, the toll road up Mt. Mansfield, an outstanding biking and hiking path, the Appalachian and Long Trails, and the historic village center.

Another Brass Lantern Inn recipe:
Anadama Bread, page 63

Zucchini Bread

Ingredients:

- 3 cups flour
- 1-1/2 cups sugar
- 4-1/2 teaspoons baking powder
- 1 teaspoon salt
- 1/2 teaspoon nutmeg
- 1-1/2 cups grated zucchini (or chop it in a food processor)
- 1-1/2 cups chopped walnuts
- 1/2 cup applesauce
- 1/2 cup vegetable oil
- 4 eggs, slightly beaten
- 2 teaspoons lemon juice

- In a large bowl, mix together flour, sugar, baking powder, salt and nutmeg.
- Stir in zucchini and walnuts.
- In a separate bowl, whisk together applesauce, oil, eggs and lemon juice.
- Pour egg mixture into flour mixture, stirring just until all ingredients are moist.
- Divide batter between two buttered and floured 9 x 5-inch loaf pans.
- Bake in a preheated oven at 350 degrees for 60 minutes or until a toothpick inserted in the middle comes out clean.
- Remove pans from oven and cool for 10 minutes before inverting to remove bread. Cool bread completely, wrap tightly in plastic wrap and store overnight before slicing.

Makes 2 loaves

from **The Tamworth Inn**
Main Street
Tamworth, NH 03886
603-323-7721
800-642-7352

"I know everyone has a recipe for Zucchini Bread, but this is absolutely the best one I have ever tasted," said Innkeeper Kathy Bender. "It was given to me by an aunt of mine, but I added the applesauce and lemon." It's often on the breakfast buffet, along with hot entrées, fruit, potatoes and cereals.

This 1833 inn, located in the town center of the village, has 16 guestrooms, a pub, a swimming pool and a restaurant that serves dinner to guests and the public. Down the lane is the oldest professional theater in the country, the Barnstormer's Summer Theater, founded by Grover Cleveland's son. The Swift River runs out in back of the inn, and guests who come to cross-country ski can ski through the village, leaving from the inn's front door.

Other Tamworth Inn recipes:
Apple Banana Syrup, page 78
Christmas Apple and Cranberry Cobbler, page 155

Preserves, Butters, Syrups & Sauces

Apple Banana Syrup

Ingredients:

2 Granny Smith apples, peeled, cored and cut into 1/2 inch slices
1/4 cup dark brown sugar, packed
1/2 cup butter
1/2 cup apple cider or apple juice
2 teaspoons lemon juice
1-1/2 teaspoons cinnamon
1/8 teaspoon nutmeg
1/2 cup raisins, optional
2 bananas, cut into 1/4 inch slices

- In a large saucepan, stir together all ingredients except the bananas.
- Simmer for 10 minutes, stirring occasionally, until apples are softened.
- Gently fold banas into apple mixture. Heat just until bananas are warm.
- Serve warm over French toast, pancakes or waffles.

Makes 2 cups

from **The Tamworth Inn**
Main Street
Tamworth, NH 03886
603-323-7721
800-642-7352

"Our chef came up with this as something different to serve with French toast, pancakes or waffles," said Innkeeper Kathy Bender. "Our guests rave about it." Guests come down to enjoy a breakfast buffet with at least one entree, potatoes, homemade muffins or breads and cereals. They gather in the inn's breakfast room, the main dining room or the screened porch, which overlooks the landscaped grounds and the Swift River. In the winter, the breakfast room has a fire crackling in the fireplace.

Kathy and her husband, Phil, purchased this inn in 1988. It was built in 1833 to serve the town's growing population, many of whom were employed by the plant that made nails. A couple decades later, the hotel was expanded by bringing two one-story buildings from about a mile away to the town center and attaching them to the existing three-story hotel. In 1894, the hotel added two more floors, giving it 28 rooms with four shared baths.

Today, the Bender's inn has 16 rooms and suites, none of which share a bath, and all of which have a sample of Kathy's quilting on the bed. Located in the center of a picturesque New England village, it draws guests who come to attend summer theater, fish or cross-country ski out the front door.

Other Tamworth Inn recipes:
Zucchini Bread, page 75
Christmas Apple and Cranberry Cobbler, page 155

Balsamic Maple Sauce

Ingredients:

1/2 cup balsamic vinegar
1/4 cup Vermont maple syrup
Juice of 1/2 lemon

- In a bowl, whisk together vinegar, syrup and lemon juice.
- Pour into a serving pitcher. Cover with plastic wrap and refrigerate.
- Serve chilled over citrus fruit, "the colder the better."

Makes 3/4 cup

from **Ardmore Inn**
23 Pleasant Street
Woodstock, VT 05091
802-457-3887
Fax 802-457-9006

Innkeeper Giorgio Ortiz has invented yet another use for Vermont maple syrup. "Mixing maple syrup in my every day cooking sometimes brings a good find, like this one," he noted. He also serves this as a salad dressing over fresh greens.

Giorgio, who opened the inn in 1994 with owner Bill Gallagher and his family, is an acclaimed breakfast chef whose fare is said to be both artistic and delicious. "I very much enjoy cooking and entertaining people," he said. "One of the things I delight in is trying new things, and that includes coming up with new menus for our guests."

Guests dine at a long English banquet table in the formal dining room, which Giorgio calls "the great room" and which is festive in its own right. The Chippendale secretary, bookcase and walnut sideboard are some of the antiques from the family collection that furnish the inn.

Bill, a native Vermonter, found this 1850 Greek Revival, built for the local mercantile owners, located just a short walk from the picturesque village center. The Gallaher family had entertained guests for years as part of their Irish tradition, and finally found this home. In the Irish language, "Ardmore" means "beautiful house." They chose to restore the home and open an inn to continue their tradition of hosting guests.

Another Ardmore Inn recipe:
Miss Fay's Brown Bread, page 71

Blueberry Champagne Sauce

Ingredients:

2 cups fresh or frozen "dry pack" blueberries
1/2 cup champagne
3 tablespoons sugar
Pinch of nutmeg, freshly grated
1 tablespoon freshly-squeezed lemon juice
1-1/2 teaspoons arrowroot powder

🍃 In a saucepan, stir together blueberries, champagne, sugar, nutmeg and lemon juice. Bring to a boil.

🍃 Dissolve the arrowroot in a little water and swish into blueberry mixture, stirring until mixture boils and thickens.

🍃 Serve warm over pancakes, waffles or French toast, or use as a dessert sauce.

Makes 2-1/2 cups

from **Red Clover Inn**
Woodward Road
Mendon, VT 05701
802-775-2290
800-752-0571

While this sauce is not especially difficult, it is delicious and unusual, and that's exactly what the innkeepers and chef at this popular country inn strive for. Guests gather in the sunlit breakfast room, helping themselves to beverages, soothed by classical music. A fresh fruit plate and a hot entrée round out the meal. Entrées might be Cinnamon Swirl French Toast (using homemade bread) or Maple Apple Walnut Pancakes.

Guests awaken in one of 14 guestrooms, seven of which are in the main inn. Built on the top of a knoll just four miles from Rutland, the inn is a former farmhouse, constructed in 1840 as a summer estate for General John Woodward of Washington, D.C.

Sue and Harris Zuckerman rescued the inn, sitting empty, from foreclosure, and gave it a new life. They had vacationed in the Green Mountains for a dozen or so years, frequenting inns whenever possible. They decided to move from New York state and enter innkeeping as "a challenging, interesting, rewarding lifestyle change," Sue said.

It has not disappointed them. They offer dinners to the public, and they have emphasized an extensive wine list and creative gourmet cuisine, such as wild mushroom ravioli with native pheasant tucked inside. Guests are only "a stone's throw" from Killington and Pico Mountain ski areas.

🏠 *Other Red Clover Inn recipes:*
Maple Butter, page 89
Maple Apple Walnut Pancakes, page 138

Blueberry Cinnamon Sauce

Ingredients:

1/2 cup sugar
4 teaspoons cornstarch
1/2 teaspoon grated lemon rind
1/4 teaspoon cinnamon
10 ounces fresh blueberries (or frozen, thawed and drained)
2/3 cup water
1 teaspoon lemon juice

- In a small bowl, stir together sugar, cornstarch, lemon rind and cinnamon. Mix well.
- In a small saucepan, combine 1/2 cup blueberries and water. Bring to a boil.
- Mash berries in saucepan. Add sugar mixture and cook, stirring constantly, until sauce thickens.
- Add remaining blueberries and lemon juice. Bring to a boil and cook 3 to 5 minutes.
- Serve warm over pancakes, French toast or waffles.

Makes 2 cups

from **Placidia Farm B&B**
R.D. 1, Box 275
Randolph, VT 05060
802-728-9883

"This is great with yeast waffles," notes Viola Frost-Laitinen, who received the recipe from a friend "in blueberry country" when she opened her B&B.

Viola now operates one of the state's smallest B&Bs, with one guest apartment. "My husband and I fell in love with Vermont and purchased our place as a weekend hideaway," she said. The hand-hewn log home is set on 81 quiet acres with a pond, babbling brook and views of the Green Mountains.

"After being widowed in 1982, I decided to try B&B. I like people and enjoy cooking and also thought it would be nice to share our idyllic spot with travelers. I re-married in 1992 and since then, Don and I have been busy." She and Don installed a new heating system and completely redecorated the B&B suite. "Don is a 'natural' for the B&B. He enjoys serving coffee and engaging in conversation while I do the cooking." Guests enjoy breakfast on the sunporch, which has mountain views.

The B&B is five miles from Randolph, home of the Vermont Castings woodstove manufacturers. Downhill ski areas are nearby, and guests can x-c ski, hike and enjoy sleigh rides on the property. Golfing, swimming, fishing, horseback riding and tennis are all popular summertime pursuits. The Chandler Music Hall offers a series of concerts, jazz and theater.

Other Placidia Farm recipes:
Islands Jam, page 88
Orange Ambrosia, page 185

Cranberry Raspberry Jam

Ingredients:

2 10-ounce packages frozen sweetened raspberries, thawed
5 cups sugar
4 cups fresh cranberries, picked over and washed
Pinch of lemon zest
1 package powdered fruit pectin

- Drain raspberries, reserving juice. Add water to juice for a total of 1-1/2 cups.
- Pour juice and water into large pot. Add raspberries, sugar, cranberries and lemon zest. Bring to full boil, stirring constantly.
- Stir in pectin and return to full rolling boil, stirring constantly, for 1 minute.
- Remove from heat and skim off any foam. Pour into six hot, sterilized jelly jars, leaving 1/2-inch space at the top. Immediately cover with sterilized tight-fitting lids and band and invert for 5 minutes.
- Turn jars upright to cool.

Makes 6 8-ounce jars

from **Birchwood Inn**
Route 45
P.O. Box 197
Temple, NH 03084
603-878-3285

Only homemade jams are served at the Birchwood Inn, and this is one of the favorites. Bright red in color, it's particularly festive around the holidays, when fresh cranberries are available.

Innkeepers Judy and Bill Wolfe bought this historic inn in 1980, after staying in dozens of New England inns on vacations. With three children ages 9 and under and a seven guestroom-inn and dining room, which serves dinner to the public as well as guests, the word "busy" took on new meaning.

But Judy and Bill fell in love with the inn, which may be the state's oldest operating inn, serving guests since around 1775. Over the years, Henry David Thoreau was a guest, and the inn housed the local post office, a small general store, a town meeting hall and an antique shop.

Bill, a former special education teacher, has a personal connection to antiques -- he has a collection of antique candy molds, handed down from his great grandfather, and each year he makes hard candy Christmas ornaments in the molds by a tricky process. They are revered by his kids and his guests.

The Monadnock Region offers a variety of recreation including hiking, alpine and cross-country skiing, riding, and leaf-peeping.

Another Birchwood Inn recipe:
Apple Pear Crisp, page 173

Decadent Praline Sauce

Ingredients:

1/2 cup butter
1-1/2 cups brown sugar, lightly packed
3/4 cup maple syrup ("the real stuff")
1/2 cup whipping cream or half -and-half
2/3 cup chopped pecans

- In a saucepan, melt butter over low heat. Blend in brown sugar until syrupy.
- Simmer over low heat for 5 minutes. Stir in maple syrup.
- Blend in cream until smooth.
- Stir in chopped pecans.
- Serve warm over French toast, pancakes, sliced apples or whatever!

Tester's Comments: Consider this to adorn bread pudding, ice cream or cheesecake -- anything that cries out for a rich caramel topping! Warning: Innkeeper Laura Simoes doubles the recipe and says it's still never enough!

Makes about 2-1/4 cups

from **The Inn at Maplewood Farm**
447 Center Road
P.O. Box 1478
Hillsborough, NH 03244
603-464-4242
800-644-6695

This recipe is so good that Innkeeper Laura Simoes has been known to catch guests spooning the last drops out of the syrup pitchers! "This recipe was inspired by the Birch Tree Inn of Flagstaff, Arizona, when we visited their area," Laura said. She uses New Hampshire pure maple syrup and has made other changes, and the sauce gets rave reviews every time it's served.

Breakfast is served in the inn's sunny dining room, but guests who have to leave earlier go with a special basket breakfast. Following their meal, guests love to savor an extra cup of coffee or tea on the porch.

Guests arrive after driving up a scenic country road from Hillsborough, pop. 4,300. The whitewashed inn and its barn appear on the top of a crest, situated on 14 acres, bordered by the Fox State Forest on one side, a field of contented cows on the other. In the spring, forsythia and daffodils line the road. In the fall, the foliage turns crimson, and in the winter, the inn's windows beckon travelers inside. Guests can fall asleep to old-time radio, piped into the four guestrooms from the inn's own transmitter. Jayme, Laura's spouse, has a huge collection of favorite shows and restored antique radios on which they are played. Requests are encouraged.

Other Inn at Maplewood Farm recipes:
Fresh Salsa, page 84
Spiced Peach Soup, page 103
Valentine Cranberry Buttermilk Scones, page 166
Maplewood Farm Granola, page 195

Fresh Salsa

Ingredients:

2 medium tomatoes, chopped
2 jalapeno peppers, seeded and chopped (you may wish to wear rubber gloves for this)
2 garlic cloves, minced
1 medium onion, chopped
1 green or red pepper, chopped
3 tablespoons fresh cilantro leaves, chopped
2 tablespoons vinegar
1 teaspoon sugar
Dash of salt

- Stir together all ingredients in a non-metal bowl and cover.
- Refrigerate for up to 10 days.

Tester's Comments: Nothing like the stuff in jars, or even in restaurants -- it's unbeatable. And, of course, you can vary the amount of any of the ingredients, including the garlic, onions or "heat" to suit personal tastes.

Makes about 2 cups

from **The Inn at Maplewood Farm**
447 Center Road
P.O. Box 1478
Hillsborough, NH 03244
603-464-4242
800-644-6695

"I usually try to make a double batch since we love it, too, with chips or on grilled fish during the summer," said Innkeeper Laura Simoes. "Fresh herbs we grow in the back garden really perk up this salsa—dill, basil and lots of fresh cilantro!" She often serves it with an Italian frittata.

Laura and Jayme Simoes bought this 14-acre farm in 1992 in order to turn it into a country inn, removing apartments and putting in four guestrooms. They had stressful jobs in public relations in Boston, and opted for life in a slower lane. Guests may hear cowbells in the morning from "our nearest neighbors" or go for a hike in the Fox State Forest, which borders the property.

Whatever their schedule, no one misses breakfast. Laura has won several cooking awards and often writes about food for regional and national publications. She also promotes New Hampshire as the state's travel office public relations director. Jayme, Laura's co-innkeeper and spouse, gladly directs guests to many area attractions and little-known spots. Summer guests often tour the homestead of Franklin Pierce, 14th U.S. President, or seek out a secluded waterfall. Mountain bikers can leave right from the inn.

Other Inn at Maplewood Farm recipes:
Decadent Praline Sauce, page 83
Spiced Peach Soup, page 103
Valentine Cranberry Buttermilk Scones, page 166
Maplewood Farm Granola, page 195

Fruit Sauce

Ingredients:

    1 cup sour cream
    1/2 cup powdered sugar
    1/2 cup orange juice
    1/3 cup finely chopped pecans

Also:

    Any fresh fruit

- Beat together sour cream, powdered sugar and orange juice until smooth.
- Stir in pecans.
- Serve over fresh fruit.

Makes 1-1/2 cups , 6 1-/4-cup servings

from **Apple Gate B&B**
199 Upland Farm Road
Peterborough, NH 03458
603-924-6543

"This sauce is the perfect complement to the fresh berries picked at our neighbor's organic farm," said Innkeeper Dianne Legenhausen. "When we start serving this sauce in the spring, we know that summer is right around the corner, and so are all the wonderful, delicious fruits of the season."

Breakfast at Dianne and Ken's B&B always includes fresh fruit, served in antique sherbet dishes. "We never dreamed when Ken's Aunt Vera gave us her Ruby red glass dishes how perfect they would be to serve our candlelight breakfasts. They really are a wonderful addition to our apple theme."

Located right smack next to a 90-acre apple orchard (guests can pick-their-own in the fall, and enjoy the blossoms in the spring), it's only natural that Dianne and Ken took the theme and ran with it. Each of their four guestrooms is named for a different variety of apple. Their friendly lab is named "Mac," short for "McIntosh." And yes, the gate really is stencilled in an apple design.

Dianne, a former music teacher, and Ken, who served as a Long Island police officer specializing in emergency rescues, found the four seasons of the Monadnock region to be the perfect place to enjoy their second careers as innkeepers. Their inn, in a restored 1832 Colonial, is only two miles from Peterborough's restaurants and the Sharon Arts Center. Temple Mountain and Windblown ski areas, a state park and other outdoor recreation is also nearby. After a day of exploring, guests enjoy the double parlors of the inn, with a collection of videos and a well-stocked library.

Other Apple Gate recipes:
Three Cheddar-Apple-Ham Bake, page 118
Apple Crisp, page 172

Grandma's Peach Chutney

Ingredients:

    2 pounds fresh peaches, peeled, pitted and chopped
    2 tart apples, cored and chopped
    1 yellow onion, diced
    1 cup raisins
    1/2 cup raspberry or cider vinegar
    1 cup sugar
    1/2 teaspoon ground allspice
    1/2 teaspoon ground ginger
    1/4 teaspoon cayenne pepper

- In a large pot, mix peaches, apples, onion, raisins, vinegar, sugar and spices.
- Cook, stirring constantly, over high heat until mixture begins to boil.
- Partially cover, reduce heat to simmer, and cook for an additional 20 minutes or until mixture thickens.
- Serve hot or cold. To store, cover and refrigerate for up to 2 weeks (reheat in microwave).

Makes 10 to 12 servings

from **Rosewood Country Inn**
67 Pleasant View Road
Bradford, NH 03221
603-938-5253 or
603-938-5220

"This recipe was found handwritten in one of my grandmother's cookbooks," said Innkeeper Lesley Marquis. "I remember her making this with peaches from our small orchard in Rhode Island." Today, Lesley serves it as a side dish with Eggs Florentine and potatoes.

Lesley grew up in Rhode Island and then worked for 23 years as a chemistry technologist in a large medical center there. As the oldest of seven children, she got plenty of experience cooking for crowds. Now she prepares "candlelight and crystal" breakfasts for guests in the 12 guestrooms, served in the dining room by the fireplace or on the one of the sunporches.

Lesley and Dick, her husband, who also worked in the medical field, decided to seek a slower-paced life with their two daughters. They restored the main inn of a former grand Victorian resort which had been sitting vacant for more than a decade, foreclosed upon and in disrepair. The home of the Edward Messers family first opened in 1896, taking guests by the week, with references only. At one time, 85 guests could be housed in the buildings and cottages. In the early 1900s, Douglas Fairbanks, Jack London, Gloria Swanson and Charlie Chaplain were among the guests. The family operated the inn as Pleasant View Farm until 1956. Lesley and Dick re-opened the inn in 1992.

Another Rosewood Country Inn recipe:
Spiced Apple Brandy, page 164

Honey Cream Sauce

Ingredients:
    2 cups sour cream
    1/4 cup honey
    1/4 cup orange juice

Also:
    Strawberries (or any fresh fruit), washed, hulled and chilled

- In a large bowl, whisk together sour cream, honey and orange juice.
- Place strawberries in dessert or fruit bowls. Pour the Honey Cream Sauce over the berries, garnish and serve.

Makes 2-1/2 cups, 10 1/4-cup servings

from **The Inn at Manchester**
Route 7A
P.O. Box 41
Manchester Village, VT 05254
802-362-1793
800-273-1793

"In the summertime, we serve fresh fruit salad, starting with June strawberries," said Innkeeper Harriet Rosenberg. "This complements the fresh fruits perfectly."

Harriet and Stan Rosenberg first saw this Queen Anne Victorian on a cold day in February 1978. They say that it looked "forlorn;" the local paper called it the "long-abandoned and derelict mansion." Still, the Rosenbergs thought "it had the possibilities we need to make a successful country inn -- perfect location in Manchester, lovely park-like setting, large entrance hall and public rooms."

So they began the undertaking of restoration of the 1880 estate. "Every inch of the house required work. We used over 500 rolls of wallpaper and countless gallons of paint to restore the house." And that was just the first time -- heading into their second decade of innkeeping, most rooms have been redone a second time. The carriage house was converted into guestrooms in 1985. It and the main inn are on the National Register of Historic Places.

In the process, the Rosenbergs raised their children here. Their business has expanded and the inn now has 18 guestrooms and four suites. "We pride ourselves on the decor and ambiance of our inn," Harriet said.

The wrap-around porch has wicker rockers. In the winter, the front parlor and library have a fire in the fireplace. Cookies and tea are available every afternoon. Guests may use the swimming pool in the back meadow, or the innkeepers can direct them to the quarry, Emerald Lake beach or the Equinox Health Club. Trout fishing and canoeing the famous Battenkill River are nearby, as are tennis, golf and touring Hildene, Robert Todd Lincoln's estate. The Manchester area has fine restaurants, outlet shops, theaters and skiing.

Islands Jam

Ingredients:

2 oranges, washed and dried
1 lemon, washed and dried
4 cups fresh pineapple, finely chopped
2 cups fresh peaches, peeled, pitted and chopped
1 6-ounce jar maraschino cherries, chopped
7 cups sugar

- Leaving rind on, cut oranges and lemon into small sections. Remove seeds.
- Place oranges and lemon in a food processor and process until finely chopped.
- In a large pot, place oranges, lemon, pineapple, peaches, cherries and sugar.
- Stirring constantly, simmer uncovered until fruit is translucent and liquid is thick.
- Remove from heat. Pour into six hot, sterilized jelly jars, leaving 1/2-inch space at the top. Immediately cover with sterilized tight-fitting lids and bands. Or pour into six jelly jars, cover and refrigerate (use within 3 weeks or store in freezer up to a year).

Makes 6 6-ounce jars

from **Placidia Farm B&B**
R.D. 1, Box 275
Randolph, VT 05060
802-728-9883

"One of my very first B&B customers enclosed this recipe and one for Orange Ambrosia in a gift box of oranges," said Innkeeper Viola Frost-Laitinen. Now this jam is often on the breakfast table for other guests to enjoy.

Guests find this secluded log home up a dirt road and tucked along a babbling brook, which lulls them to sleep. Viola and her husband, Don, have one B&B suite, which has a deck, living room, and furnished kitchen, perfect for guests on an extended stay or for families. From the deck, they may see deer grazing.

Originally purchased as a weekend retreat, this home's apartment became a B&B in 1983 after Viola was widowed a year earlier. After remarrying a decade later, the B&B is still going strong. She and Don treat guests to a hearty country breakfast on their sunporch, with views of the Green Mountains.

Guests can hike, x-c ski or have a sleigh ride at the B&B property. Located in the center of Vermont, Placidia Farm is close to skiing, biking, golf, tennis, fishing and riding. Guests also can watch maple syruping or photograph fall colors, depending on the season.

Other Placidia Farm recipes:
Blueberry Cinnamon Sauce, page 81
Orange Ambrosia, page 185

Maple Butter

Ingredients:

1/2 cup unsalted butter, softened
1/4 cup Vermont maple syrup

☛ Beat butter and syrup with an electric mixer until smooth.

☛ Serve on toast, waffles, French toast or Maple Apple Walnut Pancakes, page 138. Cover and refrigerate to store, letting maple butter soften before serving again.

Tester's Comments: Works fine with salted butter, too (but if you're thinking you can substitute fake maple-flavored pancake syrup, forget it!). This should be in everyone's repertoire. It's one of the simplest things you can do to make pancakes extra-special. Try it on cornbread or Sweet Corn Muffins, page 59.

Makes 1/2 cup

from **Red Clover Inn**
Woodward Road
Mendon, VT 05701
802-775-2290
800-752-0571

Details such as having this Maple Butter around for pancakes, or making the French toast from homemade cinnamon bread, are one of the reasons this inn has become a favorite with guests. Guests gather for breakfast in the main inn. In addition to the seven guestrooms, it has three dining rooms (one used as the breakfast room), a large common room with a fieldstone fireplace, and a pub. Originally, the inn was a farmhouse where General John Woodward escaped the heat and humidity of Washington, D.C., in the summers. Over the years, the carriage house of his summer estate had been converted and now has seven more guestrooms.

Sue and Harris Zuckerman found the inn closed down in 1993. "When we saw this property, meandering a half mile down a winding, evergreen-lined country road, we fell in love with it," Sue recalled. The inn sits on top of a knoll with Pico Mountain in the background. The 13 acres and barns are perfect for the two miniature horses. There's a pool for summer guests.

"We wanted to provide the kind of inn we would like to go to," Sue said. Each guestroom has a handmade quilt on the bed and mountain views. Harris, who used to collect sports cars, now collects fine wine and offers more than 300 selections in a 20-page wine list to dinner guests. The inn's chef creates cuisine that is not only wonderful to eat but beautiful to look at. Guests enjoy a relaxing, candlelit dinner after a day on the Killington or Pico Mountain slopes, hiking the Appalachian or Long Trails, antiquing, x-c skiing or biking.

🏠*Other Red Clover Inn recipes:*
Blueberry Champagne Sauce, page 80
Maple Apple Walnut Pancakes, page 138

Raspberry Butter

Ingredients:

1 cup frozen "dry pack" unsweetened raspberries
2 tablespoons water
1 tablespoon sugar
1/2 cup butter, at room temperature
2 tablespoons powdered sugar
1 teaspoon blackberry-flavored liqueur, such as Chambord®
1/4 teaspoon lemon juice

☛ In small saucepan over medium heat, boil raspberries, water and sugar until syrupy, stirring frequently (about 5 minutes).

☛ Strain through sieve to remove seeds. Cool.

☛ Add butter, powdered sugar, liqueur and lemon juice, stirring until smooth and well mixed.

☛ Transfer to small ramekins. Cover and chill. (Do not prepare more than one day ahead; it will separate if kept too long.)

☛ Bring to room temperature before serving.

Tester's Comments: Mmmm...wonderful on pancakes and muffins! Try it on Casco Bay Raspberry Pancakes, p. 130.

Makes 2/3 cup, or 6 to 8 servings

from **The Benjamin Prescott Inn**
Route 124 East
Jaffrey, NH 03452
603-532-6637

A simple addition to the menu, but one of the touches that makes breakfasts here special, this Raspberry Butter is served along with French toast, waffles and pancakes.

Innkeeper Barry Miller had spent 26 years traveling the country, opening hotels for various corporations. In 1988, he got one of his own, albeit small, with nine guestrooms. He and Janice, his wife, moved from Michigan to this 1853 inn, built in Greek Revival style as a home for Colonel Benjamin Prescott, who fought in the Revolutionary War.

Today, the inn sits a little over two miles from the picturesque village, neighboring a dairy farm. Old Glory hangs near the front steps, the first hint of the Early American atmosphere Jan and Barry have attempted to preserve inside. Each of the guestrooms is named after a Prescott family member and is decorated with antiques and country furnishings. Guests can cross-country ski from the inn, climb Mt. Monadnock, bike, enjoy an acclaimed concert and lecture series, or go antiquing.

🏠*Another Benjamin Prescott Inn recipe:*
Farmer's French Toast, page 122

Rhubarb Jam

Ingredients:

6 cups fresh rhubarb, chopped
4-1/2 cups sugar
1 tablespoon lemon juice

Also:

Paraffin, melted

- In a large pot, stir together rhubarb, sugar and lemon juice.
- Bring to a boil and cook for 12 minutes, stirring occasionally.
- Pour into sterilized jars. Top with paraffin.
- Let cool on counter until wax is hard.
- Screw on sterilized lids and store in cool, dry area or refrigerate.

Makes 4 8-ounce jars

from **The Inn On Golden Pond**
Route 3
P.O. Box 680
Holderness, NH 03245
603-968-7269
Fax 603-968-9226

Summer guests who arrive in the afternoon often find Innkeeper Bonnie Webb out in the inn's rhubarb patch, picking rhubarb for this jam, breakfast muffins or coffeecake. A jar of this jam is on every table at breakfast, she said.

Located across the street from Squam Lake, the setting for the Henry Fonda/Katharine Hepburn film, "On Golden Pond," the inn was built in 1879 as a private residence. Bill and Bonnie Webb left their desk jobs in Southern California in 1984 to purchase the home to turn it into an inn. They wanted to work together at their own business.

Extensive renovations were done the first year, including taking the existing attic and creating three new guestrooms. In 1988, Ricky and Becky arrived from Seoul, Korea, to complete Bonnie and Bill's family. With the arrival of two children, ages 4 and 6, more space was needed to balance inn life and personal life. A back wing was converted into living quarters for the family, a kitchen make-over was undertaken and another guestroom was added.

After breakfast in the large country dining room, guests might head to the Holderness swimming beach, hike to a mountaintop for views of the lake, or enjoy the 60-foot screened porch. The inn sits on 50 acres, mostly wooded, with trails for hikers. Squam Lake offers boating, fishing and swimming. Waterville Valley, Loon Mountain and Gunstock ski resorts are all within 30 minutes of the inn.

Spiced Tomato Jam

Ingredients:

2-1/4 pounds fully ripe tomatoes
1-1/2 teaspoons grated lemon rind
1/4 cup lemon juice
1/2 teaspoon allspice
1/2 teaspoon cinnamon
1/4 teaspoon ground cloves
1 box pectin, such as Sure-Jell® (not reduced-sugar kind)
4-1/2 cups (2 pounds) sugar

- Scald, peel and chop tomatoes. Place in saucepan.

- Bring to a boil and simmer 10 minutes, stirring occasionally.

- Measure 3 cups of prepared tomatoes into a 6 to 8 quart saucepan.

- Stir in lemon rind, lemon juice, allspice, cinnamon and cloves. Then stir in pectin.

- Place over high heat and stir constantly until mixture comes to a full boil. Immediately add sugar and stir.

- Bring to a full rolling boil and boil hard 1 minute, stirring constantly.

- Remove from heat and skim off foam with metal spoon.

- Ladle quickly into hot, sterilized jars, filling to within 1/8-inch of tops. Wipe jar rims and threads.

- Cover with sterilized two-piece lids and tighten bands.

- Invert jars for 5 minutes and then turn upright. Check seals after 1 hour. Tighten again.

Makes about 5 cups or 6 8-ounce jars

from **Watch Hill B&B**
Old Meredith Road
P.O. Box 1605
Center Harbor, NH 03226
603-253-4334

Innkeeper Barbara Lauterbach suggests this jam for English muffins or a savory muffin or scone. It's a great way to bring the taste of summer tomatoes back in the dead of winter, too.

Barbara's creative cuisine is the hallmark of her B&B. She is a certified culinary professional who has spent years teaching and doing product demonstrations. She offers occasional cooking classes for a small number of students and guests at the B&B, but all guests in the four guestrooms get to sample her hearty breakfasts. Located in the heart of New Hampshire's lakes region, there are plenty of outdoor activities to work up an appetite, no matter the season. The B&B is just up the hill from Lake Winnipesaukee and the town center.

Other Watch Hill B&B recipes:
Buttermilk Whole Wheat Bread, page 67
Mulled Cider Applesauce, page 102
Savory Christmas Bread, page 163
Firehouse Brownies, page 191

Spicy Blueberry Sauce

Ingredients:

1 cup brown sugar, packed
1 cup sugar
1 cup water (less if using frozen berries)
2 to 3 cups blueberries, fresh or frozen "dry pack"
Juice from 1/2 lemon
1/2 to 1 teaspoon nutmeg
1/2 to 1 teaspoon cloves
1 to 2 teaspoons cinnamon

Also:

Cornstarch and water

🛥 In a large saucepan, stir together brown sugar, sugar, water, blueberries, lemon juice, nutmeg, cloves and cinnamon.

🛥 Simmer mixture on low heat for approximately 30 minutes, stirring frequently. "Do not allow to cook unattended."

🛥 Mix a small amount of water with enough cornstarch to thicken to desired consistency and whisk into sauce. Continue cooking sauce, stirring constantly, until sauce thickens. Serve warm.

Makes about 3-1/2 cups

from **Small Point B&B**
312 Small Point Road
Phippsburg, ME 04562
207-389-1716

Innkeeper Jan Tingle is often stirring up this recipe for use over pancakes, waffles or French toast. "If I thicken it to the consistency of a conserve, I use it as a filling for muffins and coffeecakes. In recent years, I have also been making this blueberry sauce for a local restaurant for use over their ice cream, poundcakes and cheesecakes. I have even substituted gelatin for the cornstarch and made this into a tartlet filling."

Jan and David Tingle landed at this B&B near Bath after nine years of running week-long yacht charters, sailing guests through the Carribbean. On board, Jan prepared three meals a day, plus hors d'oeuvres and dessert, for guests. "Innkeeping was a very natural offshoot," she said. David has his own marine service business and takes charters out on their boat. Jan has permanently traded the galley for a land-locked kitchen.

When not out to sea, the Tingles have been restoring their 1890s New England farmhouse. Located close enough to the coast so the waves can lull guests to sleep, their home has three guestrooms, plus a carriage house available in July and August. Guests can explore Popham Beach State Park, Fort Popham and Fort Baldwin, hike the Morse Mountain Trail to Seawall Beach, boat, golf, or drive 35 minutes to the Freeport outlet district and L.L. Bean headquarters.

Strawberry Rhubarb Jam

Ingredients:

1 pound fresh rhubarb, cleaned and diced
1/4 cup water
1 pound frozen, sweetened and sliced strawberries
5-1/2 cups sugar
1 pouch liquid fruit pectin, such as Certo®

🥄 In a large pot or saucepan, place rhubarb and water and simmer until rhubarb is soft (about 5 minutes).

🥄 Thaw strawberries in their juice. Mash with potato masher or in food processor (pulse and chop).

🥄 Add mashed strawberries to rhubarb in pot. Stir in sugar.

🥄 On high heat, bring mixture to a full, rolling boil, stirring constantly.

🥄 Quickly stir fruit pectin into fruit mixture.

🥄 Return to full, rolling boil and boil exactly 1 minute, stirring constantly. Remove from heat.

🥄 Using a metal spoon, skim off any foam.

🥄 Immediately fill hot, sterilized jars to within 1/8-inch of the top rim and seal with hot, sterilized lids and rims. Process jars in a hot water bath or using quick-seal method following directions on pectin box.

Makes six 8-ounce jars

from **Hill Farm Inn**
RR 2, Box 2015
Arlington, VT 05250
802-375-2269
800-882-2545

Each of Innkeeper Joanne Hardy's guests goes home with a jar of jam "to remind them of the mouthwatering smells and tastes of Hill Farm Inn," she said. "We have a large rhubarb patch and I freeze enough rhubarb over the summer so that I can make the jam year 'round, something I've enjoyed doing since I grew up on a farm in Oregon many years ago."

Joanne, who had a career in early childhood education, and George, a minister and social service administrator, married, raised four children and worked in Cleveland, Ohio, for 25 years. In 1983, they "bought the farm" that had been run as Hill's Farm Inn since 1905. Nestled in a valley in the Southwest corner of Vermont, the inn's lower meadow is bordered by the Battenkill River, a world-class trout stream. Guests enjoy fishing, antiquing, or just walking the country roads or sitting in the porch rockers, enjoying the rural peace and quiet. The main inn is an 1830 post-and-beam farmhouse with seven guestrooms and a dining room serving four-course dinners as well as full country breakfasts. The Hardys also offer cabins and rooms in a guest house.

🏠 *Other Hill Farm Inn recipes:*
Oats 'n Wheat Bread, page 73
Buttermilk Blueberry Pancakes, page 129

Fruit

Cheese Cream-Filled Baked Pears

Ingredients:

4 fresh pears
8 teaspoons apple or orange juice
Dash of cinnamon or ginger
Brown sugar (enough to cover bottom of baking dish)
Butter or margarine

Cheese Cream Filling:
1 cup cottage cheese
1/3 cup sour cream
3 tablespoons powdered sugar

Also:

Nutmeg

- Halve and core each pear ("I use a melon baller"). Remove stem, but do not peel.
- Line an 8-1/2 x 11-inch baking pan (or other pan large enough to accommodate the pears laid in one layer across the bottom) with just enough brown sugar to cover the bottom.
- Lay pear halves, cut side down, over brown sugar. Pack in pear halves tightly.
- Drizzle fruit juice over pears.
- Sprinkle tops with ginger or cinnamon and dot with butter or margarine.
- Bake in an oven preheated to 350 degrees for 20 minutes or until pears are soft and lightly browned.
- For Cheese Cream Filling: Put cottage cheese, sour cream and powdered sugar into a blender and process until smooth. Set aside until pears are baked.
- Place baked pear halves cut side up on serving plates and fill the "craters" with Cheese Cream Filling.
- Sprinkle filling with nutmeg and serve pears warm.

Makes 4 servings, 2 pear-halves each

from **MapleHedge B&B Inn**
355 Main Street
P.O. Box 638
Charlestown, NH 03603
603-826-5237
1-800-9-MAPLE-9

Innkeeper Joan DeBrine loves to serve fresh fruit to her guests, but that can be problematic in a New England winter, when the variety of fresh, ripe fruit available shrinks. Pears, however, are often on hand and can be baked even if they are not yet fully ripe.

Guests might enjoy this dish at the dining room table of this Federal-style home, wich Joan and her husband, Dick, restored and redecorated before opening in 1990. Joan, who has enjoyed cooking for many years, has also wanted to open a B&B for many years, and she was deliberate and painstaking in her search for this home to convert. After narrowing their search to five New England towns, they settled on Charlestown, in part because of its historic significance and preservation efforts. The DeBrines' guests often tour The Fort at No. 4, a living history museum in Charlestown that offers a peek into life in the 1740s, complete with costumed docents.

Other MapleHedge recipes:
Banana Froth, page 21
Grandma's Fruit Bread, page 158

Dried Fruit Compote

Ingredients:
1/2 teaspoon whole cloves
1/2 teaspoon whole allspice
1 stick cinnamon
1-1/2 cups prunes, pitted
1 cup dried apricots
1/2 cup dried figs
Cold water
1/4 cup honey
1 tablespoon lemon juice

Also:
Cheesecloth and string

- Tie cloves and allspice in a piece of cheesecloth (or place in tea ball; break cinnamon stick to fit).
- In a large saucepan, place prunes, apricots and figs (see "Continue to" step below on cooking apricots first). Pour in enough cold water to cover the fruit completely.
- Stir in honey and lemon juice. Place spices in the liquid.
- Cover and bring to a boil. Immediately lower heat and simmer for approximately 5 minutes.
- Continue to "cook according to how firm you want the fruit to be. Don't overcook the prunes. You can cook the apricots first, then add the prunes and figs."
- Remove from heat. Allow to cool completely. Remove and discard spices, except cinnamon stick.
- Pour mixture into a wide mouth jar and refrigerate for 2 days before serving. Serve cold.

Makes 3 to 4 cups

from **Lakeshore Inn**
184 Lakeview Drive
Rockland, ME 04841
207-594-4209
Fax 207-596-6407

Innkeepers Joe McCluskey and Paula Nicols often serve this as a side dish on their breakfast buffet. "The recipe was adapted from a side dish served at a B&B in Ireland," Paula said. "We serve this dish at breakfast all year 'round." Breakfast is served in the formal dining room of this 1767 home. Breakfast breads such as date-nut, Danishes or rugulachs are served before the fruit dish and the main entrée. Paula, who learned very young how to cook in a family of restauranteurs, and Joe split up the breakfast duties.

They opened the Lakeshore Inn, located on the west shore of Lake Chickawaukie, after renovation in 1994. Built by Rockland's first settlers, the Tolman family, it is reported to be one of the town's earliest remaining buildings. Over the years, it has undergone several renovations and additions, and now has four guestrooms, two with decks that overlook the lake. Guests can enjoy the hot tub, swim, fish and boat on the lake, or take a short drive to Camden and Mt. Battie, or to the fishing villages of Tenants Harbor, Owls Head and Port Clyde.

Glazed Cinnamon Apples

Ingredients:

1/4 cup butter
1/2 cup dark brown sugar, packed
1/2 teaspoon cinnamon
1/4 teaspoon nutmeg, freshly grated
1/8 teaspoon allspice
1/2 tablespoon grated orange peel
1/4 cup golden raisins
1/4 cup dark raisins
2 Granny Smith apples, washed, cored and cut into 1/2-inch slices
2 Red Delicious apples, washed, cored and cut into 1/2-inch slices
2 Golden Delicious apples, washed, cored and cut into 1/2-inch slices
1/2 cup walnut halves

- In large skillet, melt butter over low heat.
- Stir in sugar, cinnamon, nutmeg, allspice and orange peel. Mix until well blended.
- Place Granny Smith apple slices in skillet. Toss well to coat with butter mixture. Do not cover.
- Sauté over medium heat 3 to 4 minutes. Add Red Delicious apples to skillet. Toss and sauté, turning occasionally, allowing apples to brown.
- Stir in Golden Delicious apples. Toss and sauté until apples are browned and soft, about 10 mintues.
- Serve hot.

Makes 6 to 8 servings

from **Foxglove, A Country Inn**
Route 117 at Lovers Lane
Sugar Hill, NH 03585
603-823-8840

"These apples are a perfect accompaniment for scrambled eggs with chives and Kielbasa, which we serve during the fall and winter season," said Innkeeper Janet Boyd. It is one of the most-frequently requested recipes by her guests. Guests gather in the dining room of this summer estate, where Janet serves breakfast on a different set of antique china each day.

Built at the turn-of-the-century atop the hill above the town of Sugar Hill, this home was converted to a country inn in 1992 and now offers six guestrooms. Janet, a former interior designer in New York, and her husband, Walter, who had a career in international marketing, turned the 18-room summer estate into their inviting inn. They serve candlelit dinners by request.

Janet and Walter can recommend activities in the little village near Franconia Notch or the surrounding White Mountains. Guests can snowshoe from the back door, take a ride in a 200-year old sleigh drawn by Belgian horses, or see Robert Frost's cottage near Sugar Hill. They can also take a scenic railroad ride, moose-watch or go antiquing.

Glazed Orange Slices

Ingredients:

2 small oranges, unpeeled
1 cup water, boiling
1 cup sugar

- Cut oranges into 1/4-inch slices and remove any seeds. Arrange in large frying pan.
- Dissolve sugar in boiling water.
- Pour sugar syrup over orange slices to cover.
- Cover pan and simmer until peels are soaked through and soft (approximately 2 hours). Add water as needed.
- Cool and arrange orange slices on platter.

Makes 6 servings

from **Grünberg Haus B&B**
RR 2, Box 1595
Route 100 South
Waterbury, VT 05676
802-244-7726
800-800-7760

Innkeeper Chris Sellers serves the colorful fruit as a side dish, a dessert or for a special holiday treat. Every breakfast at this inn is a treat. Chris, a gifted pianist, entertains quietly at the grand piano while co-innkeeper Mark Frohman serves guests seated at a table overlooking the Green Mountains. Fruit, hot muffins and Lemon Ricotta Pancakes or Vermont Cheddar Pie might be on the menu.

Chris and Mark discovered this inn in 1988, and were open for business less than a year later after buying it and beginning restoration work. George and Irene Ballschneider designed the inn from memories of their travels in Austria, and George handbuilt the inn on a hillside site they cleared by hand. After 12 years of innkeeping at the Schneider Haus, they moved to Florida. The inn fell into disrepair under its second owners, so Mark and Chris had their work cut out for them when they bought the inn.

Mark, the carpentry-plumbing-all-round-handy-guy, has done everything from rebuilding the septic system to constructing two cabins up in the woods behind the inn and a carriage house suite. His Aunt Marilyn suggested the new name, which means Green Mountain House. Chris, the chef-marketing-concierge guy, has organized concerts and festivals at the chalet-style inn. They have 11 guestrooms in the main inn, which open onto a balcony with mountain views. Guests enjoy gathering by the fieldstone fireplace.

Other Grünberg Haus recipes:
Green Mountain Lemon Bread, page 70
Lemon Ricotta Pancakes, page 135
Vermont Cheddar Pie, page 151

Lemon Cream with Berries

Ingredients:

- 1-1/2 cups sugar
- 1/4 cup cornstarch
- 1/4 cup flour
- 1-1/2 cups water
- 1 cup orange juice
- 1/2 cup lemon juice
- 4 egg yolks
- 4 tablespoons butter, softened
- 2 tablespoons lemon zest
- 2 cups heavy cream, whipped
- 2 quarts fresh mixed berries, picked over and washed
- 8 to 10 mint sprigs

- In a 3-quart saucepan, whisk together sugar, cornstarch and flour.

- Whisk in water and orange and lemon juices until smooth.

- Over medium heat, bring mixture to a gentle boil, stirring constantly with a wooden spoon.

- Simmer mixture for 1 to 2 minutes (it will be very thick).

- In a small bowl, beat egg yolks. Gradually whisk 1/2 cup of the hot sauce into the egg yolks. Whisk the yolk mixture back into the saucepan and cook mixture over low heat to a second boil.

- Remove saucepan from heat and blend in butter and zest. Transfer mixture to a bowl.

- Cover mixture with a buttered piece of wax paper and cool.

- Whip cream until firm and whisk into lemon mixture. Refrigerate until ready to use.

- Spoon berries into 8 to 10 bowls. Top each with lemon cream and a mint spring and serve with biscotti.

Tester's Comments: This is absolutely wonderful and hard to keep out of until serving time. I made "nests" with the cream in the bottoms of bowls, an excuse for me to use slightly more cream than if I'd used it as a topping.

Makes 8 to 10 servings

from Stonecrest Farm B&B
119 Christian Street
P.O. Box 504
Wilder, VT 05088
802-296-2425

Breakfast at this country inn is a leisurely affair, and Gail Sanderson has made sure there are plenty of extra touches -- not just fresh fruit, but fruit with the cream, for example, and homemade hazelnut biscotti. And that's just the first course. Many of the recipes are from her daughter-in-law, a food consultant.

Stonecrest Farm, located only 3.5 miles from Dartmouth College, was founded about 1810 as a dairy farm and owned by the Stone family until 1965. Gail has been innkeeper since 1988, offering six guestrooms.

Other Stonecrest Farm recipes:
Mascarpone Stuffed Strawberries, page 184
Fried Green Tomatoes Au Gratin, page 192

Melon Rounds with Orange Ginger Sauce

Ingredients:

1 large, ripe honeydew melon
1 cup fresh blueberries
6 fresh strawberries, sliced
1 cantaloupe
Lilac leaves

Orange Ginger Sauce:
1/2 cup fresh orange juice
1/2 teaspoon ginger
Honey to taste

- Slice honeydew into six round circles (hole in the middle is where the seeds were) and peel off rind.
- Place each circle on a fruit plate. Fill the center hole of each honeydew circle with sliced strawberries and blueberries.
- For Orange Ginger Sauce: In a saucepan, stir together orange juice, ginger and honey. Heat over medium heat until very warm but not boiling. Drizzle lightly over fruit.
- Peel cantaloupe. Slice the fruit with a paring knife from top around (like peeling an apple) into thin, 4-inch "peels."
- Use these 4-inch slices to curl into flower shapes.
- Put each flower next to the melon round. Tuck a lilac leaf next to each flower. Serve immediately.

Tester's Comments: Ginger gives this sauce a nice "bite" and keeps it from being too sweet. You can also thicken the sauce with cornstarch (mixed with water; cook, stirring constantly, until boiling and clear). When cool, stir in some poppyseed.

Makes 6 servings

from **Bufflehead Cove Inn**
P.O. Box 499
Kennebunkport, ME 04046
207-967-3879

Fresh fruit, artfully served, is always an important part of Innkeeper Harriet Gott's breakfasts. "I love to garnish. At Bufflehead Cove, no entree or fruit course goes out without some garnish to spark it." Garnishes often come from the inn's edible flower and vegetable gardens.

Bufflehead Cove was named by Harriet and her husband, Jim, for the ducks that winter there on the tide's upper reach. Their inn is a huge Dutch Colonial summer home built in woods along the shore in the 1800s by a master shipbuilder. Located on a secluded cove, Kennebunkport natives Jim and Harriet didn't even know it existed for many years.

Harriet grew up in the hotel business, her parents owning a resort. Jim, a commercial fisherman, is up early to help with breakfast, then takes the outboard from their dock out the channel to his fishing boat. The Gotts' inn opened in 1988 and has five guestrooms, with an emphasis on a light, airy feeling. Some rooms are hand-stencilled. The six acres of wooded lawn and porch invite guests to enjoy wine and cheese outside in the summer. Kennebunkport's shops, restaurants and galleries are within walking distance of the inn, and Harriet and Jim can recommend little-known spots to explore.

Mulled Cider Applesauce

Ingredients:

1 stick cinnamon, broken in half
3 whole cloves
3 whole allspice berries
1 1-inch strip orange zest
2 cups apple cider
6 to 8 tart apples, peeled, cored and coarsely diced
Pinch of salt
1/4 cup light brown sugar, firmly packed
1/4 to 1/2 cup sugar
1 tablespoon butter, softened

☛ Place cinnamon, cloves, allspice and orange zest in a spice bag or square of cheesecloth tied securely with a string.

☛ In a heavy saucepan, bring cider to a boil over high heat.

☛ Add spice bag, reduce heat to medium, and simmer until cider is reduced to 2/3 cup (about 30 minutes). Remove and discard spice bag.

☛ Add apples, salt and brown sugar to reduced cider.

☛ Cover and simmer over low heat, stirring frequently, for about 20 minutes, or until the apples become mushy.

☛ Stir in granulated sugar to taste (amount will vary depending on variety of apples used).

☛ Stir in butter until blended.

☛ Serve warm or lightly chilled. Store, covered, in the refrigerator.

Makes about 4 cups, or 8 servings

from **Watch Hill B&B**
Old Meredith Road
P.O. Box 1605
Center Harbor, NH 03226
603-253-4334

The smell of this applesauce cooking is intoxicating, says Innkeeper Barbara Lauterbach, who notes it's also a great accompaniment to roast pork or duck.

Barbara's guests fill up on a homemade breakfast featuring New Hampshire products before venturing off for a day in the Lakes Region. Just down the hill is Lake Winnipesaukee, where guests can swim, take a cruise on the *Mt. Washington,* fish or canoe. Barbara can also direct guests to arts and crafts festivals, local fairs, berry picking, horseback riding, woods to walk in, cross country or downhill skiing, or snowmobiling.

🏠 *Other Watch Hill B&B recipes:*
Buttermilk Whole Wheat Bread, page 67
Spiced Tomato Jam, page 92
Savory Christmas Bread, page 163
Firehouse Brownies, page 191

Spiced Peach Soup

Ingredients:

1 cup water
1/4 cup sugar
4 large peaches, washed, pitted and sliced
5 sticks cinnamon
Dash or 2 of nutmeg, freshly grated
2 slices fresh ginger, 1/4 inch in length

- Blend water and sugar to make a simple syrup.
- In a large saucepan, stir together syrup, peaches, one stick cinnamon, nutmeg and ginger.
- Bring to a boil and simmer for 20 minutes. Remove from heat.
- Remove ginger pieces and cinnamon stick and pour into blender. Blend until smooth.
- Place in four bowls, garnish each with a cinnamon stick and serve warm.

Makes 4 large servings

from **The Inn at Maplewood Farm**
447 Center Road
P.O. Box 1478
Hillsborough, NH 03244
603-464-4242
800-644-6695

A variation of this recipe earned second place in a national cooking contest for Innkeeper Laura Simoes. "It can also be served cool in the summer, topped with a dollop of fresh whipped cream," she suggests.

Breakfast is one of the acclaimed features of the inn. Old-time radio is another. Laura and Jayme, who collects radio programs from the 1930s to '50s as well as the vintage radios they played on, have their own low-frequency transmitter at the inn. Each night, guests can hear "The Shadow," "Fibber McGee and Molly," "The Lone Ranger" or other classics broadcast to the radios in their guestrooms. Jayme happily accommodates requests for favorite shows.

Guests return to the inn to relax after a day skiing, hiking, mountain biking, or meandering country roads in search of the perfect antique or to admire the fall foliage. Laura and Jayme and their two Boston terriers, Martha and Scollay, offer four guestrooms. Active members of the local historic society and other groups, Laura and Jayme can recommend secluded spots for picnicking or auctions only known to "the locals." An historic village, waterfalls and hiking trails in the woods are nearby.

🏠 *Other Inn at Maplewood Farm recipes:*
Decadent Praline Sauce, page 83
Fresh Salsa, page 84
Valentine Cranberry Buttermilk Scones, page 166
Maplewood Farm Granola, page 195

Strawberries with Warm Chocolate Sauce

Ingredients:

6 ounces bittersweet chocolate, finely chopped
3/4 cup heavy cream
1 tablespoon unsalted butter
1/4 vanilla bean, cut in half lengthwise
1 tablespoon blackberry-flavored liqueur, such as Chambord®
1 pint strawberries, hulled
Mint sprigs

🍓 In a medium-sized, deep bowl, place chocolate.

🍓 In a medium-sized, heavy saucepan, combine cream, butter and vanilla bean. Bring just to a boil and remove from heat.

🍓 Slowly strain the cream mixture through a sieve into the chocolate, stirring until the chocolate is completely melted and smooth.

🍓 Stir in liqueur.

🍓 Place strawberries into 6 large goblets such as those used for red wine. Spoon warm sauce over strawberries and garnish with mint leaves. Serve immediately.

Makes 6 servings

from **The Inn at Ormsby Hill**
Historic Route 7A
Manchester Center, VT 05255
802-362-1163
800-670-2841

Innkeeper/Cookbook Author Chris Sprague might serve this elegant chocolate dish as a fruit course for breakfast. Breakfast is served from a huge, carved buffet in the conservatory, where guests can look out over the Green Mountains beyond the sloping yard.

Veteran inngoers may remember Chris and Ted, her husband, as owners of a Maine inn that included a restaurant. They moved here in September 1995, transforming this large estate from a five-guestroom B&B to an elegant 10-room country inn. Major renovation was necessary before the new rooms opened in February 1996, adding double-person whirlpools (some hidden away behind cabinet doors) and gas fireplaces (some fireplaces you can see-through from the bed and whirlpool). Their challenges included adding a sprinkler system while preserving historic ceilings.

Built in 1764 the first jail in Manchester is still intact in the marble-floored basement, complete with a marble slab for a bed. The home neighbors Hildene, Robert Todd Lincoln's estate, and was once owned by a partner of Lincoln's. Some believe the home once was a hiding place for Ethan Allen.

Guests find several sitting areas, one with a TV. Special touches include a plate of Chris' cookies in their room when they arrive, and rubber duckies in all the whirlpools. Dinner is served to guests on Fridays and Saturdays.

Entrées:
*Eggs, French Toast, Pancakes,
Waffles, and Other Entrées*

Breakfast Burritos

Ingredients:

Burrito:
- 4 flour tortillas
- 1 to 2 tablespoons butter
- 8 eggs, beaten
- 2 to 4 tablespoons boiling water
- 1 cup grated Monterey Jack cheese

Also:
- 1 avocado, sliced
- Cilantro leaves
- Sour cream
- Black olives

Fresh Salsa:
- 1 cup ripe tomatoes, chopped
- Juice of 1/2 lime
- 1/2 to 1 jalapeno pepper, thinly sliced
- 1/4 to 1/2 cup cilantro, chopped
- Salt and pepper to taste

- For Salsa: Mix together tomatoes, lime juice, jalapeno, cilantro, salt and pepper. Prepare ahead of time and allow to sit to combine flavors.

- For Burritos: In a hot, cast iron pan, warm both sides of each tortilla until lightly golden.

- In a hot, buttered pan, scramble eggs, adding 2 to 4 tablespoons boiling water while scrambling to make them light and fluffy.

- Divide eggs between the four warm tortillas.

- Roll up each tortilla and place seam-side down on a cookie sheet. Sprinkle with cheese.

- Broil until cheese is melted and bubbly.

- Place 1 burrito on each of 4 warmed plates.

- Garnish with avocado slices and cilantro leaves. Serve with fresh salsa, sour cream and olives.

Makes 4 servings

from **Somerset House B&B**
24 Highland Avenue
P.O. Box 1098
Hardwick, VT 05843
802-472-5484
800-838-8074

This recipe is delicious, different and festive, notes Innkeeper Ruth Gaillard. "I usually start breakfast by serving a tropical fruit combination of mangoes, pineapples, papayas, bananas and kiwis, with lime slices, to get us into a south-of-the-border mood."

The Gaillards opened their four-guestroom B&B in 1989. Guests visit the 1894 home to enjoy the walking, hiking, mountain biking or cross-country skiing Hardwick has to offer. Hardwick, home to 2,500, is in Vermont's scenic Northeast Kingdom. Montpelier, the Canadian border and Stowe are each about a 40-minute drive from the B&B.

Another Somerset House recipe:
A Proper Cup of Tea, page 20

Cherry Tomato and Basil Omelette

Ingredients:

1 tablespoon butter
3 eggs
Splash of milk
3 to 4 cherry tomatoes, sliced
1 teaspoon fresh basil leaves, chopped (or 1/2 teaspoon dried)
2 tablespoons ricotta cheese

- Preheat broiler.
- On the stovetop, melt butter in a large omelette pan or 10-inch frying pan with oven-proof handle.
- In a medium-sized bowl, beat eggs and milk with a whisk. Set aside.
- When the butter bubbles in omelette pan, add tomatoes and basil. Sauté for 15 to 20 seconds.
- Pour in eggs. Push gently on the sides and, if possible, underneath to prevent sticking.
- When most of the underside of the omelette is cooked, remove the pan from the stovetop and place under the broiler. "It will begin to soufflé." Watch closely!
- Remove from the broiler when it has risen. Place the ricotta cheese in the middle of the omelette.
- Slide omelette onto a serving plate and fold it in half. Serve immediately while still risen.

Makes 1 omelette

from **Nereledge Inn**
River Road
P.O. Box 547
North Conway, NH 03860
603-356-2831
Fax 603-356-7085

"We offer a choice of 10 omelettes on our breakfast menu. This is one of the most popular, especially in the summer," said Innkeeper Valerie Halpin. "We use tomatoes and basil from our garden." Along with toast, muffins and breakfast meat, these three-egg omelettes assure no one goes away hungry.

The oldest section of Nereledge was built in 1787 as a homestead farm by Moses Randall. It has post-and-beam construction and wide-planked floors, and part of the granite foundation can be seen in the pub room. During the 1800s, a three-story section was moved to this location and added to the home. With views of the Moat Mountains and Cathedral Ledge, it became known as Nereledge Inn in 1922.

Valerie and David Halpin bought it in 1981, and transformed it into the kind of friendly, informal B&B Valerie remembers growing up in England. Families with children, mountain biking or climbing groups, honeymooners and outlet shoppers all come. The village center and scenic railroad and Saco River swimming, fishing and canoeing are a short walk from the inn, which is located on the road to Echo Lake State Park.

Another Nereledge Inn recipe:
Chocolate Chip Pancakes, page 131

Chicken Quiche

Ingredients:

2 cups chopped cooked chicken breast
1 medium onion, chopped
1/4 cup chopped celery
Dash of tarragon
1/4 cup grated Cheddar or Jack cheese
1 tablespoon flour
1/4 cup chopped scallions
1/4 cup chopped fresh vegetables (peas, broccoli, etc.)
1 unbaked pie shell
1 4-egg package egg substitute, such as Egg Beaters®
1/4 teaspoon white wine Worcestershire sauce
1 teaspoon Dijon mustard
1 cup half-and-half
1/4 cup chopped almonds
Salt and pepper to taste

- Sauté chicken, onion, celery and tarragon in a non-stick frying pan until chicken is tender.

- In a large bowl, combine cheese and flour. Then add cooked chicken mixture, scallions and vegetables.

- Place pie crust into quiche dish and pour chicken mixture into crust.

- In a medium bowl, whisk together egg substitute, Worcestershire, mustard, half-and-half and almonds. Pour over mixture in quiche dish. Sprinkle with almonds and salt and pepper to taste.

- Bake in a preheated oven at 325 degrees for 1 hour or until knife inserted in the center comes out clean.

- Remove from oven and allow to set for several minutes before cutting into six or eight servings.

Makes 6 to 8 servings

from **Blue Harbor House**
67 Elm Street
Camden, ME 04843
800-248-3196
Fax 207-236-6523

Guests can come to breakfast between 8 and 9:30, sitting at the sunny dining room tables that look out over Mt. Battie and the Camden Hills. Innkeeper Dennis Hayden, the kitchen whiz, might prepare this quiche, or a lobster quiche, Maine blueberry pancakes with blueberry butter, or a baked apple with homemade vanilla ice cream. He and Jody Schmoll, his spouse, believe the food should be regional, delicious, attractive and memorable. It's even FUN if you order dinner -- and the lobster one comes with a Blue Harbor House apron and is eaten with your hands (try to be stuffy during *that* meal!).

Jody and Dennis moved from California in 1989 after researching inns for several months. Their restored blue-and-cream inn, built in 1810, has eight guestrooms in the main inn and two suites in the attached carriage house. Their well-fed guests can waddle/stroll down to beautiful Camden harbor, where windjammers and yachts are anchored. Jody and Dennis know the area and will make suggestions for everything from restaurants to day sails.

Eggs Bernerhof

Ingredients:
4 eggs
1 quart water
1 quart ice water
2 bagels, toasted and lightly buttered
4 thin slices smoked Atlantic salmon (cooked salmon, not lox)
1/2 cup creme fraiche (cultured heavy cream)
1 tablespoon fresh dill, chopped

Also:
2 sprigs fresh dill
2 thin slices of lemon

- In a large saucepan, bring 1 quart water to a boil.
- Place eggs in a wire basket and set in boiling water for 5 minutes and 15 seconds.
- Remove eggs and place into ice water. Reserve boiling water to reheat eggs.
- When eggs are cooled, carefully crack shells and peel.
- Place toasted bagel halves on warm plates and arrange salmon on top.
- In a small bowl, stir together creme fraiche and dill. Spoon it over salmon.
- Place peeled boiled eggs back in boiling water for a minute, just to reheat.
- Place drained, warmed eggs on top of salmon, cut open and garnish with dill and lemon.

Makes 2 servings

from **The Bernerhof Inn**
Route 302
P.O. Box 240
Glen, NH 03838
603-383-9132
800-548-8007

A delicious and impressive meal that's not all that difficult, especially if you buy prepared creme fraiche in the dairy section, notes Chef Mark Prince.

The Bernerhof has been known for its creative cuisine at least since the mid-1950s, when the inn was renamed after the Bern region of Switzerland and began to feature fine Swiss dining. Today, the 80-seat restaurant still specializes in European, as well as American, cuisine. Guests in the nine guestrooms on the second and third floors also gather in the Black Bear Pub.

The inn is situated between Jackson, famous for its cross-country ski network, and North Conway, where tax-free outlet shopping is popular. Downhill skiing at Attitash is just two mintues away, and other ski areas are nearby.

♠ Other Bernerhof recipes:
Summer Cantaloupe Cooler, page 27
Cider Molasses Doughnuts, page 68

Farmer's Omelette

Ingredients:

3 tablespoons vegetable oil
3-1/2 cups frozen hashbrown potatoes
1/2 teaspoon salt
1/2 teaspoon pepper
1 cup chopped green onion
1 red bell pepper, seeded and chopped
4 eggs
1-1/4 cups milk
1 cup coarsely grated Swiss cheese

- In a frying pan, heat oil. Place hashbrowns in hot oil and allow to cook to golden brown.
- Spray a 9-inch pie plate with non-stick cooking spray. Remove the hashbrowns to the pie plate, patting down on bottom of plate to form a crust.
- Sprinkle hashbrowns with salt and pepper and green onions.
- Place chopped red pepper in the frying pan and cook until slightly soft.
- Meanwhile, in a large bowl, beat together eggs and milk.
- Sprinkle red pepper on top of hashbrowns, followed by the Swiss cheese.
- Pour egg mixture over all. Bake in a preheated oven at 400 degrees until golden on top and set.
- Remove from oven and allow to sit for a few minutes before cutting into wedges and serving.

Makes 4 to 6 servings

from **The Sugartree, A Country Inn**
Sugarbush Access Road
Warren, VT 05674
802-583-3211
800-666-8907

This quiche-like omelette has plenty of flavor and no soggy crust, notes Innkeeper Kathy Partsch, who is a self-taught cook, cookbook collector and recipe contest winner. She might carry this omelette out to the gazebo where breakfast is served on summer mornings, and where the chipmunks will sit up and beg for peanuts from amused guests.

Kathy and her spouse, Frank, left corporate insurance and banking careers, respectively, in Boston for the "inn life" in 1992. "We haven't looked back since. One of our rituals prior to coming here was making time for breakfast together or with friends on Sundays. We still enjoy breakfast -- we just have more people to share it with!" The Partschs serve guests in nine guestrooms.

Located on a hilltop, the inn has views of Sugarbush ski slopes, just a quarter mile away. In the summer, the inn "blooms" with flowers. Covered bridges, swimming holes, canoeing the Mad River and hiking the Long Trail are nearby.

Another Sugartree recipe:
Ham and Pineapple Stuffed French Toast, page 123

Grandma Wilkin's Baked Eggs

Ingredients:

    2 slices bacon
    1 egg

- Partially cook bacon. Reserve grease.
- Wrap bacon slices around the sides (but not across the bottom) of a muffin cup, overlapping if necessary.
- Drop a couple of drops bacon grease into bottom of cup.
- Break egg directly into cup, inside the bacon.
- If desired, repeat with enough eggs and bacon to serve the number desired.
- Bake in a preheated oven at 350 degrees for 15 to 20 minutes, or until done to taste. "They don't look done when they are. A knife inserted beside the yolk is the best test."
- To remove from pan, loosen with table knife, if necessary, and slide out. Serve hot.

Makes 1 serving

from **Black Friar Inn**
10 Summer Street
Bar Harbor, ME 04609
207-288-5091

"I learned how to do this when I was about 4 years old -- lots of years ago," said Innkeeper Perry Risley. "My grandmother used to make them as a special breakfast for us. They can be varied in 'doneness' depending on your desires for soft eggs or hard-as-rubber eggs." Today, he and Sharon, his spouse, serve these to guests who gather in the sunroom for breakfast.

This house on a quiet Bar Harbor street was built circa 1900 and survived the 1947 fires that leveled much of Bar Harbor. It fell into disrepair, and Freddie Pooler bought it as a condemned building in 1976. He planned a restaurant, so added the sunroom and a room across the back. Various features, such as mantels of Victorian summer estates on the island, were incorporated and put to new uses here. The previous library was converted into a replica of a British pub. About 1978, he opened it as a B&B. Barbara and Jim Kelly bought it in 1986, added private baths and did more remodeling.

Perry and Sharon, looking to settle in one place after Perry's U.S. Air Force career, fell for the inn's woodwork, design and the good care the previous owners had taken. Falke, their Brittany, immediately fell into his role as the inn dog. The Risleys added a seventh guestroom and did more remodeling. They welcome guests with refreshments in the pub. The harbor, with lobster boats, schooners, yachts and cruise ships (including the QE2), is only a short walk. Guests can park their car at the inn and leave it while in town. Acadia National Park, the second most visited park in the U.S. system, is a short drive.

Another Black Friar Inn recipe:
Sourdough Stuffed French Toast, page 125

Green One-Eyed Jacks

Ingredients:

1 slice favorite bread
1 egg
1/2 to 1 teaspoon butter
Salsa verde
Sharp Cheddar cheese, shredded

- Using a biscuit cutter, cut a hole out of center of bread.
- In a non-stick skillet, heat butter (use as much as you need/want) on medium-high heat.
- When butter is sizzling, put the bread in pan. Gently crack the egg over the hole in the bread, keeping the yolk intact, as you would for a fried egg.
- Fry for a few minutes on medium heat.
- Turn gently and fry other side until all the egg white is cooked and yolk is desired doneness.
- Place on a plate. Add salsa verde in a circle around yolk. Sprinkle with cheese and serve hot.

Makes 1 serving

from **The Old Iron Inn B&B**
155 High Street
Caribou, ME 04736
207-492-IRON (4766)

Also known as "Eggs in a Frame," this dish is a spiced up Southwestern version with salsa verde. Innkeeper Kate McCartney's Arizona-based sister-in-law brought her the recipe. "Salsa verde is made from green chilies and tomatillos and is a mildly spicy/slightly sweet salsa, very different from the tomato salsa we all know -- it is delicious!" Kate serves it to guests who have a fondness for Mexican food.

Kate and Kevin McCartney host guests from all over the world, who visit Aroostook County for business or pleasure. The McCartneys' home is an 80-year-old house boasting interior oak woodwork, which they complement with their antique furnishings. The B&B also showcases their collection of antique irons, the use of which Kevin has researched and can share with guests.

Kate, who is working on her master's degree in English literature, traveled in B&Bs in Great Britain. She and Kevin decided to open their home as a B&B when Kevin, a paleontologist, came to Caribou to teach at the University of Maine Presque Isle. They both enjoy sharing their home with travelers who have chosen to visit the largest county east of the Mississippi. At the same time, "The County," as it is known, has one of the smallest populations, and half the residents' native language is French. Caribou has shops, restaurants and historical and natural science museums. Guests are welcome to enjoy the large selection of books and magazines in the McCartneys' libraries.

Other Old Iron Inn recipes:
Sunshine Punch, page 28
Chocolate Cheesecake Muffins, page 49

Herbed Cheese Soufflé

Ingredients:

2 tablespoons butter
12 eggs, separated
1/4 cup water
3 tablespoons flour
1 teaspoon ground tarragon
3 tablespoons grated Parmesan cheese
1/2 teaspoon salt, divided
Dash of hot cayenne pepper sauce, such as Tabasco®
4 tablespoons finely chopped chives
1 cup grated sharp Cheddar cheese
1 teaspoon cream of tartar
1/4 teaspoon salt

Also:

Tarragon sprig

🥄 Place butter in a 2-quart soufflé dish. Put the dish into the oven as it preheats to 400 degrees. Remove when butter is melted and swirl it around the pan.

🥄 In a large bowl, whisk together egg yolks, water, flour, tarragon, Parmesan cheese, 1/4 teaspoon salt, pepper sauce and chives. Stir in Cheddar cheese.

🥄 With an electric mixer, beat the egg whites, cream of tartar and salt until stiff peaks form.

🥄 Fold a small amount of beaten egg whites into cheese mixture, then fold in remaining egg whites.

🥄 Spoon mixture into the hot, buttered dish. Bake until the soufflé puffs and is firm in the center, 15 to 20 minutes. "This dish cannot sit too long. It will hold its loft for 5 to 10 minutes in the warm oven."

🥄 Remove from oven, quickly garnish with a tarragon sprig and serve by using two serving forks to "cut" the soufflé into portions.

Makes 6 to 8 servings

from **The Inn on South Street**
5 South Street
P.O. Box 478A
Kennebunkport, ME 04046
207-967-5151
800-963-5151

When Eva Downs rushes this soufflé to the table from the oven, guests are already seated and have been enjoying conversation with her and Jack, her husband, in the eat-in kitchen that overlooks the river and ocean. A comfortable ambiance was the aim of Eva and Jack, her husband, when they turned their long-time home into a B&B. The 200-year-old Greek Revival house was owned by a succession of sea captains. Eva and Jack raised three children here, then redecorated to offer three guestrooms and an apartment-like suite. Located in the town's historic district, the inn is a short walk to the popular restaurants, galleries and shops, and just a short drive from beaches.

🏠 *Other Inn on South Street recipes:*
Minted Watermelon Refresher, page 23
Zucchini Apple Coffeecake, page 41

Herbed Shirred Eggs

Ingredients:

1/2 teaspoon butter
5 teaspoons shredded cheese (Monterey Jack or Cheddar)
Dash of tarragon leaves
Dash of ground thyme
Dash of ground marjoram
Dash of chopped parsley, dried or fresh
Dash of oregano
Dash of cumin
2 large eggs
2 teaspoons cream or half-and-half
Dash of paprika

- Melt butter in two small ramekins or custard cups.
- In bottom of each cup, place 2 teaspoons cheese.
- Add a dash of tarragon, thyme, marjoram, parsley, oregano and cumin.
- Break an egg into each cup (do not break yolk).
- Sprinkle the rest of cheese over egg.
- Pour 1 teaspoon cream over each egg and sprinkle each with paprika.
- Bake in a preheated oven at 325 degrees for 25 minutes. Remove from oven and serve hot.

Tester's Comments: Rich and delicious. Don't judge doneness by the yolk since it doesn't change color!

Makes 1 serving

from **The Crab Apple Inn B&B**
P.O. Box 188
Plymouth, NH 03264
603-536-4476

Innkeeper Christine DeCamp serves these eggs often with toasted English muffins and a selection of local jams and jellies. Guests in the five guestrooms gather in the cheery breakfast room to see what Chris has created. She experiments often and has several courses, including fruit, muffins or coffeecakes and an entrée such as this.

This brick Federal-style home was built as a farmhouse in 1835. Over the years, it had several owners and became a B&B in the 1980s. Chris bought it in 1994, after a long career in personnel. She has gardened, stenciled, redecorated and cooked like crazy to make her venture "a go."

Guests are welcome to enjoy homebaked goodies by the fire in the parlor or to enjoy the grounds, complete with a brook and views of Tenney Mountain in the back. Located in the White Mountains and lakes region, the inn often hosts people who want to ski, hike, boat, fish, golf or antique. Lake Winnipesaukee, Franconia Notch and the Flume Gorge and other activities are nearby.

Lobster Omelette

Ingredients:

2 tablespoons extra light olive oil
1/2 green pepper, chopped
1 small onion, chopped
1/2 cup chopped mushrooms
3/4 cup cooked lobster, cut into small pieces
6 eggs, beaten
1/2 teaspoon salt
1/4 teaspoon pepper
1/4 teaspoon dill
1/4 teaspoon sage
1/4 teaspoon garlic powder
1/3 cup milk
1/2 cup Cheddar cheese, shredded

🦞 Pour olive oil in an electric skillet and heat to 300 degrees.

🦞 Place pepper, onion, mushrooms and lobster in olive oil and sauté.

🦞 In a medium bowl, whisk together eggs, salt, pepper, dill, sage, garlic powder and milk.

🦞 Remove sautéed mixture from skillet with a slotted spoon and place into egg mixture.

🦞 Pour all ingredients back into skillet and cook for 5 minutes.

🦞 Add cheese and cook for an additional 5 minutes.

🦞 Run a narrow spatula around rim of skillet to loosen, lift up and fold omelette onto itself. Cook an additional 2 minutes.

🦞 Flip onto other side and cook for 2 minutes. Then cut into six servings and place on serving plates.

Makes 6 servings

from **Bethel Point B&B**
RR 5 Bethel Point Road
P.O. Box 2387
Brunswick, ME 04011
207-725-1115
888-238-8262

The lobster for the omelette comes fresh from the lobster boats that the guests at this B&B might watch at work during breakfast. Betsy and Peter Packard's inn's view of Casco Bay is so spectacular that many guests return often, Betsy notes. For lunches and dinners, the Packards steer their guests to the best seafood restaurants in Brunswick, about eight miles from their home and B&B.

Betsy and Peter worked as a social worker and nurse, respectively, and retired back to Maine after 30 years in Kansas. The home "is one that the family has always dreamed about owning, and we were lucky to be in the right place at the right time," Betsy said. Summertime breakfasts might be served outdoors.

🏠*Another Bethel Point recipe:*
Maine Blueberry Muffins, page 53

The Maine Quiche

Ingredients:

Unbaked pie crust for a one-crust pie
5 ounces mushrooms, sautéed and drained
1 cup shredded Cheddar cheese
1/2 medium onion, chopped and sautéed
4 eggs, beaten
1/2 cup heavy cream
1 teaspoon paprika
1 teaspoon nutmeg
Salt and pepper to taste

Also:

Lobster (cubed), shrimp (shelled) or crabmeat (flaked)
Grated Romano cheese

🖝 Place homemade or store-bought pie crust in a 9 or 10-inch pie plate.

🖝 Layer the mushrooms, cheddar cheese and onions in pie crust.

🖝 In a blender, blend eggs, cream, paprika, nutmeg, salt and pepper. Pour over onions.

🖝 Top with seafood. Sprinkle top with Romano cheese. (Can cover and refrigerate overnight at this point.)

🖝 Bake in a preheated oven at 350 degrees for 1 hour or until a knife inserted in the center comes out clean. Cool for 10 minutes before cutting into wedges and serving.

Makes 6 servings

from The Galen C. Moses House
1009 Washington Street
Bath, ME 04530
888-442-8771

This quiche, using fresh Maine seafood, is always a hit with Innkeeper Jim Haught's guests. "I serve it often to my guests on Sunday mornings or whenever there is a newlywed couple staying." Breakfast is served in the wood-paneled dining room with a fire in the fireplace.

Jim and Larry Kieft purchased this home in 1994 to transform it into a B&B. The house earned something of local celebrity status when the co-innkeepers had it painted in vivid plum, pink and teal. The three-story Italianate deserved more notice and recognition of its grand stature, they thought.

In addition to creating four guestrooms, Jim and Larry have restored the formal parlors, originally used by the Galen Clapp Moses family for entertaining. Outside, guests can enjoy the porches and garden. Don't leave without asking to see the third floor theater, once used to entertain officers from the nearby Naval air station during WWII. The innkeepers will recommend the best local seafood restaurants, as well as sandy beaches, antique shops, museums, galleries and other day trips.

Savory Eggs

Ingredients:

1 8-ounce package Kraft Old English® cheese slices
3 tablespoons butter, cubed
1 cup half-and-half
1/2 teaspoon salt
1/4 teaspoon pepper
1 tablespoon Dijon mustard
14 eggs
1 tablespoon chives, chopped
2 cups sharp Cheddar cheese, grated
Dash or 2 of paprika

- Butter a 9 x 13-inch casserole dish. Cover bottom with cheese slices. Top cheese with dots of butter.
- In a small bowl, whisk together half-and-half, salt, pepper and mustard. Set aside.
- In a separate bowl, beat eggs with chives.
- Pour half of cream mixture over cheese.
- Pour eggs over cream mixture, then top with remaining cream mixture.
- Sprinkle with grated Cheddar and paprika. (May be covered and refrigerated overnight at this point.)
- Bake in a preheated oven at 325 degrees for 40 minutes. Cut in squares and serve immediately.

Makes 14 to 16 servings

from **Maine Stay Inn**
22 High Street
Camden, ME 04843
207-236-9636
Fax 207-236-0621

Rushing this hot dish to the large breakfast table is not the only special part of breakfast here. Innkeepers Diana Robson, her twin sister Donny Smith, and Donny's husband, Peter, have most likely been chatting up the guests during its preparation, as the kitchen is not off-limits to guests here. Then, before breakfast is over, lucky guests might be serenaded in a bit of three-part harmony by the trio (the sisters have won old-time singing contests).

If the innkeepers seem enthusiastic, it is genuine. The family landed here in 1988 after Peter retired from 36 years in the Navy, ready to start a new career -- in one spot. Their 1802 house and attached carriage house have eight guestrooms, a deck, two guest parlors, a TV room, and a whopping forested garden in the back with paths. The often-photographed town harbor is a 5-minute walk past other homes in the historic district. Peter or the sisters will print out detailed trip itineraries from the computer so departing guests can make the most of their Maine stay.

*Another Maine Stay Inn recipe:
Mom's Shortbread, page 198*

Three Cheddar-Apple-Ham Bake

Ingredients:

2 cups apple slices, peeled before slicing
1 tablespoon sugar
1 cup shredded "Three Cheddar Cheese" mixture, such as Sargento® or 1 cup shredded Cheddar
1-1/2 cups chopped ham
2 eggs
3/4 cup milk
3/4 cup buttermilk biscuit mix
1/4 teaspoon nutmeg, optional

- In a large bowl, toss apple slices with sugar.
- Place apple slices evenly in a lightly-buttered 9 x 9-inch baking dish.
- Sprinkle cheese and ham over the apples.
- Beat the eggs. Add milk and biscuit mix, beating or whisking until smooth.
- Pour the egg mixture evenly over the apples, cheese and ham. Sprinkle with optional nutmeg.
- Bake in a preheated oven at 375 degrees for about 30 minutes or until golden brown.

Tester's Comments: I made this and refrigerated it unbaked, covered with plastic wrap, for about seven hours before baking -- it was still wonderful. The apples make a delicious difference in this crustless ham quiche.

Makes 6 servings

from Apple Gate B&B
199 Upland Farm Road
Peterborough, NH 03458
603-924-6543

"This recipe is adapted from one given to us by a guest from Arlington, Virginia," said Innkeeper Dianne Legenhausen. "Knowing how much we love apples here at the Apple Gate, Jane Diehl was kind enough to share it with us. It was an instant success!" Dianne often makes it in six individual ramekins instead of the 9 x 9-inch baking pan.

Dianne and her husband, Ken, opened their B&B in 1990 in an 1832 house. The four upstairs guestrooms all have views of the gardens and the 90-acre apple orchard next door, and each guestroom is named after a different variety of apple. Guests will find a complimentary apple-themed basket in their guestrooms. In spring, the scent from the apple blossoms is intoxicating.

Though Dianne and Ken each enjoyed long careers in the Long Island, New York, area, they decided to move here and begin a new career working together at innkeeping. Called "the Currier and Ives corner of New Hampshire," the Monadnock region boasts many outdoor activities.

Other Apple Gate recipes:
Fruit Sauce, page 85
Apple Crisp, page 172

Almond French Toast

Ingredients:

5 eggs
1 cup light cream or milk
1 teaspoon cinnamon
Dash nutmeg
2 tablespoons almond-flavored
   liqueur, such as Amaretto®

Syrup:
1 pint real maple syrup
2 tablespoons almond-
   flavored liqueur
1/2 cup slivered, blanched almonds
1/3 cup raisins

Also:

French bread, sliced into six 1/2-inch slices
Powdered sugar
Whole strawberries

- For Syrup: In a saucepan, stir together syrup, liqueur, almonds and raisins. Warm over low heat.
- For Batter: Whisk eggs until whites and yolks are blended.
- Stir in cream, cinnamon, nutmeg and liqueur.
- Dip one slice of bread at a time into mixture, coating each piece.
- Grill coated bread on a buttered griddle preheated to 325 degrees (medium-high heat). Turn bread when first side is a medium golden brown. Grill second side.
- Place three slices of bread on a warm plate and ladle with syrup.
- Sprinkle tops with powdered sugar, and garnish with a sliced whole strawberry on the side.

Makes 2 servings of 3 slices each

from **The Blue Hill Inn**
P.O. Box 403
Route 177, Union Street
Blue Hill, ME 04614
207-374-2844
Fax 207-374-2829

"This recipe evolved over six years in our kitchen by our breakfast cook, Debra Smith," said Innkeeper Mary Hartley. "It is a regular offering at breakfast, where we feature four or five entrées each morning. Hints are warming the syrup and the serving plates and turning the toast only once while cooking. The Amaretto® can be adjusted to taste."

The breakfast entrées might include blueberry pancakes, waffles with fresh strawberries and two egg dishes, as well. There's also Canadian bacon, homemade sweet breads and fresh fruit, all enjoyed at the lace-covered tables in the sunny dining room. Then, guests may enjoy dinner at the inn, too.

Guests have been coming to the Blue Hill Inn since 1840, a decade after it was built by a blacksmith. Mary and Don Hartley left careers as administrators in the mental health and mental retardation fields to buy the 11-guestroom inn in 1987. They note that Blue Hill, where the inn is in the historic district, "is home to talented musicians, artists, craftspeople, authors and other nice people."

*Another Blue Hill Inn recipe:
Brown Sugar Coffeecake, page 33*

Banana Almond French Toast

Ingredients:

2 very ripe bananas, well mashed
6 eggs
1-1/2 cups milk
1 tablespoon rum
1/2 teaspoon nutmeg
Pinch of salt
Pinch of sugar
1/4 cup sliced almonds
6 to 8 slices day-old French or challah bread

Also:

Maple syrup

- In a large bowl, whisk together mashed bananas, eggs, milk, rum, nutmeg, salt and sugar.
- Dip bread slices in batter, allowing it to sit for a minute or two to absorb the liquid.
- Place slices on a hot, buttered griddle. Sprinkle slices with almonds.
- Cook for 2 to 3 minutes on each side, until lightly browned. Serve hot with maple syrup.

Makes 6 to 8 slices

from **By the Old Mill Stream**
RR 2, Box 543
Hinesburg, VT 05446
802-482-3613

"I enjoy making something guests have never had," said Innkeeper Michelle Fischer, and this French toast might fit the bill. "I know I've succeeded in delighting them at breakfast when they ask for the recipe." The "teaching kitchen" is large enough so guests often sit at the counter with their morning coffee and observe breakfast being prepared.

Michelle and Steve Fischer's home and inn has a fascinating history. In this section of Hinesburg, known as Mechanicsville, 34 mills were built along Pond Brook, to saw wood, press cider, make flour and to power a number of other businesses. One was a large woolen mill owned by Isaiah Dow and his father. His prosperity allowed him to build this house at the top of the hill, just above the woolen mill. He is perhaps best remembered because in 1884, nearly 30 years after he and his father opened their mill, Isaiah had the mill begin producing flannel for the general market -- and saw his business take off.

Guests can see the waterfall that powered Dow's mill from the back porch, and they can walk down a path to the ruins of the mill itself. The home was built in the 1860s with all the nooks and crannies common in those days. Three guestrooms, a double living room and the dining room are open to guests.

Another By the Old Mill Stream recipe:
Banana Praline Waffles, page 142

Blueberry Stuffed French Toast

Ingredients:

1 8-ounce package cream cheese
1/4 cup sugar
1/8 teaspoon nutmeg
Splash of orange-flavored liqueur
16 slices of 9-grain bread
2 eggs
4 tablespoons sugar
1 teaspoon cinnamon
Splash of vanilla extract

Blueberry Sauce:
2 cups blueberries
1/4 cup sugar
1 tablespoon raspberry vinegar
1/4 teaspoon cinnamon
1/8 teaspoon nutmeg
1/8 teaspoon cloves

🐝 With an electric mixer, beat cream cheese, sugar, nutmeg and liqueur until creamy.

🐝 Spread filling evenly onto 8 slices of bread and cover with remaining 8 slices to form sandwiches.

🐝 For Blueberry Sauce: In a medium pan, place blueberries, sugar, vinegar, cinnamon, nutmeg and cloves. Bring sauce to a boil, stirring occasionally. Boil for 5 minutes. Reduce heat to medium and heat sauce for an additional 10 minutes, or until it begins to thicken. Keep warm.

🐝 In a shallow bowl, mix eggs, 4 tablespoons sugar, cinnamon and vanilla.

🐝 Dunk each sandwich into the egg mixture, coating both sides, and place on a hot griddle.

🐝 Cook each sandwich until golden brown on both sides (about 5 minutes each side). To serve, cut sandwiches into four triangles and arrange them on a plate with the points up, leaning on each other.

🐝 Spoon warm Blueberry Sauce over the French toast points and serve immediately.

Makes 8 servings

from **Applebrook B&B**
Route 115A
Jefferson, NH 03583
603-586-7713
800-545-6504

This is one of the hearty breakfasts that might be served to guests heading off for a day at the White Mountains ski slopes or x-c trails, or canoeing, kayaking or biking. Most of Applebrook's guests are active, outdoorsy types and many families come to the inn, said Innkeepers Martin Kelly and Sandra Conley.

This husband-and-wife team offers 14 guestrooms in this Queen Anne Victorian farmhouse. They also have a dormitory and can accommodate groups up to 30. It is a favorite with the Appalachian Mountain Club members, who come a couple of times a year.

Sandra and Martin bought this old farmhouse after Sandra spent 12 years as a geologist. They opted for a career move into innkeeping. The farmhouse had served as a ski lodge and nursing home and needed major work, much of which was scrubbing. They emphasize friendly, informal accommodations where kids and dogs are welcome.

Farmer's French Toast

Ingredients:

 1 8-ounce package cream cheese
 1/4 teaspoon cinnamon
 1/4 cup apple juice
 12 slices white bread
 1-1/2 apples, cut into quarters and cored
 4 eggs, beaten
 1 teaspoon vanilla extract

Also:

 Salt and pepper
 Powdered sugar
 Pure maple syrup

 ➤ Cream the cream cheese, cinnamon and apple juice. Spread on 6 slices of bread.

 ➤ Slice each apple quarter into 8 thin slices and place on top of cream cheese mixture.

 ➤ Place other slice of bread on top to make a sandwich.

 ➤ Repeat with rest of ingredients to make six sandwiches. (At this point, the sandwiches can be tightly wrapped in plastic wrap and refrigerated overnight.)

 ➤ In a large bowl, whisk together eggs and vanilla. Add salt and pepper to taste.

 ➤ Dip each sandwich in the egg mixture, then flip and dip other side.

 ➤ Fry on a hot, buttered griddle until golden brown. Flip and fry other side until golden.

 ➤ Serve hot, dusted with powdered sugar, and with warmed maple syrup.

Makes 6 servings

from **The Benjamin Prescott Inn**
Route 124 East
Jaffrey, NH 03452
603-532-6637

Innkeepers Janice and Barry Miller use apples from a local orchard in this French toast, a favorite with guests. It is served with syrup made by the Millers from their own maple trees and is the result of experimenting with local foods in order to showcase them while serving guests. Breakfast here is served in the cheery yellow dining room. The French toast would be accompanied by a freshly-baked coffeecake or specialty bread.

The inn, originally built for Revolutionary War Col. Benjamin Prescott, was purchased by the Millers in 1988. Barry had spent nearly three decades opening hotels for major corporations, and it was time to own and operate their own enterprise. The Millers offer nine guestrooms, each named after a member of Prescott's family.

🏠 *Another Benjamin Prescott Inn recipe:*
Raspberry Butter, page 90

Ham and Pineapple Stuffed French Toast

Ingredients:

    3 eggs
    1 cup milk
    3 tablespoons sugar
    1 8-ounce package cream cheese, softened (low-fat is OK)
    1 8-ounce can crushed pineapple, drained
    12 1-inch thick slices of French bread
    6 medium-thick slices boneless ham

Also:

    Maple syrup, warmed

- In a medium bowl, whisk together eggs, milk and sugar. Set aside.
- In a separate bowl, mix cream cheese and drained pineapple with a fork. Set aside.
- Trim ham to fit bread slices.
- Spread cream cheese mixture on one side of 6 bread slices. Top with a slice of ham and another slice of bread to make a sandwich.
- Dip each sandwich in the egg mixture, coating both sides as you would for French toast.
- Place dipped bread in a buttered 9 x 13-inch baking pan. Cover and refrigerate overnight.
- In the morning, remove pan from refrigerator while preheating oven to 400 degrees.
- Bake, uncovered, for 20 minutes or until bread is golden brown. Serve hot with warmed maple syrup.

Makes 6 servings

from The Sugartree, A Country Inn
Sugarbush Access Road
Warren, VT 05674
802-583-3211
800-666-8907

A second-prize winner in the 1995 Jones Dairy Farm B&B Recipe Contest, this recipe continues to please guests at Kathy and Frank Partsch's inn. Kathy may have to triple the recipe to serve guests in the nine guestrooms, but she appreciates that most of the work can be done the night before. While the ham flavor is delicious, those who don't eat meat can make it without the ham.

Kathy and Frank left corporate careers in Boston in 1992 and bought this operating inn, once a ski lodge. They decorated as they envisioned a country inn should be, with Waverly wallpapers and ruffled curtains.

The hillside gazebo is the site of summer breakfasts, afternoon refreshments and an occasional wedding. Covered bridges, white steepled churches, antique and craft shops are close by, as is golf, biking, tennis, hiking the Long Trail and swimming. Sugarbush ski resort's famed slopes are only a quarter mile away.

Another Sugartree recipe:
Farmer's Omelette, page 110

Orange French Toast

Ingredients:

3 medium eggs, beaten
1/3 cup orange juice
1/2 teaspoon vanilla extract
1 teaspoon grated orange peel
4 slices bread ("Day old is better")

Also:

Butter
Maple syrup
Grated orange peel

- In a bowl large enough to hold a slice of bread, whisk together eggs, orange juice, vanilla and orange peel.
- Dip bread slices into mixture until all liquid is absorbed.
- Spray a preheated frying pan or griddle with non-stick cooking spray (remove from heat when spraying).
- Lightly brown bread on both sides.
- Serve immediately with butter, warm maple syrup and a garnish of grated orange peel on top.

Makes 2 servings

from **Bass Cove Farm B & B**
Route 185, Box 132
Sorrento, ME 04677
207-422-3564

After eating an orange omelette, Innkeeper Mary Ann Solet was so inspired she came home and devised this recipe for French toast. It's often on the menu and guests enjoy it while looking out on Bass Cove from the dining room or porch.

Mary Ann and Mike Tansey have been hosting Downeast visitors in their 1840s farmhouse since 1992. They turned their empty nest into their dream of B&B innkeeping, converting a former "mother-in-law apartment" with a separate entrance into the B&B. Mary Ann is an editor, writer, gardener and fiber craftsperson. Mike is a teacher, group-home counselor and photographer, plus two-time "Harry S. Truman Manure Pitchoff" champ at Maine's Common Ground Country Fair.

Sorrento, pop. 250, is about halfway between Ellsworth and Milbridge, and the B&B is only a mile off Route 1. Sorrento's working harbor is shared by lobster boats and pleasure craft. The shore is open to beachcombers looking for shells.

An oceanside golf course is a half-mile away, and Mt. Desert Island's Cadillac Mountain in Acadia National Park can be seen from the harbor at the village green. Restaurants serving lobster, studios of potters and artists, flea markets and antique shops are found throughout the area.

Sourdough Stuffed French Toast

Ingredients:

6 slices sourdough bread, crust removed, cut into 1/4-inch cubes
4 ounces cream cheese, cubed (low-fat is OK)
1 to 2 cups blueberries or other fresh berries
6 eggs
1/4 cup maple syrup
1 cup milk
Cinnamon and nutmeg to taste

Fruit Sauce:
2 cups fresh blueberries
2 cups fresh strawberries
1/2 cup sugar
1/2 cup orange juice
2-3 tablespoons lemon juice.

- In a lightly-buttered 8 x 8-inch baking dish, place half of the bread cubes.
- Place cream cheese cubes on top, followed by fruit. Top with remaining bread cubes.
- In a medium bowl, whisk together eggs, syrup, milk, cinnamon and nutmeg. Pour over bread.
- Cover dish with plastic wrap and refrigerate overnight.
- In the morning, remove plastic wrap and bake in a preheated oven at 350 degrees for 45 minutes, or until set.
- For Fruit Sauce: In a large saucepan, stir together berries, sugar, orange juice and lemon juice. Cook over medium heat, stirring often, for about 5 minutes. Pour mixture into a blender and pureé. Return it to the saucepan and heat until warm. Serve Fruit Sauce in a pitcher or poured on top of French toast.

Makes 6 servings

from **Black Friar Inn**
10 Summer Street
Bar Harbor, ME 04609
207-288-5091

"Like many other innkeepers, this is a recipe I created because I wasn't satisfied with the flavor of other Stuffed French Toasts," said Perry Risley. He prefers to use wild Maine blueberries and Maine maple syrup. "I find that if I freeze the bread and cream cheese, it makes it easier to cube them."

Perry and Sharon, his wife, serve this for breakfast in the sunroom at a large breakfast table that seats 10 guests. Guests meet in the sunroom to eat and chat before heading out for a day exploring Acadia National Park, whale watching, sailing, touring the harbor, or stuffing themselves with delicious local lobster.

The Risleys acquired this operating inn in 1995, having searched for the right inn to buy after Perry's 20-year career in the Air Force (which meant moving every three years). The inn is in a 1900 home which has been completely rebuilt, remodeled and redecorated by various owners over the years. They offer seven guestrooms, plenty of parking, and a replica of a British pub in the former library, where guests enjoy afternoon refreshments and swap stories of what to do on Mt. Desert Island. Falke, the inn's Brittany spaniel, enjoys the guests almost as much as the Risleys do.

Another Black Friar Inn recipe:
Grandma Wilkin's Baked Eggs, page 111

Applesauce Spice Pancakes

Ingredients:

2 cups flour
3 tablespoons sugar
3 teaspoons baking powder
3/4 teaspoon salt
1 teaspoon cinnamon
1/4 teaspoon nutmeg
1/4 teaspoon allspice
1 cup milk or buttermilk plus some extra
2 eggs
2 tablespoons vegetable oil
1 teaspoon vanilla extract
1 cup applesauce

- In a large bowl, sift together flour, sugar, baking powder, salt, cinnamon, nutmeg and allspice.
- In a separate bowl, whisk together milk, eggs, oil, vanilla and applesauce.
- Pour milk mixture into flour mixture. Stir until all ingredients are well-moistened.
- Heat griddle to 375 degrees and brush with vegetable oil. Stir pancake batter, adding more milk "until the batter is the consistency of heavy cream."
- Pour 1/4 cup of the batter onto the hot griddle. Cook until the pancakes are bubbly, then flip and cook until golden brown on the other side.
- "You will need to keep adding milk to the batter to maintain the appropriate consistency of cream."
- Serve pancakes hot with warmed maple syrup.

Tester's Comments: Thin the batter with more applesauce for more apple taste! Top with whipped cream and syrup.

Makes about 22 pancakes

from **Maine Stay Inn & Cottages**
34 Maine Street
P.O. Box 500-A
Kennebunkport, ME 04046
207-967-2117
800-950-2117

One of Carol Copeland's guests gave her this recipe "and it has become one of our most popular breakfast dishes." Guests in the six guestrooms might descend the flying staircase in this circa 1860 home to gather for breakfast. Homemade muffins or scones, granola, yogurt and fruit might accompany an entrée such as this. Then guests head off for a day shopping and browsing art galleries or exploring the local beaches, along the bike path or breakwater, or at the wildlife refuge. A lobsterboat cruise, where guests see traps pulled and learn about lobstering, is a popular option.

Other Maine Stay Inn & Cottages recipes:
Apricot Scones, page 46
Pumpkin Ginger Muffins, page 56
Christmas Prelude Gingersnaps, page 156
Mrs. Miild's Oatmeal Cookies, page 199

Banana Oat Pancakes

Ingredients:
    3 bananas
    1-1/4 cups milk
    2 eggs
    2 teaspoons sugar
    1 teaspoon salt
    3 tablespoons vegetable oil
    2 cups flour
    5 teaspoons baking powder
    1 cup old-fashioned rolled oats

Also:
    Maple syrup, warmed

- Purée bananas with milk and pour into a large bowl.
- Whisk together eggs, sugar, salt and oil. Stir into banana mixture.
- Stir in flour and baking powder and mix thoroughly.
- Stir in oats.
- Ladle by heaping tablespoons onto a hot, buttered griddle. Cook on medium-high heat for 1 to 2 minutes per side, until bubbles appear, and the pancakes are golden brown.
- Serve hot with Vermont butter and maple syrup.

Tester's Comments: Fragrant! These filling pancakes would be great before a day on the slopes at Stowe or Sugarbush. They are even better with a little cinnamon or nutmeg added to the batter.

Makes 22 to 24 3-inch pancakes

from Thatcher Brook Inn
Route 100 North
P.O. Box 490
Waterbury, VT 05676
802-244-5911
800-292-5911

Inn guests might enjoy these pancakes in one of four dining rooms at this inn, one of which is reserved as a romantic, fireside dining room for couples only. That's one of the things Kelly and Pete Varty have done to try to make their inn live up to its billing as one of Vermont's most romantic inns.

While the address says Waterbury, and Ben & Jerry's Ice Cream headquarters is just down the road a piece, historians would argue that the town is really Colbyville. Here, Stedman Wheeler, the local lumber baron, built a grand Queen Anne Victorian mansion along Thatcher Brook. When Pete and Kelly bought this inn in 1986, they began renovations. In 1989, the inn was completely restored and a covered walkway was built to connect the Wheeler's house to the inn, and more guestrooms (24 total) and a small conference center were added to complement the restaurant. Located just eight miles from the popular village of Stowe, guests find a wide variety of area activities.

Blueberry Cornmeal Pancakes

Ingredients:

1-1/2 cups coarse yellow cornmeal
1/4 cup whole wheat flour
1/4 cup oat bran
1 teaspoon baking soda
1/2 teaspoon salt
2 tablespoons maple syrup
2 tablespoons vegetable oil
1 egg, lightly beaten
2 cups low-fat buttermilk
1-1/2 cups small blueberries, fresh or frozen "dry pack"

 In a medium bowl, stir together cornmeal, flour, oat bran, baking soda and salt.

 In a small bowl, whisk together syrup, oil, egg and buttermilk. Stir well.

 Add syrup mixture to cornmeal mixture.

 Let batter stand for 15 minutes to soften cornmeal. Add additional milk if required for a thin enough consistency.

 Pour batter on a preheated griddle and sprinkle with blueberries. Flip when tops are bubbly and golden brown other side. Serve with warmed maple syrup or blueberry sauce.

Makes about 15 4-inch pancakes

from **The Elms B&B**
84 Elm Street
Camden, ME 04843
207-236-6250
800-755-ELMS

Innkeeper Ted Panayotoff serves these pancakes often, using fresh wild Maine blueberries whenever possible. "Next to lobster, blueberries and cornmeal are traditional Maine foods," he said. This recipe combines them beautifully for the candlelit breakfasts served in the Elms' dining room.

Ted and Jo, his spouse, came to Camden in July 1994 for a windjammer cruise. "Our only intent was to spend a few days relaxing aboard the schooner," Ted said. After the cruise and a trip exploring the coast's lighthouses, they returned to New Jersey, quit their jobs, sold their house and bought The Elms. Their heads still swimming, they hosted their first guests Oct. 21, 1994, just two days after closing the sale and three months after first setting foot in Maine.

Lighthouse enthusiasts, the Panayotoffs have decorated their inn in nautical themes, and they are happy to suggest lighthouse tours to guests. Their 1806 home, built by sea Captain Calvin Curtis, is four blocks from the harbor where their adventure began. Guests can sightsee on a lobsterboat, kayak, hike, bike, ski, swim, antique, shop and enjoy lobster and other seafood.

Another Elms recipe:
The Megunticookie, page 196

Buttermilk Blueberry Pancakes

Ingredients:

1 egg
1 cup buttermilk
2 tablespoons vegetable oil
1 cup flour
1 tablespoon sugar
1 teaspoon baking powder
1/2 teaspoon baking soda
1/2 teaspoon salt
Wild blueberries, frozen

Also:

Vermont maple syrup

🍂 In a large bowl, beat egg. Beat in buttermilk, vegetable oil, flour, sugar, baking powder, baking soda and salt until smooth.

🍂 Ladle about 1/4 cup batter onto hot, buttered griddle.

🍂 Sprinkle 1 tablespoon frozen blueberries onto each pancake. Cook until golden brown, then flip and cook on other side.

🍂 Serve hot with warm pure maple syrup.

Tester's Comments: These are just fabulous (and easy) from-scratch pancakes, with or without the berries.

Makes 12 4-inch pancakes

from **Hill Farm Inn**
RR 2, Box 2015
Arlington, VT 05250
802-375-2269
800-882-2545

"We've discovered the secret to nice-looking blueberry pancakes is to sprinkle the frozen blueberries into the batter already on the griddle," said Joanne Hardy. "Never stir them in ahead of time or you'll have purple pancakes."

Joanne and George Hardy's inn is so popular that breakfast cook Sharon Knight is making enough of this recipe to serve as many as 36 guests a day during summer and fall seasons. She comes in early to make homemade muffins, pancakes, bacon or sausage and eggs any style, served 7:30-9:30 in the inn's dining room. Home-cooked meals (with produce from the garden) are extended to dinner, when a four-course feast is served. Seven guestrooms are located upstairs in the 1830 main inn, plus six rooms in the 1790 guest house next door and another four seasonal cabins. Families, couples and individuals have been coming since 1905 to enjoy the inn's quiet 50 acres along the Battenkill River. They can hike, bike, antique, shop, fish or ski.

🏠 *Other Hill Farm Inn recipes:*
Oats 'n Wheat Bread, page 73
Strawberry Rhubarb Jam, page 94

Casco Bay Raspberry Pancakes

Ingredients:
- 1 cup flour
- 2 tablespoons sugar
- 3/4 cup milk
- 2 tablespoons vegetable oil
- 2 tablespoon vinegar
- 1 teaspoon baking soda
- 1 egg, beaten
- 1 cup raspberries, fresh (if using frozen berries, defrost for 1-1/2 minutes in microwave, drain and add just before cooking)

Also:
- Maple syrup
- Whipped cream
- Additional raspberries

- In a large bowl, stir together flour and sugar.
- In a separate bowl, mix milk, oil and vinegar. Stir in baking soda.
- When milk mixture foams, pour it into flour mixture and mix well. Stir in beaten egg.
- Fold in raspberries.
- Ladle batter onto a hot griddle, cooking until bubbles appear and top dries. Then flip and cook on other side until golden brown.
- Garnish with a dab of whipped cream and a raspberry on the top. Serve with warm Maine maple syrup.

Tester's Comments: Slather on the Raspberry Butter, p. 90, add whipped cream and you won't miss the syrup!

Makes 8 to 10 4-inch pancakes

from **Andrews Lodging B&B**
417 Auburn Street
Portland, ME 04103
207-797-9157
Fax 207-797-9040

"This is my best recipe," says Innkeeper Elizabeth Andrews. "It's been in my husband's family forever. I do not know where it came from, but when we visited the family summer cottage in Casco Bay every summer, we always made this recipe." The island version usually was blueberry, but Elizabeth uses raspberries from her garden patch for this version.

Elizabeth, a former college professor, and Doug, a veterinarian, turned their family home into a six-guestroom B&B. Located just five minutes from downtown Portland and the historic district, their Colonial home is convenient to Portland's attractions and restaurants. Elizabeth, a Maine native, believes "we have it all right here in our own backyard" (given her beautiful gardens, she means that literally!).

Chocolate Chip Pancakes

Ingredients:

    2 cups self-rising flour
    1 tablespoon baking powder
    2 eggs, separated
    1 cup milk

Also:

    Semi-sweet chocolate chips or miniature chips

- In a large bowl, combine flour and baking powder.
- Add egg yokes and milk, mixing thoroughly with a whisk.
- In the bowl of an electric mixer, beat egg whites until stiff. Fold into flour mixture.
- Grease a preheated grill or griddle and ladle about 1/3 cup of pancake batter at once onto it.
- Sprinkle with chocolate chips.
- When pancakes begin to rise and form little holes on top, flip over and leave on grill until cooked.
- Serve on plate with real maple syrup.

Makes about 8 pancakes

from **Nereledge Inn**
River Road
P.O. Box 547
North Conway, NH 03860
603-356-2831
Fax 603-356-7085

This recipe is adapted from David Halpin's grandmother's recipe. It is very popular at the inn, especially when children are staying. Families with children find the inn a great choice, with an informal atmosphere and the Saco River swimming hole just a short walk. The village center is also a short walk, with the Conway Scenic Railroad depot and a playground. Many guests also come to hike, mountain bike (David is a biker and can offer suggestions), climb rock ledges, ski, shop outlet malls, fly fish, or enjoy the fall foliage. The old-fashioned inn is just past the railroad bridge on River Road.

Valerie and David bought the inn in 1981 and offer 11 guestrooms in their large home. The inn is designed to be friendly, and guests can have one of David's home brews by the fireplace in the pub room. There are three sitting rooms, games, a bike shed, a place to wax skis, and the Halpins will arrange for babysitting or pack a picnic lunch. Those arriving on the Trailways bus from Logan airport are transported to and from the bus by the Halpins. Part of the inn was built in 1787, and a three-story addition was moved to the site during the next decade. It has served as an inn for most of the 1900s. Valerie, a native of England, and David, North Conway's deputy fire chief, will make suggestions for dining and exploring the area.

Another Nereledge Inn recipe:
Cherry Tomato and Basil Omelettes, page 107

German Crown Pancakes

Ingredients:

3 eggs
1/2 cup milk
1/2 cup or more flour, sifted
1/2 teaspoon salt
2 tablespoons butter, melted
Vegetable oil

Raspberry Sauce:
1/2 to 2/3 cup raspberry preserves
Cold water

Also:

Powdered sugar
Whipped cream
Sliced almonds

Fruit Filling:
1/2 cantaloupe, peeled and diced
1 apple, cored and thinly sliced
1 orange, peeled, cut into bite-size pieces
1 pear, peeled, cored and sliced
1 small bunch grapes
1 kiwi, peeled and sliced
2 bananas, peeled and sliced
1/2 cup or more blueberries, strawberries
or cherries

🍃 For Pancakes: In medium size bowl, whisk eggs until frothy. Add milk and whisk again.

🍃 Sift flour and salt onto a piece of waxed paper. Bring edges of paper together to form funnel and gradually shake flour into egg mixture while whisking. Whisk entire mixture thoroughly.

🍃 Blend in melted butter with whisk. Batter should be creamy, not runny (you may add 1 to 2 tablespoons more flour, depending on size of eggs used).

🍃 Coat insides of four 6-inch cast iron skillets with vegetable oil. Divide batter among four skillets.

🍃 Bake in a preheated oven at 425 degrees for approximately 20 minutes, or until top edges are browned and very firm ("they will fall apart if not cooked enough").

🍃 For Raspberry Sauce: Whisk raspberry preserves with enough cold water to make a fairly thick sauce.

🍃 For Fruit Filling: In a large bowl, mix together cantaloupe, apple, orange, pear, grapes and kiwi.

🍃 Remove pancakes from their pans to a large plate and dust pancake with powdered sugar.

🍃 Move to serving plate and place sliced bananas on each pancake. Next, scoop mixed fruit on top of bananas. Add desired berries.

🍃 Top with whipped cream. Spoon Raspberry Sauce over cream and sprinkle with sliced almonds.

Makes 4 servings

from **The Jeweled Turret Inn**
40 Pearl Street
Belfast, ME 04915
207-338-2304
800-696-2304

German Crown Pancakes are one of the signature breakfasts of this 1898 inn, which Cathy and Carl Heffentrager opened in 1987. The young couple moved here from Alaska after vacationing on the coast and discovering Belfast. They spent a year restoring the home themselves before opening seven guestrooms. Guests come to sail Penobscot Bay or take a walking tour of the historic district.

🏠 *Other Jeweled Turret Inn recipes:*
Chocolate Mint Scones, page 50
Sourdough Gingerbread Belgian Waffles, page 143

Good Morning Fruit Crepes

Ingredients:

2-1/2 cups milk
4 tablespoons butter, cubed
2 cups flour, sifted and swept level with knife
1/4 teaspoon salt
4 eggs

Also:

Vegetable oil
Sugar or sweetener

Fruit Filling:

Fresh mango, papaya, blueberries,
   peaches or strawberries to serve 10
2 8-ounce packages cream cheese
3 tablespoons sugar
1/4 cup skim milk
1 teaspoon vanilla extract

- In a small saucepan, heat milk and butter until butter has melted.
- Combine flour and salt in food processor. With motor running, add milk mixture and eggs until just blended. Let stand 30 minutes.
- Brush 10-inch crepe pan with vegetable oil. Set over medium heat and heat until smoking.
- Pour 1/4 cup batter into pan, tilting and turning pan immediately so batter will coat evenly.
- Turn the crepe in 3 to 4 minutes, or when underside is brown. Crepe may have a few holes. Brown other side 2 to 3 minutes. Slide onto towel to cool.
- Repeat process until all batter is used. Prepare crepes the evening before, if desired. Refrigerate flat with wax paper between each crepe.
- For Fruit Filling: Dice fruit and set aside. Blend cream cheese, sugar, milk and vanilla extract with an electric mixer or in a food processor until smooth and spreadable. Spread cream cheese mixture on each crepe and sprinkle with diced fruit. Roll up and place on serving platter seam side down.
- Process remaining fruit mixture in food processor, adding sweetener to taste. Drizzle across crepes before serving.

Makes 10 crepes

from **University Guest House**
47 Mill Road
Durham, NH 03824
603-868-2728
Fax 603-868-2744

You can be sure these crepes won't be popping up at every B&B in New England. "This recipe was created by our intern, Anna, who learned it from her Ukranian mother," said Innkeeper Elizabeth Fischer.

Beth's four-guestroom B&B is located smack dab across the street from the University of New Hampshire, hence its name, and hence the availability of wonderful interns, like Anna, from the hospitality program. Guests often include visiting professors or lecturers or parents visiting their kids. Beth aims to make her 1930 Dutch Colonial home a home-away-from-home for visitors. Breakfast always includes homemade muffins or scones, fruit and an entrée such as this, served in the airy dining room. Beth, a builder and real estate broker, opened the B&B in 1994 in response to a need for B&B lodging for University travelers and visitors to the seacoast.

Hannah's Baked Apple Puff

Ingredients:

2 Granny Smith apples, peeled, cored and cut to 1/4-inch slices
1/4 cup butter
Heaping 1/4 cup sugar
1-1/2 teaspoons cinnamon
Zest of 1 orange, minced
1 cup flour
6 eggs
1/4 teaspoon salt
1 cup milk
1/4 cup orange juice
1/2 cup sugar

Strawberry Sauce:
    1 10-ounce package frozen sweetened
      strawberries, defrosted
    1 tablespoon orange juice

Topping:
    3 ounces cream cheese, softened
    2 tablespoons powdered sugar
    1/3 cup sour cream

 Sauté the apples in butter until tender. Remove from heat.

 Stir together the heaping 1/4 cup sugar and cinnamon and add to apples. Stir until sugar is incorporated into the butter.

 Spray a 9 x 13-inch pan with non-stick cooking spray and spread apples evenly on bottom.

 Cover with aluminum foil and bake in a preheated oven at 425 degrees for 15 minutes or until bubbly.

 With an electric mixer, beat orange zest, flour, eggs, salt, milk, orange juice and sugar.

 Pour over bubbling apples and return to oven for 15 minutes. Reduce heat to 350 degrees and bake for an additional 15 to 20 minutes, or until puffed and golden.

 For Strawberry Sauce: Place strawberries and orange juice in blender and purée. Warm on stovetop.

 For Topping: Beat together cream cheese, powdered sugar, and then the sour cream.

 Cut puff into six squares. Sprinkle with powdered sugar. Top with warmed purée, and place a dollop of topping on top.

Makes 6 servings

from **Hannah Davis House**
186 Depot Rd
Fitzwilliam, NH 03447
603-585-3344

Innkeeper Kaye Terpstra "played with" this recipe for weeks before it became a standard at her B&B, served with scrambled eggs, homemade turkey sausage and a green vegetable (yes, vegetables at breakfast!). Guests always gather before breakfast by the hearth in the kitchen to talk to Kaye and each other.

Kaye and Mike, her husband, ran a small grocery store in a nearby village for 10 years before beginning restoration of this circa 1820 Federal-style home. "We worked for a year together tearing out walls, adding insulation, installing bathrooms, stripping woodwork." Their B&B opened with one guestroom in 1990 and now has six. The home is located near the town common.

Another Hannah Davis House recipe:
Spanikopita, page 149

Lemon Ricotta Pancakes

Ingredients:
- 3/4 cup flour
- 1/2 teaspoon nutmeg
- 1 cup ricotta cheese
- 1 tablespoon sugar
- 1 teaspoon baking powder
- Grated peel of 1 lemon (about 1 tablespoon)
- 2 eggs
- 2/3 cup milk
- Juice of 1 lemon (2 to 3 tablespoons)

Also:
- Powdered sugar
- Vermont maple syrup

- In a large bowl, stir together flour, nutmeg, ricotta cheese, sugar, baking powder and lemon peel.

- In a separate bowl, whisk together eggs, milk and lemon juice.

- Stir egg mixture into flour mixture.

- Pour approximately 1/4 cup batter per pancake onto a hot, oiled grill. Cook pancakes until golden brown, flip once and cook the other side.

- Arrange finished pancakes on a warm platter and dust with powdered sugar.

- Serve with Vermont maple syrup.

Makes 10 pancakes

from **Grünberg Haus B&B**
RR 2, Box 1595
Route 100 South
Waterbury, VT 05676
802-244-7726
800-800-7760

"Returning guests claim they dream about these pancakes," said Innkeeper Chris Sellers. Fortunately for a busy innkeeper, the pancakes are simple. He might have to double or triple the recipe to serve guests in the 11 guestrooms.

Guests here end up at the dining room table with huge appetites. Skiers find Stowe is just up the road, and cross-country ski trails leave from the property. Hiking, biking and canoeing are popular summer pursuits, as is tennis on the inn's court. Ben and Jerry's ice cream factory tours, Green Mountain Coffee Roasters and Green Mountain Chocolates shops are nearby.

The sauna and fireplace welcome guests home after a busy day. Guests like to visit with the chickens (perhaps gather eggs before breakfast) and ducks. Chris often plays a little Bach on the Steinway during breakfast.

Other Grünberg Haus recipes:
Green Mountain Lemon Bread, page 70
Glazed Orange Slices, page 99
Vermont Cheddar Pie, page 151

Light and Fluffy Pancakes

Ingredients:

1 cup sour milk or buttermilk
1 egg, separated
1 cup flour
1 teaspoon sugar
3/4 teaspoon baking powder
1/2 teaspoon salt
1/2 teaspoon baking soda
1 tablespoon melted butter or vegetable oil
1/2 cup mashed banana, optional
2 tablespoons chopped walnuts, optional

🍂 For sour milk: Add 1/4 cup plain yogurt to 3/4 cup milk or 1 tablespoon vinegar to 7/8 cup milk, stir and then set aside.

🍂 With an electric mixer, beat egg white until stiff peaks form. Set aside.

🍂 In a large bowl, mix flour, sugar, salt, baking powder, salt and baking soda.

🍂 In a separate bowl, whisk together egg yolk, soured milk, melted butter and optional mashed banana.

🍂 Add milk mixture to dry ingredients and add optional walnuts. Stir just until all ingredients are blended (over-stirring "toughens" pancakes).

🍂 Fold in beaten egg white. Batter will be thick.

🍂 Heat lightly-buttered griddle to medium hot. Spoon 1 to 2 heaping tablespoons batter onto griddle, spread batter out with the back of the spoon, and cook until bubbles appear and just start to break. Flip and cook other side until golden brown.

Tester's Comments: These are light and fluffy, yet filling -- and very low-fat, too. Add cinnamon if you wish.

Makes 8 4-inch pancakes

from **The Country Porch B&B**
281 Moran Road
Hopkinton, NH 03229
603-746-6391

"One of our guests commented, 'This is the first time I've had pancakes that didn't need syrup!'"said Innkeeper Tom Solomon, who often makes this recipe. "The beaten egg white and the sour milk are our secrets." There's no secret as to why guests seek out this B&B -- the food, the location, and, of course, the wrap-around porch, where many a guest settles into a rocker for a longer time than originally intended. Tom and Wendy Solomon opened their 18th century reproduction home in 1994. Guests come to relax and enjoy the surrounding area, with plenty of country attractions like auctions, fishing and skiing.

🏠 *Other Country Porch B&B recipes:*
This is Such Good Punch, page 29
Buttery Orange Pecan Scones, page 48

Maine Wild Blueberry Pancakes

Ingredients:

    1 cup milk
    1 egg
    1/4 cup sour cream
    1 cup flour
    1 tablespoon baking powder
    1 tablespoon sugar
    1/4 teaspon salt
    2 tablespoons butter, melted
    1/2 to 3/4 cup fresh Maine blueberries, washed and picked over

Also:

    About 1 tablespoon flour

- In a large bowl, whisk together milk, egg and sour cream.
- In a separate bowl, stir together flour, baking powder, sugar and salt.
- Add flour mixture all at once to milk. Stir only until large lumps disappear.
- Mix in butter.
- In a separate bowl, "dust" blueberries with flour. Fold them gently into batter.
- Ladle about 1/4 cup batter onto a hot, buttered griddle and cook for 2 to 3 minutes per side. Flip and cook on other side until golden brown. Serve hot with pure maple syrup.

Makes 12 4-inch pancakes

from **Admiral Peary House B&B**
9 Elm Street
Fryeburg, ME 04037
207-935-3365
800-237-8080

These unusual sour cream pancakes with flavor-packed wild blueberries are a special treat for guests in the six guestrooms here. Innkeeper Nancy Greenberg has been cooking and baking since she was a girl spending summers with her family and grandparents at a cottage in Michigan. Guests gather in the large country kitchen for a full, homemade breakfast.

Whether Admiral Peary did make it to the North Pole is debatable, but he surely spent a number of years in this house. He lived here with his mother before he began surveying for the Panama Canal. Nancy and Ed, avid tennis players, enjoy the home's red clay tennis court and invite guests to practice or even schedule a lesson. Billiards, an outdoor hot tub, fishing, swimming and canoeing the nearby Saco River, biking around the village and climbing up Jockey Cap to enjoy the views are other favorite pursuits. Winters guests snowhose on the inn's eight acres. Nancy and Ed, who formerly taught school in Canada, decided innkeeping would be a good career change. Now, 14 years and two B&Bs later, they are still enjoying innkeeping.

Another Admiral Peary House recipe:
Carrot Spice Cake, page 179

Maple Apple Walnut Pancakes

Ingredients:

1 cup flour
1-1/2 cups whole wheat flour
1 tablespoon baking powder
Pinch of salt
2 eggs, beaten
1 cup buttermilk
1-1/2 cups milk
4 tablespoons melted butter or vegetable oil
2 tablespoons Vermont maple syrup
1 apple, chopped (and/or banana, strawberries, blueberries, kiwi)
1/2 cup chopped walnuts

Also:

Cinnamon

- In a large bowl, stir together flour, whole wheat flour, baking powder and salt.

- In a separate bowl, whisk together eggs, buttermilk, milk, butter and maple syrup.

- Pour egg mixture into flour mixture and stir until combined. Then let sit for at least 10 minutes.

- Pour about 1/4 cup batter per pancake onto a hot, buttered griddle.

- Drop some chopped apple (and/or other fruit) and walnuts onto each pancake, and sprinkle with cinnamon.

- Flip pancake over when it begins to bubble and appear dry on top. Cook on other side until golden brown. Serve warm with pure maple syrup and Maple Butter, page 89.

Makes 12 pancakes

from **Red Clover Inn**
Woodward Road
Mendon, VT 05701
802-775-2290
800-752-0571

This is one of the favorite entrées served at this country inn, set on 13 pastoral acres overlooking Pico Mountain. Guests always get to choose from a variety of fruit combinations in the recipe since some of each are made.

A hearty breakfast sends guests on their way to explore the attractions of the Green Mountains. In the summer, they can lounge by the pool, hike the Appalachian or Long Trails, or mountain bike. In the winter, Killington and Pico Mountain ski areas are less than five miles away, and a number of x-c trails are available. Then guests return for a drink in the pub and a superb gourmet dinner, accompanied by their choice of 300 wines, in the two candlelit dining rooms. A dessert tray to die for puts the perfect end on the day.

Other Red Clover Inn recipes:
Blueberry Champagne Sauce, page 80
Maple Butter, page 89

Marilyn's Fruit Pancake

Ingredients:

3/4 cup flour
3 tablespoons sugar
1/4 teaspoon salt
3 eggs, beaten
3/4 cup light cream (buttermilk can be substituted)
2 tablespoons butter, melted

Topping:
2 tablespoons brown sugar
1/2 teaspoon cinnamon
1/4 teaspoon ginger

Also:

Any fruit combination--peaches or nectarines and blueberries, pears and raspberries
Mint leaves

- In a large bowl, stir together flour, sugar and salt.
- Beat in eggs, cream and melted butter.
- Heat a 10-inch oven-proof frying pan on the stove and brush with oil. Ladle in batter and cook on stovetop until light brown on bottom. "Watch carefully to prevent burning."
- Remove from heat and arrange fruit on top.
- Stir together brown sugar, cinnamon and ginger and sprinkle over fruit.
- Bake in a preheated oven at 400 degrees for 10 minutes. Remove from oven.
- Remove pancake from pan by running a spatula around the edge and lifting out to serving plate. Cut into wedges, garnish with mint leaves and serve immediately.

Makes 4 servings

from **Candlelite Inn B&B**
5 Greenhouse Lane
Bradford, NH 03221
603-938-5571
888-812-5571

Breakfast here is, of course, served by candlelight. Innkeeper Marilyn Gordon loves serving this dish to a crowd and makes it all year 'round, changing the fruit topping from one season to the next.

Marilyn and her spouse, Les, decided to pursue innkeeping as a new career after their kids graduated from high school. They had traveled extensively in New England inns, so they sold their New Jersey house, quit their jobs and started looking. "The first time we saw the Candlelite Inn, we knew it was the inn for us," Marilyn said. It needed lots of cosmetic work, but they bought it, rolled up their sleeves and opened in 1993, offering six guestrooms.

The inn was built as the Gillis House in 1897, hosting summer boarders. By 1933, it was known as Green Shutters, and in 1954 it became the Candlelite Inn. After a decade as apartments, it was restored as a B&B in the '80s. Located in the Lake Sunapee Region, the inn is minutes from fishing, boating and skiing.

Another Candlelite Inn recipe:
Bread Pudding with Custard, page 178

Spicy Apple Pancakes with Cider Sauce

Ingredients:

1 cup flour
1 cup whole wheat flour
1/4 cup sugar
2 tablespoons baking powder
1 teaspoon cinnamon
Dash of salt
2 cups milk
2 eggs
1/4 cup vegetable oil
2 medium-sized apples, peeled, cored and chopped

Cider Sauce:
1/2 cup sugar
2 tablespoons cornstarch
1/4 teaspoon cinnamon
1/4 teaspoon nutmeg
2 cups apple cider
2 tablespoons lemon juice

☛ In a large bowl, stir together flour, whole wheat flour, sugar, baking powder, cinnamon and salt.

☛ In a separate bowl, whisk together milk, eggs and oil.

☛ Pour milk mixture into flour mixture and stir until all ingredients are moist and fairly lump-free. Stir in apples.

☛ Spoon batter on a buttered griddle (preheated to 350 degrees). Turn when bubbles form and cook until golden brown.

☛ For Cider Sauce: In a large saucepan, stir together sugar, cornstarch, cinnamon and nutmeg. Whisk in cider and lemon juice. Cook, stirring constantly, until sauce thickens and boils. Boil and stir for 1 minute. Serve hot over hot pancakes.

Makes 20 3- to 4-inch pancakes and 2-1/2 cups of sauce

from **Brunswick B&B**
165 Park Row
Brunswick, ME 04011
207-729-4914
800-299-4914

"These pancakes are light and fluffy and chock-full of wonderful soft apple pieces, delicious on a cool autumn morning," said Innkeeper Mercie Normand. Steve, her husband, lights a fire in the parlor fireplace where guests enjoy their breakfast looking out at the fall colors in the town green across the street.

Built in 1849 by carriage builder Robert H. Bowker, the home passed through a number of prominent Brunswick families. In 1934, Daniel Stanwood, professor of International Law at nearby Bowdoin College, added the large living room to house his law library. Guests of the well-traveled Stanwood family included Edna St. Vincent Millay, Thornton Wilder and Admiral Richard Byrd.

Mercie, a quilter and occupational therapist, and Steve, an architect, purchased this operating B&B in 1991. They spent six years restoring the B&B and offer eight guestrooms. Shopping in Freeport's outlet stores is only 10 miles away, and guests can ice skate at the town park across the street in the winter. Antiquing, state parks and other Mid-Coast Maine attractions are nearby.

🏠 *Another Brunswick B&B recipe:*
Overnight Crunch Coffeecake, page 37

Sweet Potato and Apple Johnnycakes

Ingredients:
> 3/4 cup flour
> 1-1/2 cups yellow cornmeal
> 3 teaspoons baking powder
> 1 teaspoon salt
> 1/4 cup vegetable oil
> 2 cups peeled and grated sweet potatoes
> 1/2 cup diced scallions
> 1 cup chopped apple, such as McIntosh
> 3 eggs, beaten
> 1-1/2 cups milk

Also:
> Clarified butter
> 1 apple, julienned
> Maple syrup
> Cheddar cheese, sliced

* In a large bowl, stir together the flour, cornmeal, baking powder and salt.

* In a skillet, heat the oil and sauté the sweet potatoes, scallions and chopped apple until the sweet potato is soft. Set aside to cool.

* Stir the cooled sweet potato-apple mixture into the flour mixture. Then stir in eggs and milk.

* Heat skillet and brush with clarified butter (Editor's Note: Clarified butter does not burn; if you are using a non-stick griddle, you may not need butter, or you may use non-stick cooking spray.)

* Drop spoonfuls of the johnnycake batter into the butter. When bubbles appear, flip and cook other side until golden brown.

* Keep cooked johnnycakes warm in the oven. Serve 3 pancakes per plate, topped with julienned apple, Vermont maple syrup and slices of cheese.

Makes 12 3-inch pancakes

from **The Battenkill Inn**
Route 7A
P.O. Box 948
Manchester, VT 05254
802-362-4213
Fax 802-362-0975

Guests at this 11-guestroom inn might fortify themselves with a hearty breakfast featuring these pancakes before a day on the inn's namesake river. The inn is located on seven acres along this world-class trout stream, so many guests enjoy fishing from the banks. Right next door is a canoe rental, as well.

Laine and Yoshi Akiyama bought this inn in 1996, giving up the corporate life in Southern California to spend more time together. Both had worked for Disney Imagineering. They fell in love with this 1840 Victorian farmhouse when they were guests here looking for the "right" inn to purchase. They and their two golden retrievers began welcoming guests in October 1996.

Banana Praline Waffles

Ingredients:

3 eggs
1-1/2 cups milk
1 tablespoon rum
1/2 cup sour cream (or plain yogurt)
2 to 3 bananas
2 tablespoons brown sugar, packed
1 cup flour
1 cup whole wheat flour
1 tablespoon baking powder
1/2 teaspoon salt
1 teaspoon cinnamon
1/2 teaspoon nutmeg
6 tablespoons unsalted butter, melted (or flavorless oil)

Also:

Brown sugar
Chopped pecans (or walnuts)
Whipped cream or ice cream

- In a large bowl, whisk together eggs, milk, rum and sour cream.

- Mash bananas and combine with egg mixture.

- In a separate bowl, combine brown sugar, flour, whole wheat flour, baking powder, salt, cinnamon and nutmeg. Form a well in center of ingredients and add egg mixture, stirring only until mixed.

- Let stand 1 or 2 minutes. Gently stir in butter.

- Ladle about 1/3 cup batter onto a preheated, lightly-oiled waffle iron and cook for about 1 minute.

- Gently lift top of waffle iron. Sprinkle some brown sugar and nuts on top. Close cover and cook until done (usually when steaming stops).

- Remove from waffle iron. Wipe iron and oil lightly before cooking next waffle (it'll be messy!).

- Serve topped with whipped cream or ice cream.

Makes 10 waffles

from **By the Old Mill Stream**
RR 2, Box 543
Hinesburg, VT 05446
802-482-3613

These sweet waffles can be served as a dessert, too. Innkeepers Michelle and Steve Fischer were encouraged to open a B&B by friends who visited them in Vermont. While expecting their first child, they looked for a house large enough for a baby and B&B. The waterfall out back made this house irresistible. They have three guestrooms in the Dow home, built in the 1860s for the owner of a large woolen mill. Half of a mill stone from the waterwheel that powered his plant is part of the stone wall in front of the home.

Another By the Old Mill Stream recipe:
Banana Almond French Toast, page 120

Sourdough Gingerbread Belgian Waffles

Ingredients:

- 3 cups flour
- 3/8 cup sugar
- 3 teaspoons baking powder
- 3/4 teaspoon baking soda
- 1-1/2 teaspoons salt
- 1-1/2 teaspoons ginger
- 3/4 teaspoon cinnamon
- 3 eggs
- 3/4 cup sourdough starter, at room temperature (available as a mix in some baking sections, may require from 9 to 48 hours to make)
- 3/4 cup molasses
- 1/2 cup vegetable oil
- 1-1/2 cups milk

☛ In a large bowl (do not use copper or aluminum; it reacts with sourdough starter), stir together flour, sugar, baking powder, baking soda, salt, ginger and cinnamon with a wooden or plastic utensil.

☛ In a medium plastic bowl, whisk eggs. With a plastic spatula, stir in sourdough starter, molasses, vegetable oil and milk.

☛ Pour sourdough mixture into flour, stirring with plastic utensil. Let batter rest for 5 to 10 minutes.

☛ Brush top and bottom of Belgian waffle iron with vegetable oil to coat well. Pour enough batter onto preheated waffler to cover grid pattern evenly.

☛ Close waffle iron and bake as directed, or until steaming stops. Serve with maple syrup.

Makes 5 large waffles

from **The Jeweled Turret Inn**
40 Pearl Street
Belfast, ME 04915
207-338-2304
800-696-2304

Alaskan by birth, Cathy Heffentrager uses sourdough starter (brought to Alaska by the gold miners) in some of her breakfasts. These get rave reviews. New England, with its emphasis on history and its charming coastal villages, "hooked" Cathy and Carl when they vacationed here in 1981. In April 1986, they bought this 1898 Queen Anne Victorian, located in the heart of town and within walking distance of Belfast's Penobscot Bay harbor, shops and restaurants. They spent a year restoring it and opened seven guestrooms, each named after a particular jewel. The inn itself is named after the staircase in the turret with "jewel-like embellishments." Guests are free to enjoy the common rooms. Belfast offers walking tours, summer theater, concerts, lobster picnics, train excursions and four state parks within 20 miles.

🏠 *Other Jeweled Turret Inn recipes:*
Chocolate Mint Scones, page 50
German Crown Pancakes, page 132

Crab Potato Bake

Ingredients:

8 large white potatoes, peeled
1/2 cup butter
1 to 1-1/2 cups light cream or half-and-half
Cayenne pepper sauce to taste
1/2 teaspoon garlic powder
1/4 cup chopped fresh parsley
1/4 cup chopped green onions
1/2 teaspoon salt
2 cups sharp Cheddar cheese, grated
8 ounces fresh crab meat or 1 6-ounce can white crab meat

Also:

Paprika

- Boil the potatoes until tender.
- Drain potatoes. Mash with the butter and cream until smooth and not stiff.
- Stir in cayenne pepper, garlic powder, parsley, green onion, salt and cheese.
- Wash and drain crab meat (squeeze dry). Gently fold crab into potato mixture.
- Spread potato-crab mixture into a buttered 9 x 13-inch baking dish. Sprinkle with paprika.
- Bake in a preheated oven at 400 degrees for 20 to 25 minutes or until cheese melts.
- Remove from oven, cool for 5 minutes, cut into squares and serve.

Makes 8 servings

from **The Inn at Southwest**
371 Main Street
P.O. Box 593
Southwest Harbor, ME 04679
207-244-3835
Fax 207-244-9879

"The first time I wanted to make this dish, I went looking for crab meat at the grocery store," admits transplanted Midwesterner/Innkeeper Jill Lewis. "A friendly Mainer told me about a place down the road where they picked crab fresh every day." Jill notes that canned crab from the grocery store will do for those who can't find fresh crab. She might serve this dish with bananas foster, blueberry corn muffins and plenty of friendly conversation.

Guests may have crab for breakfast, but chances are they are eating lobster for dinner, fresh from Southwest Harbor's lobster wharves. Jill's Second Empire-style inn, situated at the edge of town, is walking distance to the wharves and marina, restaurant and shops. Located on Mt. Desert Island only minutes from Acadia National Park, the inn has welcomed guests since 1884. Nine guestrooms on the second and third floors are each named after an historic Maine lighthouse. Guests enjoy the fresh sea air on the wrap-around porch.

Another Inn at Southwest recipe:
Blueberry Apple Crisp, page 175

Croissant á la Orange

Ingredients:

6 large croissants
1 18-ounce jar orange marmalade
1/3 cup orange juice
5 eggs
1 cup heavy cream
1 teaspoon almond extract
Grated rind of 1 orange

Also:

3 orange slices
Creme fraiche or unsweetened whipped cream
Strawberries

- Butter three oven-proof dishes ("We use round Dansk shallow soup bowls, each of which holds 2 croissants, serving two guests").
- Cut croissants in half lengthwise and place 2 bottom halves in each dish.
- Thin the marmalade with orange juice and spoon it over each bottom half so that each bottom is evenly covered (saving some to glaze the top). Replace croissant tops.
- In a small bowl, whisk together eggs, cream, almond extract and orange rind.
- Pour mixture over the top of croissants until half is submerged in the cream mixture.
- Spoon the remaining thinned marmalade on top of each croissant. Cover and refrigerate overnight.
- Bake in a preheated oven at 350 degrees for approximately 25 minutes.
- Serve hot, but allow to set a few minutes before cutting.
- Garnish with a half slice of orange and creme fraiche or whipped cream, topped with a strawberry.

Makes 6 servings

from **Cornucopia of Dorset**
Route 30
P.O. Box 307
Dorset, VT 05251
802-867-5751
800-566-5751

Travellers seeking that storybook village -- the one with the white clapboard houses with dark green shutters, white-steepled churches and tree-lined streets that look as though horse-drawn carriages are just around the corner today -- will think they've died and gone to heaven when they get to Dorset. Linda and Bill Ley did. They fell in love with the town, pop. 2,000, where the sidewalks and a church are constructed of Dorset marble from some of the nation's oldest quarries, ones that produced marble for the New York City Public Library. The Leys bought this 1880 inn six weeks after seeing it for the first time. Guests have the use of the entire first floor of this turn-of-the-century home. Four guestrooms are on the second floor and a separate cottage behind the inn also is popular. Located right in town with clapboard siding (vinyl siding is illegal here) and a marble porch, fine restaurants are a stroll away. Guests are only 10 minutes from Manchester. They can fish the Battenkill or Mettowee rivers, ski, canoe, swim in the defunct quarries, bike, golf and attend professional theater.

Kathy's Spinach Pie

Ingredients:

7/8 cup milk
3 eggs
1/2 cup Basic Mix
1/2 package (5 ounces) frozen chopped spinach, thawed and squeezed dry
2/3 cup cottage cheese
3 ounces white Cheddar cheese, grated
1/4 teaspoon caraway seeds
Dash of nutmeg

Basic Mix:
4-1/4 cups flour
3/4 cup instant non-fat dry milk
1-1/2 teaspoons baking powder
1 teaspoon salt
1 teaspoon cream of tartar
1/2 teaspoon baking soda
1-1/8 cups solid vegetable shortening

Also:

Powdered sugar or Maine maple syrup, optional

🐖 For Basic Mix: In a large bowl, sift together flour, dry milk, baking powder, salt, cream of tartar and baking soda. With a pastry cutter, cut in shortening. Store in an airtight container in a cool, dry place and use within three months. (Tester notes that packaged biscuit mix can be used if you're short of time.)

🐖 In a blender, mix milk, eggs and Basic Mix.

🐖 Pour mixture into a large bowl. Stir in spinach, cottage cheese, Cheddar cheese, caraway seeds and nutmeg.

🐖 Pour into a buttered 9-inch pie plate.

🐖 Bake in a preheated oven at 375 degrees for 40 minutes.

🐖 Remove from oven. Cool a little before cutting. Serve sprinkled with powdered sugar or maple syrup.

Makes 6 to 8 servings

from **Captain Swift Inn**
72 Elm Street
Camden, ME 04843
207-236-8113
800-251-0865

Innkeepers Kathy and Tom Filip started their B&B adventures just up the street at the Blue Harbor House, the first inn in which they ever stayed. A dozen years and some 50 more B&Bs later, they still wanted a B&B of their own, and in 1992 they returned to Camden and restored this 1810 Federal house. "Breakfast" is an important part of "B&B" for them, so they serve a healthy, full breakfast in front of the old kitchen fireplace and beehive oven.

Captain Frank Swift is credited with bringing the schooner business to Camden, where he began offering cruises to passengers in 1935. He bought this house in 1942 and lived here for more than 30 years. The house, which once was the Camden Home for Aged Women, was vacant and dilapidated when the Filips bought it (when they looked at it, their neighbor next door yelled out her window, "Buy it!"). After two years of work, they opened four guestrooms. Guests have use of three common rooms and a patio.

Sausage with Cider Cranberry Glaze

Ingredients:

2 cups apple cider
1/2 cup sugar
1/2 cup brown sugar, packed
1 tablespoon raspberry or cider vinegar
1-1/2 teaspoons minced garlic
1/2 teaspoon whole cloves
1 cup cranberries, fresh or frozen
2 tablespoons cornstarch
2 tablespoons water

Also:

Smoked, cooked sausage, cut diagonally into bite-sized pieces
Sautéed onions

- In a medium saucepan, stir together cider, sugar, brown sugar, vinegar, garlic, cloves and cranberries.
- When mixture boils, reduce heat to simmer and cook for 20 minutes.
- In a small bowl, whisk together cornstarch and water. Pour into cranberry mixture and cook, stirring constantly, until thickened and clear.
- Heat sausage and onions together. Place a helping on each plate, top with sauce and serve.

Tester's Comments: Those who love tart cranberries will enjoy this unusual glaze over kielbasa or polish sausage.

Makes 2-1/2 cups of glaze, about 5 servings

from **The Ram in the Thicket**
24 Maple Street
Milford, NH 03055
603-654-6440

Innkeeper/Restaurateur Priscilla Tempelman is constantly reading about food, devising new recipes and changing the menu at her inn and restaurant, which prides itself on using seasonal ingredients. This sausage recipes combines two fall products, cider and cranberries, in a colorful sauce.

Priscilla, her husband, Dr. Andrew Tempelman, and their three sons moved here from the Midwest in 1977. Andrew was a minister, and he and Priscilla had fallen in love with New England. They bought this mansion from a textile milling company and the family that once lived here.

Restoration and renovation took many years. They turned the 10 upstairs bedrooms into guestrooms and the music room, library and parlors into two dining rooms, a small lounge and a sitting room. Priscilla runs the kitchen and Andrew is the bartender, among other duties. Breakfast maight include hot and cold cereals, fruit and homemade scones, muffins or coffeecake.

▲Another Ram in the Thicket recipe:
Indian Pudding, page 183

Smoked Salmon Quesadilla

Ingredients:

1 10-inch flour tortilla
2 ounces Boursin cheese
1 ripe plum tomato or other fresh tomato
1 tablespoon plus 1/2 teaspoon fresh dill, chopped
1/2 teaspoon capers
2 ounces smoked salmon
1 cup sour cream
2 tablespoons olive oil
1 red onion, cut in half and sliced crosswise

Bring tortilla to room temperature. Spread cheese on half of tortilla.

Top with tomato, 1/2 teaspoon dill, capers and flaked salmon.

Fold tortilla in half and press lightly.

Stir together sour cream and remaining 1 tablespoon dill. Set aside.

Heat olive oil in sauté pan over medium heat. Sauté tortilla until golden brown. Turn tortilla over and brown other side.

Serve warm topped with sour cream mixture and red onion slices.

Makes 1 serving

from **Molly Stark Inn**
1067 Main Street
Bennington, VT 05201
802-442-9631
800-356-3076

Entrees such as this -- spicy, creative, unusual and tasty -- are how Innkeeper Reed Fendler likes to cook. Guests in the seven guestrooms and the garden cottage enjoy breakfast in the sun room or on the wrap-around porch.

In 1988, while working in retail, the 30-year-old Reed saw an ad in the New York Times listing this operating inn for sale. He found the inn, a grand Queen Anne Victorian on an acre of landscaped grounds, in the perfect location in town. "So I sold my house in Hartford, Connecticut, and took the plunge, truly not knowing what I was getting myself into at the time." Turned out, he loves being his own boss and meeting new guests or welcoming old ones back. "I have never been happier with any decision I have ever made in my life."

Just a year later, another big event at the inn: Reed met Cammi, a guest on vacation, and, Reed says, "I guess you could say it was love at first sight." Since then, they married and Cammi attended Bennington College, just five miles away. Many guests come to Bennington for summer theater or festivals, winter sports, or hiking the Appalachian or Green Mountain trails.

Other Molly Stark Inn recipes:
Almond and Dried Cherry Muffins, page 44
Granola Trail Mix Cookies, page 193

Spanikopita

Ingredients:

1 box phyllo dough (found in freezer section)
3 medium yellow onions, coarsely chopped
1/4 cup butter or margarine
5 10-ounce packages frozen chopped spinach, thawed, drained and squeezed dry
2 tablespoons dill
2 pounds Feta cheese, crumbled
4 eggs, beaten
1/4 to 1/2 pound butter, melted

☛ Thaw phyllo dough in refrigerator 4 to 6 hours or overnight. Let sit at room temperature for 2 hours.

☛ Sauté onions in 1/4 cup butter until tender. Add the squeezed spinach and toss well. Cook for 4 minutes, and let cool slightly.

☛ Mix in dill, Feta and eggs. Stir until well combined ("I use my hands").

☛ Unroll phyllo and cover with a slightly damp towel (important-it dries out quickly). Brush with melted butter. Keep unused phyllo stack covered with damp towel.

☛ Lay one sheet of phyllo in the bottom of a 9 x 13-inch pan (edges will hang over pan). Repeat with 5 more layers of buttered phyllo. Carefully spread half of the filling over layers.

☛ Pull edges over filling and brush edges with butter.

☛ Top with another 2 or 3 buttered layers of phyllo, folded in half. Repeat with a second pan, which can be frozen after baking. (Thaw pan at room temperature before reheating, uncovered, at 200 degrees.)

☛ Bake in a preheated oven at 375 degrees for 30 minutes or until golden. Cut into squares and serve.

Makes two pans, 8 to 10 servings each

from **Hannah Davis House**
186 Depot Rd
Fitzwilliam, NH 03447
603-585-3344

"Mike and I have always traveled on our stomachs and find ourselves expecting the rest of you to do the same," notes Innkeeper Kaye Terpstra in her inn's brochure. "Breakfast is therefore a priority." No kidding. This Greek dish might be on the menu with two types of bread, homemade granola, scrambled eggs, bacon, fruit, and zucchini and onions.

Kaye, a former social worker, and Mike, an engineer by training, ran a grocery store before they decided to restore this private home as a B&B. They named it after a 19th-century woman who lived in Jaffrey. After a year of restoration work they did themselves, they opened their B&B in 1990 with one guestroom; now it's grown to six. The Terpstras often help guests plan antiquing intineraries or pursue outdoor activities in the Monadnock region.

🏠 *Another Hannah Davis House recipe:*
Hannah's Baked Apple Puff, page 134

149

Vegetable Hash

Ingredients:

1 pound new potatoes, washed, peeled and diced into pieces about the size of a quarter
1 or 2 parsnips, washed and diced
1 or 2 carrots, washed and diced
1 piece butternut squash, diced
1/2 medium rutabaga, diced
Salt and pepper to taste
1 medium onion, diced
1 to 2 tablespoons olive oil
1/4 red bell pepper, diced

- Place potatoes, parsnips, carrots, squash and rutabaga in a large saucepan, cover almost completely with water, and parboil until just tender. Then drain and season with salt and pepper.
- In a separate pan, sauté onion in oil until transparent.
- Add red pepper and the parboiled vegetables to sauté pan and sauté until crispy.
- Serve hash alongside eggs or egg dishes or top the hash with a poached egg and rosemary-flavored Hollandaise sauce.

Makes 4 to 6 servings

from **Fairhaven Inn**
North Bath Road
Bath, ME 04530
888-443-4391
Fax 207-443-6412

"I usually make this when I have left-over baked potatoes and other root vegetables," said Innkeeper Susie Reed. "The quantities given here are not exact as I usually just throw in whatever I have in the fridge!" She also makes an oven-roasted version with garlic and rosemary, omitting the red pepper. She shakes the vegetables in a plastic bag with olive oil, spreads them on a prepared baking sheet or two, and roasts at 400 degrees for 50 minutes or so.

Creative cooking is one of Susie's specialties. She studied with Rolland Messinier, the White House pastry chef. Along with David, her husband, she owned and operated a D.C.-based pastry shop. "Since we moved to Bath (in 1995), we have had the time to do many of the things that we couldn't squeeze into 12-hour, 6-day weeks at the bakery," Susie notes. She taught a Life Skills class to low-income mothers, offering ways to feed children healthy, well-balanced meals on a budget. Susie also gardens, growing the inn's herbs and spinach, and they pick strawberries and blueberries at the many area pick-your-own farms. Guests in the 1790 Colonial, which offers eight guestrooms, often enjoy her efforts in the full breakfasts.

Other Fairhaven Inn recipes:
Gaye's Currant Scones, page 52
David's Gingerbread, page 69
Cranberry Bars, page 190

Vermont Cheddar Pie

Ingredients:
2 cups frozen hash brown potatoes, thawed
1 medium onion, finely chopped
1 teaspoon seasoned pepper
1/3 cup grated Romano cheese
2 teaspoons garlic powder
1/3 cup frozen chopped spinach, thawed and squeezed dry
1/3 cup Feta cheese, crumbled
1 cup grated sharp Vermont Cheddar cheese
2 eggs
1/2 cup milk
2 tablespoons dried parsley flakes
2 teaspoons paprika

Also:
Favorite red salsa

- In a medium bowl, combine hash browns with all but 1/8 cup of the onion.
- Press mixture into a buttered 9-inch glass pie plate to form a crust.
- Sprinkle crust with pepper, Romano cheese and garlic powder. Dot with spinach and Feta cheese.
- Top evenly with Cheddar cheese.
- Whisk together eggs and milk and pour over pie, working from edges to middle.
- Position remaining 1/8 cup onions on top of cheddar cheese in center of pie.
- Sprinkle parsley in a ring around the onion. Sprinkle paprika around parsley to make an outside ring.
- Bake in a preheated oven at 325 degrees for approximately 1 hour, or until lightly browned, "and respond to everyone asking, 'What smells so good?'"
- Let cool, then cut into six slices. Reheat slices in microwave oven.

Makes 6 servings

from **Grünberg Haus B&B**
RR 2, Box 1595
Route 100 South
Waterbury, VT 05676
802-244-7726
800-800-7760

This dish has become the favorite entrée, not only because it is delicious, but because it fills the inn with a wonderful savory aroma, said Innkeeper Chris Sellers. Chris might be playing a little classical music on the Steinway while co-innkeeper Mark Frohman serves guests at the dining room table, which has views of the surrounding Green Mountains. Their inn, tucked into a forested hillside, was handbuilt as a chalet in 1972. Mark and Chris have restored and improved the inn, serving guests who come to ski, hike, or tour Ben & Jerry's.

Other Grünberg Haus recipes:
Green Mountain Lemon Bread, page 70
Glazed Orange Slices, page 99
Lemon Ricotta Pancakes, page 135

Holiday Fare

Boiled Fruit Cake

Ingredients:

1 cup sugar
1 cup mixed dried fruit
1 cup water
1 bottle whiskey (wine may be substituted)
1 cup butter
4 large eggs
1 tablespoon brown sugar
1 teaspoon salt
1 teaspoon baking soda

- Place 1/2 cup of the sugar, dried fruit and water in a small sauce pan. Boil for 2 minutes.
- Pour whiskey into shot glass, sample to check quality.
- Get large mixing bowl. Check whiskey again. Pour one level cup and drink. Repeat previous step.
- Turn on electric mixer and beat butter in a large fluffy bowl.
- Add one spoontea of baking soda, other half cup of sugar and beat again.
- Turn off mixer brake two leggs, add to bowl. Chuck in fried druit.
- Mix on the turner. If fruit gets stuck in the beaters, pry loose with a drewscrier.
- Sample whiskey to check tonsisticity.
- Next, sift two cups of salt, two cups of salt, or something --who cares what! Check the whiskey!
- Add one babblespoon of brown sugar, or which ever color you can find. Wix mell.
- Grease the oven. Turn pan cake to 350 gredeedles. Don't forget to off beat the turner.
- Pour mix into pan and over bench. Throw bowl out the window.
- Stagger to laundry, put pan cake in oven, set to hot rinse.
- Continue sampling whiskey til bottle is empty. Bo to ged.

Tester's Comments: This will teech me to reed ALL the instrucshuns befour I start to make a receipe!

from **The Notchland Inn**
Route 302
Hart's Location, NH 03812
603-374-6131
800-866-6131

Humor (or what some may call the staff's vain attempt at it) is alive and (arguably) well at the Notchland. One might argue that the inn's relatively remote location, just east of Crawford Notch in the White Mountains, and the region's relatively long winters, compared to, say, Miami's, are to blame for this silliness. One might argue that, but one would be wasting one's breath. Blame it on Innkeepers Les Schoof and Ed Butler, who blatantly encourage both their staff and guests to ham it up (but not to really *drink* it up, seriously folks) whenever possible. They hope this tickled your funny bone.

Other Notchland Inn recipes:
Notchland 'Muddled' Cider, page 24
Favorite Popovers, page 51
Cranberry Bread Pudding, page 181

Christmas Apple and Cranberry Cobbler

Ingredients:

1/2 cup apple juice (or water)
1/2 cup sugar
1 tablespoon cornstarch
1-1/2 cups cranberries (fresh or frozen)
2 Granny Smith apples, peeled and sliced
1/2 cup raisins, optional

Streusel Topping:
3/4 cup flour
1/2 cup sugar
1/3 cup butter or margarine
1 cup rolled oats
1/4 cup applesauce

- Butter a 9-inch baking dish.
- In medium saucepan, stir together apple juice, sugar and cornstarch. Stir in cranberries.
- Heat to boiling, reduce heat and simmer about 5 minutes or until cranberries pop.
- Stir in apples and optional raisins. Pour into baking dish.
- For Streusel Topping: In a medium bowl, stir together flour and sugar.
- Cut in butter with a pastry cutter until mixture resembles coarse crumbs.
- Stir in oats and applesauce and mix well.
- Crumble mixture evenly over top of fruit.
- Bake in a preheated oven at 400 degrees for 35 to 40 minutes, or until top is golden brown.

Tester's Comments: This appears to make too much topping, but it turns out to be exactly right. The red color is lovely! Serve warm topped with whipped or ice cream and, if you dare, sprinkled with green sugar sprinkles!

Makes 8 servings

from **The Tamworth Inn**
Main Street
Tamworth, NH 03886
603-323-7721
800-642-7352

"My mother used to make this Apple and Cranberry Cobbler at Christmas time and I continued it with my family, gradually adding and changing it a little over the years," said Innkeeper Kathy Bender. Since 1988, when Kathy and her husband, Phil, purchased this inn, Kathy has had more than cooking for family to do. Among other duties, she oversees the inn's kitchen, which serves breakfasts to guests in the 16 guestrooms and dinner to guests and the public, as well. She was an executive in a landscape architecture firm, and Phil was a commercial banker before they changed careers and moved from California to this hamlet, where the inn has been welcoming travelers since 1833.

Many guests come to bike or x-c ski between this inn and two others in the White Mountains. Others come to attend the Barnstormer's Summer Theater, fish the Swift River, swim in the pool or just relax in this quiet village.

Other Tamworth Inn recipes:
Zucchini Bread, page 75
Apple Banana Syrup, page 78

Christmas Prelude Gingersnaps

Ingredients:
    3/4 cup shortening
    1 egg
    1/4 cup molasses
    2-1/4 cups flour
    1 cup brown sugar, packed
    2 teaspoons baking soda
    1 teaspoon ginger
    1 teaspoon cinnamon
    1/2 teaspoon cloves

Also:
    Additional sugar

- With an electric mixer, beat together shortening, egg and molasses.

- Beat in flour, brown sugar, baking soda, ginger, cinnamon and cloves.

- Shape mixture into balls approximately 1-1/2 inches round. Roll balls in sugar.

- Place balls on a lightly-buttered cookie sheet and bake in a preheated oven at 375 degrees for approximately 10 minutes or until tops "crack" and set.

- Remove from the oven and allow pans to set for a few minutes before removing cookies to wire racks.

Tester's Comments: Save this recipe just for the holidays and you'll be sorry! Double this batch and freeze some.

Makes about 2 dozen cookies

from **Maine Stay Inn & Cottages**
34 Maine Street
P.O. Box 500-A
Kennebunkport, ME 04046
207-967-2117
800-950-2117

"We offer Gingersnap Cookies at tea time during Kennebunkport's Christmas Prelude festival, which is held over the first two weekends in December," said Innkeeper Carol Copeland. "One of our kitchen assistants, Margo Grady, shared this recipe with me." Guests often find something special here at tea time, and occassionally Carol and her husband, Lindsay, will offer a special wine tasting or other event at the inn. Carol and Lindsay purchased this operating inn in 1989, aiming at working together and raising their daughters here. The square block Italianate-style home, listed on the National Register of Historic Places and in Kennebunkport's historic district, features a wrap-around porch and white cupola, with panoramic views. Guests can choose from six rooms here or 11 cottage accommodations.

Other Maine Stay Inn & Cottages recipes:
Apricot Scones, page 46
Pumpkin Ginger Muffins, page 56
Applesauce Spice Pancakes, page 126
Mrs. Milld's Oatmeal Cookies, page 199

Cranberry Eggnog Tea Bread

Ingredients:

2 eggs
1 cup sugar
1 cup dairy eggnog (without rum or rum flavor added)
1/2 cup butter, melted
1-1/2 teaspoons rum extract
1 teaspoon vanilla extract
1-1/4 cups flour
1 cup whole wheat flour
2 teaspoons baking powder
1/2 teaspoon salt
3/4 teaspoon nutmeg (freshly ground is best)
3/4 cup fresh cranberries, rinsed
1 teaspoon flour

🍂 In a food processor, beat eggs. Add sugar, eggnog, butter, rum extract and vanilla extract. Blend well.

🍂 In a large bowl, stir together flour, whole wheat flour, baking powder, salt and nutmeg. Blend well.

🍂 By hand, stir egg mixture into flour mixture just until all ingredients are moist.

🍂 In a medium bowl, stir together cranberries with 1 teaspoon flour. Fold cranberries into the mixture.

🍂 Bake in a preheated oven at 350 degrees for 45 minutes. Allow to cool completely before removing from pan and serving.

Makes 1 loaf

from **The Inn at The Round Barn Farm**
East Warren Road
RR 1, Box 247
Waitsfield, VT 05673
802-496-2276
800-326-7038

Innkeeper Anne Marie DeFreest might have this bread on the breakfast menu during the holidays, or guests might enjoy it as an afternoon treat. Breakfasts are served in the sunroom with a view of the hills.

Anne Marie's parents, Doreen and Jack Simko, sold their successful floral business in New Jersey when this 85-acre farm came on the market. They were smitten with the 1910 round barn and the idea of a slower-paced life in the country. Countless dollars and several months later, the three Simkos had restored the farmhouse and interconnected buildings into an elegant, but unpretentious, B&B inn. Eventually the three-story barn itself was redone, lifted in the air so a new foundation could be poured. The top floor is now the site of many weddings, and guests use the 60-foot lap pool, ending in a greenhouse, in the lower level. Cross-country skiiers have 30 km of groomed trails, with rentals and instruction available at the inn.

🏠 *Another Inn at the Round Barn Farm recipe:*
Southwestern Fiesta Cheesecake, page 188

Grandma's Fruit Bread

Ingredients:

2 cups sugar
1 cup butter (do not substitute margarine)
4 eggs, separated
4 cups flour
2 tablespoons baking powder
1 cup milk
2 cups raisins
1/2 cup candied pineapple
1/2 cup maraschino cherries
1/3 cup candied citron
1 cup chopped nuts

- With an electric mixer, cream sugar and butter.

- Add egg yolks and beat until well combined.

- In another bowl, sift flour and baking powder together.

- Alternate beating flour mixture and milk into batter with an electric mixer. Stir in fruit and nuts by hand.

- With an electric mixer, beat egg whites until stiff peaks form, then fold into batter.

- Spread the batter into two buttered 9 x 5-inch bread loaf pans, or four buttered small loaf pans, and bake in an oven preheated to 325 degrees until a toothpick inserted in the center comes out clean (60 to 65 minutes for large loaves, 40 to 45 minutes for small loaves).

Makes 2 large or 4 small loaves

from **MapleHedge B&B Inn**
355 Main Street
P.O. Box 638
Charlestown, NH 03603
603-826-5237
1-800-9-MAPLE-9

"This recipe has been part of my Christmas since I was a youngster and first enjoyed it at Grandma Beale's home in Buffalo, New York," recalls Joan DeBrine. "My mother has made it every year since and it now has become a tradition at MapleHedge during the holidays." Joan doubles the recipe and serves slices of the bread with the fruit course at her inn.

Breakfast at MapleHedge is served at the large dining room table, set with linens, china and Joan's collection of 1895 French opalescent blue water goblets. Joan tries to be creative with recipes and even long-term guests never dine on the same three-course breakfast twice. Joan and Dick took nearly three years to find this 18th-century Federal-style home in historic Charlestown on the Connecticut River. Joan wanted to run an inn April through December, after Dick retired and their youngest son was off to college. Restoration took another two-and-a-half years.

Other MapleHedge recipes:
Banana Froth, page 21
Cheese Cream-Filled Baked Pears, page 96

"High Hat" Irish Soda Bread

Ingredients:

2 eggs
1-1/2 cups sour cream
3-1/2 cups sifted flour
1/2 cup sugar
2 teaspoons baking powder
1 teaspoon salt
1/2 teaspoon baking soda
1 cup golden raisins

🥄 With an electric mixer, beat eggs slightly. Then beat in sour cream.

🥄 In a separate bowl, mix together flour, sugar, baking powder, salt and baking soda.

🥄 Beat flour mixture into egg mixture. Stir in raisins by hand.

🥄 Place dough in a buttered 8-inch soufflé pan or round casserole dish. With a sharp knife, cut a cross in the top of the dough.

🥄 Bake in a preheated oven at 350 degrees for 60 minutes. "Be careful when you peek in the oven so your bread doesn't fall! It will puff up and brown on top."

🥄 Remove bread from oven and let sit for 10 minutes. Then remove from pan. Serve warm with butter or honey-butter.

Makes 10 servings

from **Abigail's B&B by the Sea**
8 High Street
Camden, ME 04843
207-236-2501
800-292-2501

Called "high hat" because of the way it puffs up, this bread is a family favorite of Innkeepers Donna and Ed Misner. Donna suggests it for St. Patrick's Day, and she has served it with a traditional Irish dinner, as well as during breakfast for her B&B guests. Whenever it's served, she notes there are no leftovers!

The Misner's four-guestroom inn is an 1847 Greek Revival home within walking distance of Camden and its popular harbor. Built for a member of Congress, the home frequently was an overnight destination for Jefferson Davis. Today, guests still enjoy the wide front porch, cozy parlors, sunny dining room and gardens. But today's guests also luxuriate in four-poster beds and feast on a full, homemade breakfast. The two carriage house suites also have mini-kitchens, designed for extended stays.

Ed, a former commercial pilot, and Donna, who owned her own retail clothing store, first got into innkeeping at Abigail Adams B&B in Cape May, New Jersey. Their love of restoring historic homes brought them to Camden for their next B&B adventure. They opened this inn in 1990.

🏠 *Another Abigail's recipe:*
Strawberry Orange Juice, page 26

Julekakke

Ingredients:

2 packets active dry yeast
1/2 cup warm water, 105 to 115 degrees F
1-3/4 cups milk, scalded
1/2 cup butter, melted
2/3 cup sugar
1 teaspoon salt
1/4 teaspoon ground cardamom
1 teaspoon cinnamon
2 eggs, beaten
8 cups flour, divided
1-1/2 cups raisins
1-1/2 cups mixed candied fruit

Also:

1 egg, beaten
Cinnamon and sugar

🔹 Dissolve yeast in warm water. Set aside.

🔹 In a very large mixing bowl, place milk and butter. One at a time, beat in sugar, salt, cardamom, cinnamon, yeast, eggs and 4 cups flour.

🔹 Stir in raisins and fruit. Stir in final 4 cups of flour gradually, mixing well.

🔹 Cover bowl with a towel and allow to double in size in a warm place, about 90 minutes. (Since this makes so much dough, it may be necessary to divide dough in thirds before rising, and place it in three separate, covered bowls.)

🔹 Punch down. Divide into three equal amounts (if you have not done so already). Place dough into three buttered 9 x 5-inch loaf pans and cover with towels. Allow dough to rise until pans are almost full.

🔹 Brush tops with beaten egg and sprinkle with cinnamon and sugar. Bake in a preheated oven at 350 degrees for 45 minutes. Loaves are done if they sound hollow when tapped. Remove and cool on wire racks. Serve with butter.

Makes 3 loaves

from **Packard House**
45 Pearl Street
Bath, ME 04530
207-443-6069
800-516-4578

Innkeeper Debby Hayden, who has Norwegian ancestry on both sides of her family, notes that "no Christmas would be possible" without Julekakke. She loves this recipe because it yields consistent results and requires no kneading. Debby and Bill moved to Mid-Coast Maine to open a B&B and be near Debby's family after they both had careers with American Airlines. They sold their home July 12, 1996, bought this inn July 14, and had the first guests July 16.

🏠*Another Packard House recipe:*
Apple Torte, page 174

Pumpkin Spice Bread

Ingredients:

2 cups sugar
1/2 cup vegetable oil
1-1/2 cups cooked pumpkin
2-1/4 cups flour
1 teaspoon cinnamon
1/2 teaspoon cloves
1/4 teaspoon nutmeg
1/4 teaspoon salt
1 teaspoon baking soda
1/2 cup chopped nuts, "more or less to your own liking"
1/2 cup raisins

- With an electric mixer or by hand, beat together sugar, oil and pumpkin.

- Beat in flour, cinnamon, cloves, nutmeg, salt and baking soda. Stir in nuts and raisins by hand.

- Turn batter into two well-buttered 9 x 5-inch loaf pans or four small loaf pans.

- Bake in a preheated oven at 350 degrees for 1 hour (less for small pans) or until a toothpick inserted in the center comes out clean. Cool on wire racks at least 10 minutes before inverting pans.

Makes 2 loaves

from **The Whispering Pines B&B**
Route 113 A and Hemenway Road
Tamworth, NH 03886
603-323-7337

Rich, dark and spicy, this bread is popular with Innkeeper Karen Erickson's guests any time of year. It makes a welcome treat or gift at the holidays.

Karen's family owned this large farmhouse since the 1940s, where she vacationed as a child. In 1989, she and her husband, Kim, left their careers in California to buy the farm and turn it into a B&B. Situated on more than 20 acres of pines and moose trails next to the Hemenway State Forest, the farmhouse had an ideal location for a B&B, just 20 minutes to North Conway and a short drive to Tamworth's Barnstormer's Summer Theater.

"Believe me, we had our work cut out for us," Karen recalls, working on heating, wiring, insulation, plumbing, painting, re-roofing and other improvements. They opened four guestrooms in 1992. Turns out the house had been an inn in the early 1900s, named "The Pines," and the original sign is mounted in one of the gardens. The clay tennis courts are now a fir and balsam grove, but that's about the only change in the setting. Moose often come through the yard. Guests can x-c ski on the inn's acreage at no charge.

Another Whispering Pines recipes:
Old-Fashioned Hermits, page 200

Red, White and Blueberry Pancakes

Ingredients:
3 cups flour
1 tablespoon sugar
4 teaspoons baking powder
Pinch of salt
4 eggs
2 cups milk
1-1/2 cups low-fat plain yogurt
6 tablespoons vegetable oil
2 cups fresh blueberries
1 cup fresh raspberries or sliced strawberries

Also:
1 cup low-fat yogurt
1 tablespoon maple syrup, plus syrup to pass

- In a large mixing bowl, stir together flour, sugar, baking powder and salt.
- In a separate bowl, whisk together eggs, milk, 1-1/2 cups yogurt and oil.
- Stir eggs into flour mixture and mix just until smooth. Gently fold berries into batter.
- Spoon batter onto a hot griddle and cook until golden on both sides.
- While pancakes are cooking, whisk together additional yogurt and maple syrup.
- Serve pancakes with a dollop of yogurt mixture on top, and more warm maple syrup on the side.

Makes about 15 4-inch pancakes

from **Manchester Highlands Inn**
Highland Avenue
P.O. Box 1754
Manchester, VT 05255
802-362-4565
800-743-4565

"We developed this recipe to serve on the Fourth of July 1988, our first Fourth at the Inn," recalls Innkeeper Patricia Eichorn. "We garnished the plates with miniature flags stuck into strawberries." Guests can expect a choice of an entrée, such as this or an omelette, as part of their breakfast.

Patricia and Robert, her husband, after careers with international airlines, bought this operating inn in 1988. Their inn originally was built by Joseph Fowler, a lawyer and member of an old Manchester family. The stone for the foundation was quarried on the hill behind the house.

The Eichorns now offer 15 guestrooms in the Queen Anne Victorian inn and carriage house, located on a quiet street. The hilltop view, the pool, the pub with full liquor license, homebaked afternoon treats and Humphrey, the inn cat, are some of the reasons guests keep coming back. Skiing, Green Mountain hiking, fishing the Battenkill, shopping outlets, theater, golfing and other Manchester-area pursuits are all nearby.

Savory Christmas Bread

Ingredients:

3 cups flour
2 teaspoons baking powder
1 teaspoon salt
8 ounces Provolone cheese, grated (approximately 2 cups)
4 eggs, beaten
1/2 cup evaporated milk
3 large garlic cloves, crushed
1/4 cup green pepper, chopped (may substitute fresh chives or green part of scallions)
1/4 cup sun-dried tomatoes, chopped (or drained pimentos or red bell pepper, chopped)

Also:

Additional flour

- In a large bowl, stir together flour, baking powder, salt and cheese.
- Reserve 2 tablespoons of beaten eggs for glazing bread before baking. Stir in rest of eggs.
- Stir in evaporated milk, garlic and vegetables to make a soft dough.
- Turn dough out on a well-floured surface and form into a smooth ball.
- Roll ball into a log shape about 10 inches long.
- Place log on a buttered cookie sheet and brush with the reserved beaten egg.
- Bake in a preheated oven at 350 degrees for 30 to 35 minutes, or until loaf is golden brown.
- Remove from the oven and cool thoroughly. Cut into very thin slices, fanning onto a plate. Eat as is, or spread with butter or herb butter.

Makes 8 to 10 servings

from **Watch Hill B&B**
Old Meredith Road
P.O. Box 1605
Center Harbor, NH 03226
603-253-4334

Innkeeper Barbara Lauterbach knows her breads. As a spokesperson for King Arthur flour, made in Norwich, Vermont, she has tested and developed plenty of bread recipes over the years. This one "stuck" as a holiday favorite.

Barbara opened a four-guestroom B&B in 1989. The circa 1772 house is one of the oldest in Center Harbor, built as a summer home up on the hill overlooking Lake Winnipesaukee. Guests in the upstairs guestrooms often are awakened by the aroma of Barbara's breakfasts wafting up the stairs. They join her in the dining room downstairs for homemade breads, sausage or bacon, fruit and brown eggs. Many guests come for Barbara's occasional cooking classes.

🏠 Other Watch Hill B&B recipes:
Buttermilk Whole Wheat Bread, page 67
Spiced Tomato Jam, page 92
Mulled Cider Applesauce, page 102
Firehouse Brownies, page 191

Spiced Apple Brandy

Ingredients:

8 medium tart apples, peeled, cored and quartered
4 cinnamon sticks
2 teaspoons whole cloves
2 teaspoons whole allspice
1 bottle dry white wine
4 cups sugar
4 cups brandy
1/2 teaspoon grated lemon rind

🍂 In a medium saucepan, mix together the apples, cinnamon sticks, cloves, allspice and 1/2 cup wine.

🍂 Cook, stirring constantly, over medium heat, then simmer, loosely covered, for about 7 minutes or until the apples begin to soften slightly.

🍂 Stir in the sugar and cook, stirring constantly, until the sugar dissolves.

🍂 In a large glass container, mix the apple mixture, the remaining wine and brandy. Cover tightly and store in a cool, dark place. Shake the container every 2 or 3 days for 3 weeks.

🍂 After 3 weeks, strain through a double thickness of cheesecloth. (You'll need to repeat the process at least once until the liquid is clear. Reserve the "drunken apples" to serve over ice cream or gingerbread.)

🍂 Pour the Spiced Apple Brandy into decanters and place in a dark place for 1 to 2 weeks before serving.

Makes 8 cups

from **Rosewood Country Inn**
67 Pleasant View Road
Bradford, NH 03221
603-938-5253 or
603-938-5220

"We make this liqueur every fall with our local apples," said Lesley Marquis. "It is left handy for our guests to enjoy while sitting by the fire on a chilly evening." An old friend gets together with Lesley and Dick, her spouse, to make a few batches as Christmas gifts.

The brandy makes a perfect nightcap after a day spent skiing at Mt. Sunapee or Pat's Peak, or x-c skiing on the wooded trails that start from the front door. There's also ice skating, and sleigh rides can be arranged.

Lesley and Dick left hospital jobs in Rhode Island to raise their two teenaged daughters here. They restored a former 1896 resort, offering 12 guestrooms in the three-story inn, with room to expand. Today the inn, with rose-colored shutters, has gardens, croquet, stone walls and a little brook along a country lane in the popular Dartmouth/Sunapee Lakes region of New Hampshire. Lesley and Dick specialize in themed weekends.

🏠*Another Rosewood Country Inn recipe:*
Grandma's Peach Chutney, page 86

Sweet Potato Latkes with Cranberry Relish

Ingredients:

1 small sweet potato, peeled and grated
1 medium carrot, peeled and grated
2 eggs
6 tablespoons flour
1/4 teaspoon salt
1/4 teaspoon nutmeg
Pinch of cayenne
2 tablespoons vegetable oil

Cranberry Relish:
1 orange, unpeeled, cut into 8ths and seeded
1 lemon, unpeeled, cut into 4ths and seeded
1 tart apple, peeled, cored, seeded and cut
    into 8ths
2 cups fresh cranberries
1/2 cup sugar
1/2 cup chopped walnuts

For Relish: In a food processor finely chop (but do not purée) orange, lemon and apple chunks. Add cranberries and pulse until chopped. Place mixture in a bowl. Add sugar and walnuts. Mix well and chill in the refrigerator.

For Latkes: Place potato and carrot in a towel and squeeze out liquid.

In a medium bowl, stir together egg, flour, salt, nutmeg and cayenne. Stir in carrot-potato mixture.

In a heavy skillet, heat 1 tablespoon oil over medium heat.

For each latke, place 2 tablespoons batter on skillet and spread with a spoon. Add remaining oil as needed. Cook each side for 2 to 3 minutes, or until brown. Drain on paper towels.

Serve with Cranberry Relish.

Makes 8 latkes

from **Shire Inn**
Main Street
P.O. Box 37
Chelsea, VT 05038
802-685-3031
Fax 802-685-3871

"The secret to crisp latkes is getting moisture out of the vegetables before cooking them," notes Innkeeper/Chef Karen Keller. "Sweet potatoes and carrots make a lovely pairing." These might be served for either breakfast or dinner to inn guests (dinner is served at 7 p.m. each night).

Karen and Jay, her husband, spent more than 20 years in sales and marketing in the information technology industry before deciding to buy a business in Vermont. "We were the first to see the property for sale and fell in love with it. It took us all of 48 hours to say, 'Yes!'," Karen said.

Built in 1832, the red brick Federal-style house was owned by the Davis family until it became an inn in 1977. Karen and Jay had no trouble relocating from Chicago to Chelsea, pop. 900. It is the county seat, also known as "the domain of an earl," thus a "shire town." Located on Main Street, the inn is set on 23 acres on which guests can sled, fish in the stream (a branch of the White River) or ski cross-country. Many explore the quintessential New England village, which appears untouched by time. A favorite place for weddings is on the inn's country bridge over the river. The Central Vermont location is popular with hikers, bikers and skiiers, as well as those who just want to be close to Vermont's attractions. Maps are provided to many self-guided tours.

Valentine Cranberry Buttermilk Scones

Ingredients:

2 cups flour
1/3 cup sugar
1-1/2 teaspoons baking powder
1/2 teaspoon baking soda
1/4 teaspoon salt
6 tablespoons unsalted butter, chilled
1/2 cup buttermilk
1 large egg
1-1/2 teaspoons vanilla extract
2/3 cup dried cranberries, chopped (or any dried fruit)

🍴 In a large bowl, stir together flour, sugar, baking powder, baking soda and salt.

🍴 Cut butter into 1/2 inch cubes and distribute over the flour mixture.

🍴 With a pastry blender, cut in butter until the mixture resembles course crumbs.

🍴 In a small bowl, stir together buttermilk, egg and vanilla extract. Add this mixture to the flour mixture and stir to combine. Stir in the dried fruit.

🍴 With lightly floured hands, pat the dough into a circle on an ungreased baking sheet and cut into 8 wedges.

🍴 Bake in an oven preheated to 400 degrees for 20 minutes, or until the tops are slightly brown.

🍴 Cool on a wire rack. Serve with butter and jam.

Makes 8 scones

from **The Inn at Maplewood Farm**
447 Center Road
P.O. Box 1478
Hillsborough, NH 03244
603-464-4242
800-644-6695

These pretty scones, speckled with red cranberries, are beautiful served for Valentine's breakfast or tea, especially with strawberry or raspberry jam. Innkeeper Laura Simoes, who always makes good use of fresh produce, makes her own jam from locally-grown peaches and blueberries, too.

Laura and Jayme, her husband, restored this 1794 farmhouse, located just 2.5 miles up a country lane from the town of Hillsborough. In 1992, they opened four guestrooms to travelers, and they serve an award-winning breakfast in the sunny breakfast room. The inn is surrounded by pasture and the Fox State Forest, yet is close to good restaurants and attractions.

🏠 *Other Inn at Maplewood Farm recipes:*
Decadent Praline Sauce, page 83
Fresh Salsa, page 84
Spiced Peach Soup, page 103
Maplewood Farm Granola, page 195

Vermont Challah

Ingredients:
1-1/2 cups potato water
2 tablespoons active dry yeast
2 tablespoons maple syrup
2 teaspoons salt
2 eggs
2 tablespoons vegetable oil
5 to 5 1/2 cups white flour, sifted
2 tablespoons melted butter

For Potato Water: Boil some clean white potatoes until tender. Pour off potato water and let cool to 105 to 115 degrees.

Sprinkle yeast in potato water and let sit for 5 minutes.

Stir in maple syrup, salt, eggs, oil and approximately 3 cups of the flour. Beat until texture is smooth.

Add the remaining flour. Turn out onto a floured board. Knead until the dough is smooth and elastic.

Place dough in a buttered bowl and turn once. Cover with a damp cloth and let rise in a warm place until it doubles in size (about 90 minutes).

Punch down and divide in half.

Divide each half into thirds. Roll each third into a log up to 9 inches long.

Braid the three strands and tuck the ends under to secure them. Place in a buttered 9 x 5-inch loaf pan and brush with 1 tablespoon of the melted butter.

Repeat with second half of dough.

Bake in a preheated oven at 350 degrees for 25 to 30 minutes. Serve with honey.

Makes 2 loaves

from **The Quail's Nest B&B**
Main Street
P.O. Box 221
Danby, VT 05739
802-293-5099
800-599-6444

"This is an egg-yeast bread served on Jewish holidays and the highest of Jewish holidays, the Sabbath," said Innkeeper Nancy Diaz. She modified her mother's recipe to use Vermont maple syrup in place of sugar.

Nancy and Greg, her spouse, opened this six-guestroom B&B in 1994. The inn, circa 1835, served as the town's post office, among other things, and is located along the town's main street. Greg, a doctor of philosophy and computer programmer, and Nancy, a quilter and seamstress, met on the job, but opted out of the corporate life. Nancy's quilts and other crafts adorn each room. In back of the blue-and-white B&B is a gift shop, featuring works of area artists and craftspeople, as well as Nancy's own sewing.

Other Quail's Nest recipes:
Apple Blueberry Breakfast Pie, page 171
Rugalach, page 202

Wassail

Ingredients:

1 46-ounce can apple juice
1 46-ounce can pineapple juice
2 46-ounce cans apricot nectar
2 cups orange juice
1 pot (approximately 6 cups) strong tea, such as Earl Grey
3/4 cup honey
3 to 4 cinnamon sticks
1/2 teaspoon nutmeg
6 to 7 whole cloves

- In a large pot, stir together all ingredients.
- Bring to a boil, then reduce heat and simmer for 2 to 3 hours.
- Remove cinnamon sticks and whole cloves. Serve steaming hot.

Makes about 30 cups

from **The Maples Inn**
16 Roberts Avenue
Bar Harbor, ME 04609
207-288-3443
Fax 207-288-0356

When Innkeeper Susan Sinclair makes this recipe at Christmas time, the whole three stories of her inn smell wonderful. "We have a tree-trimming weekend package that we do the first weekend in December each year in conjunction with another local inn, and I serve this to our guests on that weekend. They really go nuts over it and always ask for a copy of the recipe."

Susan's recipes have been in such demand that she finally compiled a cookbook, which she "co-authored" with her miniature schnauzer, Bailey, who gets alot of attention from adoring guests. Breakfast, served in the sunny dining room, might include Soufflé á la Orange, Banana Clafouti or Chilled Strawberry Soup, plus muffins or breads. Afternoon treats are served on the front porch in the summer or the parlor in the winter, in front of the fire.

No one is more surprised (yet pleased) by the success of these breakfasts than Susan. "I had never made breakfast in my life until I bought the inn! In the beginning, I relied upon friends to give me recipes and to coach me on what to prepare. After awhile, however, it became much simpler and I now really do enjoy coming up with some of my own creations," some of which have been featured in Gourmet and Bon Appetit magazines.

Susan, who worked in banking in California, apprenticed with a local innkeeper while thinking about innkeeping. In 1991, she bought this circa 1900 home on a quiet residential street. The inn has six guestrooms, each named after a local tree. Guests are an easy walk from Bar Harbor restaurants and shops and only a five-minute drive to Acadia National Park.

Dessert for Breakfast

Almond Butter Cake

Ingredients:

1 cup butter, softened
1 cup sugar
Dash of salt
1 egg, beaten
2 cups flour

Also:

1 egg, beaten
Milk
Sliced almonds

Filling:
1 cup almond paste
1/2 cup sugar
1 egg

☛ In a large bowl, stir together butter, sugar, salt, egg and flour. Turn out onto a floured board and knead until all ingredients are well mixed.

☛ Pat half of dough into the bottom of a buttered 9-inch cake pan.

☛ For Filling: Beat together almond paste, sugar and egg (add a little water if it's too stiff to spread) and spread on top of dough.

☛ Pat remaining dough out on top of filling.

☛ Beat remaining egg with a little milk and brush egg-milk mixture over top of dough. Sprinkle with sliced almonds.

☛ Bake in a preheated oven at 350 degrees for 1 hour. Cool before cutting,

Makes 6 to 8 servings

from **Liberty Hill Farm**
RR 1, Box 158
Rochester, VT 05767
802-767-3926

Guests who gather for breakfast at Beth Kennet's two dining room tables might be treated to this cake, as well as bacon and eggs, or pancakes and sausage. She serves a farm breakfast to guests, including those who have been up early to help her husband, Bob, and sons, Tom and David, milk the cows.

Milking is optional, but there's rarely a guest who doesn't want to try milking by hand, or perhaps many of the other chores involved in operating a dairy farm with 115 registered Holsteins, two horses, chickens, ducks and turkeys, and Lassie, the collie. Kids, always welcome in the seven-guestroom farmhouse, love the hay loft, where there may be a new litter of kittens.

Beth and Bob opened their 150-year-old farmhouse to guests in 1984 after milk prices dropped. Today, having guests living with them has become a way of life. Their farm vacations include breakfast and dinner, served family-style at 6 p.m. Guests also enjoy tubing the White River, which borders the farm.

🏠 Another Liberty Hill Farm recipe:
Rhubarb Custard Kuchen, page 187

Apple Blueberry Breakfast Pie

Ingredients:

4 large apples, peeled and sliced
3 cups blueberries, fresh or frozen "dry-pack"
1 cup sugar
1/2 teaspoon salt
1 teaspoon cinnamon
1/2 teaspoon nutmeg
2 tablespoons flour
1 tablespoon lemon juice
2 tablespoons butter, cubed

Also:

2 unbaked 9-inch pie crusts
Cinnamon and sugar mixture (1 tablespoon sugar, 1/2 teaspoon cinnamon)

- In a large bowl, toss apples and blueberries.
- Add sugar, salt, cinnamon, nutmeg and flour and toss again. Sprinkle on lemon juice.
- Line pie pan with bottom crust and pour in apple-blueberry mixture. Dot with butter.
- Cover with top crust and crimp edges.
- Poke top crust with fork to vent steam. Sprinkle with cinnamon and sugar.
- Bake in a preheated oven at 425 degrees for 15 minutes.
- Reduce heat to 350 degrees and bake for an additional 45 minutes, or until crust is golden brown. Cool on a wire rack for at least 15 minutes before serving.

Tester's Comments: Unusual combination of fruit? Yes. Unusual dish for breakfast? Yes! Delicious? Yes!!

Makes 6 to 8 servings

from **The Quail's Nest B&B**
Main Street
P.O. Box 221
Danby, VT 05739
802-293-5099
800-599-6444

Innkeeper Nancy Diaz doesn't shy away from serving dessert for breakfast, especially when it features local produce. She can cook, however, just about anything guests want or need, including a macrobiotic diet. Breakfast is served by Nancy, dressed in clothing from the same era the inn was built (1835).

Nancy and Greg, her husband, aim to have fun at their B&B. They chose quiet Danby, 13 miles from Manchester, surrounded by the Green Mountains, in which to open a six-guestroom B&B in 1994, after leaving the corporate world. Nancy, an accomplished seamstress, made the curtains and the quilts, and can lead a piano sing-a-long. Greg, the Mr. Fixit, is also a computer programmer. They direct guests to skiing, hiking, dining, fishing and shopping.

Other Quail's Nest recipes:
Vermont Challah, page 167
Rugalach, page 202

Apple Crisp

Ingredients:

6 apples, peeled, cored and sliced
1/3 cup sugar
1 teaspoon cinnamon
1/2 teaspoon nutmeg
1 teaspoon vanilla extract

Also:

Whipped cream or vanilla or cinnamon ice cream

Topping:
1/2 cup walnuts, chopped
3/4 cup flour
1/2 cup dark brown sugar, packed
3/4 cup rolled oats
1/4 teaspoon salt
1 teaspoon cinnamon
1 teaspoon nutmeg
2 teaspoons vanilla extract
1/2 cup cold butter, cut into chunks

- In a large bowl, toss together apples, sugar, cinnamon, nutmeg and vanilla extract.
- Spoon mixture into a buttered 9 x 9-inch baking pan.
- For Topping: In a separate bowl, stir together walnuts, flour, brown sugar, oats, salt, cinnamon, nutmeg and 2 teaspoons vanilla. Cut in butter with a fork or pastry cutter.
- Sprinkle the Topping over the apple mixture.
- Bake in a preheated oven at 350 degrees for about 50 minutes, or until the top is crisp and brown.
- Remove from oven and let cool slightly. Serve warm with ice cream or whipped cream.

Makes 9 servings

from **Apple Gate B&B**
199 Upland Farm Road
Peterborough, NH 03458
603-924-6543

An old-fashioned comfort food, there's nothing more aromatic, soothing and satisfying than traditional apple crisp. Innkeepers Dianne and Ken Legenhausen serve it often, especially in the fall and winter, as part of their candlelit breakfasts served fireside. The apples most likely came from the 90-acre orchard next door. In the fall, many guests love to wander over to the orchard, talk to the owners and be directed to a pick-your-own area.

The Legenhausen's B&B is located down a country lane, two miles from downtown Peterborough. Ken and Dianne are happy to help guests find a restaurant, shop or outdoor pursuit to their liking. Whether they choose a long walk in the summer, a book to read in the double parlor or on the porch, or skiing and mountain biking, they appreciate the four comfortable guestrooms upstairs and the hearty breakfasts each morning. Those who wish can meet Mac, the 100-pound yellow lab named after an apple variety, McIntosh, as are the guestrooms. Jessie the cat is Mac's buddy who also shares the Legenhausen's quarters.

Other Apple Gate recipes:
Fruit Sauce, page 85
Three Cheddar-Apple-Ham Bake, page 118

Apple Pear Crisp

Ingredients:

3 cups apples, peeled and sliced
3 cups pears, peeled and sliced
1/4 cup sugar
2 tablespoons flour
1 teaspoon cinnamon
Pinch of nutmeg

Crumb Topping:
3/4 cup flour
1 cup müesli or granola
3/4 cup brown sugar, packed
1/2 cup butter

Also:

Whipped cream or ice cream

- In a large bowl, toss together apples and pears.
- In a separate bowl, stir together sugar, 2 tablespoons flour, cinnamon and nutmeg. Sprinkle over the fruit and mix.
- Place fruit mixture in an ungreased 9 x 13-inch pan.
- For Crumb Topping: In a medium bowl, stir together 3/4 cup flour, müesli and brown sugar.
- With pastry cutter, cut in butter until mixture resembles crumbs. Sprinkle crumb mixture over fruit.
- Bake in a preheated oven at 375 degrees for 40 minutes. Serve with whipped cream or ice cream.

Tester's Comments: A delicious change from apple crisp. Next time I'll try it with ginger instead of cinnamon.

Makes 12 servings

from **Birchwood Inn**
Route 45
P.O. Box 197
Temple, NH 03084
603-878-3285

"The Apple Pear Crisp is great on a brunch buffet or a nice autumn dessert choice," said Innkeeper Judy Wolfe. Judy is in charge of all the desserts at the inn, which serves breakfast to inn guests and dinner to guests and the public, as well. Judy and Bill, her spouse, offer seven guestrooms.

Guests enjoy breakfast in the historic inn's dining room, beside a mural painted by Rufus Porter. Porter, a New England itinerant painter, worked on the mural between 1825 and 1833. His works can also be found at Old Sturbridge Village in Sturbridge, Mass.

Judy and Bill bought the inn in 1980. "We do all the work ourselves," Judy said. "Our children have been wait persons to serve evening meals." Their inn may be the oldest operating inn in the state, serving guests since 1775. The inn once hosted Henry David Thoreau and is now listed on the National Register of Historic Places. It also served as the town's post office, general store and an antique shop.

Another Birchwood Inn recipe:
Cranberry Raspberry Jam, page 82

Apple Torte

Ingredients:

1 cup sugar
1/2 cup flour
1 teaspoon baking powder
1/2 teaspoon salt
1 cup apple, chopped (do not need to peel)
1/2 cup nuts, chopped
1 teaspoon almond extract
1 egg

☛ In a large bowl, stir together sugar, flour, baking powder, salt, apple, nuts and almond extract by hand.

☛ Crack in unbeaten egg and mix well.

☛ Turn into a lightly-buttered 8 or 9-inch pie pan. Bake in a preheated oven at 350 degrees for 30 minutes.

☛ Cool on wire rack completely before cutting. Serve plain or with whipped cream or ice cream.

Makes 6 servings

from **Packard House**
45 Pearl Street
Bath, ME 04530
207-443-6069
800-516-4578

"I find that I always have the ingredients on hand for this so it's a perfect 'emergency' dessert," said Innkeeper Debby Hayden. This cake might finish off a breakfast featuring New England foods, served in the dining room.

Debby and her husband, Bill, opened a B&B just six weeks after Bill retired from American Airlines, where Debby also worked for 21 years. "I have wanted to open a B&B forever," Debby said. "My maternal grandmother had tourist cabins and did four rooms in the house until the mid-sixties. I worked with her and we often imagined having an inn together." Unfortunately, she did not live to see Debby's B&B open in 1995.

The Packard House is a 1790 Georgian-style home in Bath's historic district. It was purchased in the mid-19th century by Benjamin F. Packard, a partner in a shipbuilding company. Packard House is on the walking tour of historic sea captain's homes, and guests are invited to take that neighborhood tour.

Debby and Bill offer three guestrooms. Bath's "Mid-Coast location is loaded with interesting things to see and do," Debby said. "This area is an ideal spot for a multi-day stay." Two state parks with ocean beaches, Freeport's L.L. Bean, Wiscasset Village and Boothbay Harbor are all favorite places to visit.

🏠*Another Packard House recipe:*
Julekakke, page 160

Blueberry Apple Crisp

Ingredients:

    4 cups Granny Smith apples, peeled and sliced
    1 cup fresh or frozen "dry pack" blueberries
    2/3 cup brown sugar, lightly packed
    1/2 cup flour
    1/2 cup rolled oats
    3/4 teaspoon cinnamon
    3/4 teaspoon nutmeg
    1/3 cup butter, softened

Also:

    Whipped cream
    Lemon zest

- Toss together apples and blueberries and place in a buttered 8 x 8-inch baking dish.
- In a separate bowl, stir together sugar, flour, oats, cinnamon and nutmeg.
- Cut in softened butter until coarse crumbs form.
- Sprinkle topping over fruit.
- Bake in a preheated oven at 350 degrees for 25 to 35 minutes, until bubbly around the edge.
- Cool for a few minutes before dishing into serving bowls and garnishing with whipped cream and lemon zest.

Makes 6 servings

from **The Inn at Southwest**
371 Main Street
P.O. Box 593
Southwest Harbor, ME 04679
207-244-3835
Fax 207-244-9879

"I decided to start serving this for breakfast when I saw it on the dessert menu of a local restaurant," said Innkeeper Jill Lewis. "Serving this with whipped cream and lemon zest changes it from a basic dessert to a gourmet dish!" Guests might finish a breakfast of eggs Florentine, bacon and lemon poppyseed bread with a bowl of this steaming dessert.

This inn was built in 1884 as an annex to the Ashmont Hotel. The first floor was the dining room, the kitchen was in the basement, and the second and third floors had guestrooms, but no bathrooms or central heat. After the hotel burned down in the early 1900s, the annex continued hosting guests. In 1939, it was named Harbor Lights Tourist Home, and bathrooms and heating were added. In 1986, it was converted to a B&B, and Jill bought it in 1995, again making several improvements. Jill, a former manager of a computing services company, fell in love with the area while looking for a B&B. She lives in Michigan in the winter and works as a computer consultant.

Another Inn at Southwest recipe:
Crab Potato Bake, page 144

Blueberry Peach Cobbler

Ingredients:

3 cups peeled and sliced fresh peaches or frozen "dry pack" peach slices
3 cups blueberries, fresh or frozen "dry pack"
1/2 cup sugar
2 teaspoons cinnamon
2 eggs
1/2 cup vegetable oil
1 cup sugar
1 cup flour
1 teaspoon baking powder
2 tablespoons grated orange peel
1 cup chopped pecans
2 tablespoons sugar
1/2 teaspoon cinnamon

☛ In a large bowl, toss peaches and blueberries with 1/2 cup sugar and 2 teaspoons cinnamon.

☛ Turn the fruit into a buttered 9 x 13-inch pan.

☛ In a separate bowl, beat eggs. Stir in oil, sugar, flour, baking powder and orange peel. Pour and spread on top of fruit.

☛ Sprinkle with chopped pecans. Mix sugar and cinnamon and sprinkle on top of cobbler.

☛ Bake in a preheated oven at 350 degrees for 30 minutes or until fruit is tender and cobbler is "set."

☛ Remove from oven and let cool 5 to 10 minutes. Serve warm in bowls topped with whipped cream or ice cream.

Makes 12 to 16 servings

from **The Village House**
P.O. Box 359
Route 16A
Jackson, NH 03846
800-972-8343
Fax 603-383-6464

This cobbler is an old family recipe that Innkeeper Robin Crocker now serves to guests in the 10 guestrooms in the main inn. In the summer, they gather at linen-covered tables on the front porch, where they can eat a leisurely meal while watching the activity along the main street of the village of Jackson.

Many of Robin's guests, however, love the picture-perfect village in the winter. Renowned for its snowfall and ski resorts, Jackson is home to Black Mountain for downhill skiing and some 167 kilometers of x-c trails, which can be accessed right from the inn. Ice skating and sleigh rides under the stars, snowshoeing and ice climbing are also popular winter pursuits.

Robin, who has renovated the inn and converted the barn to five guest suites, has a special interest in dog training. One of the three inn dogs is a Service Dog in Training Puppy. Several guestrooms welcome pets (and kids, too).

🏠 *Another Village House recipe:*
Raspberry Cream Cheese Coffeecake, page 38

Blueberry Shortcakes

Ingredients:

   1-3/4 cups flour
   1/2 cup sugar
   3 tablespoons baking powder
   1/4 teaspoon salt
   4 tablespoons butter or margarine
   3/4 cup milk
   2 cups fresh blueberries, washed and picked over
   3/4 cup sugar

Also:

   About 2 more cups blueberries
   6 to 8 scoops vanilla ice cream
   Whipped Cream

- For shortcake biscuits, in a medium bowl, stir together flour, sugar, baking powder and salt.

- With a pastry cutter or forks, cut in butter or margarine "until corn-sized nuggets appear."

- With a wooden spoon, stir in milk. Mix for 30 seconds.

- Spread dough onto a well-floured board and knead for 15 seconds. Roll out to 1/2-inch thick.

- Cut into 6 to 8 3-inch circles with a biscuit cutter or jar cap. Place on a lightly-buttered cookie sheet.

- Bake in a preheated oven at 425 degrees for 12 or more minutes or until golden in color.

- Remove cookie sheet from oven and cool shortcakes. Meanwhile, in a blender, place fresh blueberries and 3/4 cup sugar. Blend until a thick purée forms.

- On each of 6 (or 7 or 8, depending on number of shortcakes) dessert plates, pour 3 tablespoons of blueberry purée.

- Slice biscuits in half horizontally and place the bottom halves on top of the purée.

- Place additional blueberries and a scoop of ice cream on the bottom half of biscuit.

- Top with top half of biscuit and additional purée, blueberries and whipped cream. Serve immediately.

Makes 6 to 8 servings

from **Deerhill Inn**
Valley View Road
P.O. Box 136
West Dover, VT 05356
802-464-3100

Chef/co-innkeeper Michael Anelli insists on using fresh regional ingredients, and many times guests will find these blueberries are served the same summer day they are picked. Michael and Linda, his spouse, opened this 17-guestroom inn in 1994, serving both breakfast and dinner to guests who come to ski ("Mount Snow and Haystack are at your feet, Stratton and Bromley just up the road"), fish the Battenkill, golf, mountain bike or laze by the pool. Michael and Linda bought this inn after they sold a local restaurant and spent seven years of traveling, indulging their wanderlust. The restaurant specializes in wines from North and South America, a variety of seafood selections and a dynamic dessert tray. Breakfasts might include a memorable omelette. Linda and Michael plan several special interest packages during the year.

Bread Pudding with Custard

Ingredients:

1/3 cup raisins
5 slices of bread, cubed ("I use a cinnamon swirl bread")
1/4 cup butter, melted
2 eggs
2/3 cup sugar
2 cups milk
1/2 teaspoon vanilla extract

Also:

Cinnamon

🥄 Line the bottom of a buttered 9-inch casserole with raisins.

🥄 Place cubed bread in casserole, pour melted butter over and toss.

🥄 Beat eggs, sugar, milk and vanilla extract together and pour over bread. Sprinkle with cinnamon.

🥄 Set dish in a larger baking pan of hot water so that water goes about 3/4-inch up the sides of the casserole.

🥄 Bake in a preheated oven at 375 degrees for 45 minutes, or until bread is browned and knife blade comes out clean. Do not overcook "or it will be too dry."

Makes 6 servings

from **Candlelite Inn B&B**
5 Greenhouse Lane
Bradford, NH 03221
603-938-5571
888-812-5571

"This recipe was handed down from my mother, and it's the only bread pudding I'll eat," said Innkeeper Marilyn Gordon. Breakfast always includes dessert at her inn, perhaps this or an apple crisp. Breakfast might be served in the sun room overlooking the brook and pond.

Marilyn, a former bank teller and customer service manager, knew how to work with people, and Les, a machinist, knew how to fix stuff. When their kids graduated from high school, they sold their New Jersey home and began to pursue their second careers as innkeepers. Five years later, Marilyn notes that "it's still the best job either of us has ever had!" They love Bradford, where Marilyn is now the deputy town clerk/tax collector.

Their six-guestroom inn was built as a boarding house in 1897. Over the years, it was winterized, had a succession of owners, was converted into apartments and back to a B&B again. Les and Marilyn redecorated and did other work on the inn and opened in 1993. The Gordons can recommend barn sales and auctions, boating and fishing, ski areas and restaurants and other activities in the scenic Lake Sunapee Region of New Hampshire.

🏠 *Another Candlelite Inn recipe:*
Marilyn's Fruit Pancake, page 139

Carrot Spice Cake

Ingredients:

3 eggs
2 cups sugar
1 cup canola oil
2 teaspoons vanilla extract
4 medium carrots, grated (2 cups)
2 cups flour
2 teaspoons baking soda
1 teaspoon baking powder
1/2 teaspoon salt
1 tablespoon cinnamon
1/4 teaspoon allspice
1 cup chopped walnuts
1 cup raisins

Also:

Powdered sugar

🥄 In a food processor with a steel blade, process eggs and sugar for 1 minute.

🥄 While machine is running, add oil and vanilla through the feeder tube and process for about 45 additional seconds. Add carrots and process for 10 seconds.

🥄 In a separate bowl, stir together flour, baking soda, baking powder, salt, cinnamon and allspice.

🥄 Add carrot mixture all at once to flour mixture. Stir until blended, about 45 seconds.

🥄 Stir in nuts and raisins.

🥄 Pour batter into a buttered and floured 9 x 13-inch baking pan or Bundt pan.

🥄 Bake in a preheated oven at 350 degrees for 55 to 60 minutes. Cool completely before inverting. Dust with powdered sugar before serving.

Makes 12 to 15 servings

from **Admiral Peary House B&B**
9 Elm Street
Fryeburg, ME 04037
207-935-3365
800-237-8080

This is a favorite at Nancy and Ed Greenberg's B&B, once owned by the famous American explorer and named after him. Peary lived here for several years with his mother.

This is the Greenberg's second B&B after careers as school teachers. They used to vacation here and loved the area "mainly because of all the beauty and activities it offers," Nancy said. Guests can play tennis on their red clay court, snowshoe on the inn's eight acres of trails, canoe and swim in the Saco River, or shop in North Conway, N.H., outlet stores, only 15 minutes away.

🏠*Another Admiral Peary House recipe:*
Maine Wild Blueberry Pancakes, page 137

Cheesecake Squares

Ingredients:

5 tablespoons butter or margarine
1/2 cup brown sugar, packed
1 cup flour
1/3 cup walnuts, chopped
1/2 cup sugar
1 8-ounce package cream cheese (not low-fat)
1 egg
2 tablespoons milk
1 tablespoon fresh lemon juice
1/2 teaspoon vanilla extract

- With an electric mixer, cream together butter or margarine and brown sugar.
- Add flour and walnuts. Mix well. Set aside 1 cup of the mixture for a streusel topping.
- Press remaining mixture in an unbuttered 8 x 8-inch pan.
- Bake in a preheated oven at 350 degrees for 12 to 15 minutes, until lightly browned. Keep oven on.
- With an electric mixer, beat sugar and cream cheese until smooth.
- Add egg, milk, lemon juice and vanilla. Beat well.
- Pour mixture over baked crust and sprinkle top with reserved cup of topping.
- Return to oven and bake for an additional 25 minutes.
- Allow pan to come to room temperature and refrigerate. Cut into squares.

Tester's Comments: Two neighbors with whom this test was shared immediately requested the recipe. If you wish, instead of the streusel, top with fresh raspberries after baking, then brush with raspberry jelly that has been melted and thinned with water. Beautiful and delicious!

Makes about 16 servings

from Swan House B&B
49 Mountain Street
Camden, ME 04843
207-236-8275
800-207-8275

Innkeeper Lyn Kohl's Cheesecake Squares are served as "pastry of the day" on the expansive breakfast buffet. "As a variation, I add one-third cup of drained, crushed pineapple to the cheese filling before baking," Lyn notes.

Lyn and Ken Kohl's six-guestroom inn is located a short walk up the hill from the heart of Camden, where guests might book a cruise on a schooner or a lobster boat. One of the trails in Camden Hills State Park and up Mt. Battie starts behind the inn, and many guests enjoy the hike, some even before breakfast. Two of the guestrooms are in the main house, a Victorian built by the Swan family in 1870, and four are in the Cygnet Annex.

▲Another Swan House recipe:
French Almond Coffeecake, page 35

Cranberry Bread Pudding

Ingredients:

2 cups milk, scalded and cooled
1/2 cup butter, melted
2 eggs, beaten
1/2 cup sugar
1 teaspoon cinnamon
1/2 teaspoon nutmeg
6 cups bread cubes, made from buttered toast
1/2 cup dried cranberries

Also:

"Hard sauce," whipped cream or ice cream

- Mix together milk, butter, eggs, sugar, cinnamon and nutmeg.
- Place bread cubes and cranberries in a well-buttered, 2-quart casserole dish.
- Pour liquid mixture over the bread and fruit.
- Place casserole dish into a larger pan and fill the larger pan with hot water until the water is 1/2-inch up the sides of the casserole dish.
- Bake in an oven preheated to 350 degrees for 40 to 45 minutes or until a knife inserted in the center comes out clean. Serve warm with your favorite topping.

Makes 8 servings

from **The Notchland Inn**
Route 302
Hart's Location, NH 03812
603-374-6131
800-866-6131

The Notchland Inn's chef, Laurel Tessier, developed this dish. "We have served it to raves morning, noon and night," said Innkeeper Les Schoof. "Guests have always purred after its consumption."

Guests who can tear themselves away from the breakfast table will find much to do before their five-course dinner that night. Notchland Inn is just east of Crawford Notch on 100 acres in the White Mountains, including 8,000 feet of Saco River frontage. Guests can climb Mt. Crawford, fish, visit Dolly, the Belgian draft horse, soak in the outdoor hot tub, read in front of the parlor fire or work a jigsaw puzzle in the music room. That's just at the inn. The attractions of North Conway are a 25-minute drive.

Les and Ed Butler found this 1862 granite mansion on "one last trip" after a three-year search for the perfect inn. With seven guestrooms, five suites, several friendly resident animals, a pond, a gazebo and perennial gardens, they believe they found the "right" place.

Other Notchland Inn recipes:
Notchland 'Muddled' Cider, page 24
Favorite Popovers, page 51
Boiled Fruit Cake, page 154

Grandma's Applesauce Cake

Ingredients:

2-1/2 cups flour
2 cups sugar
1-1/2 teaspoons baking soda
1/2 teaspoon baking powder
1-1/2 teaspoons salt
3/4 teaspoon cinnamon
1/2 teaspoon cloves
1/2 teaspoon allspice
1 cup raisins
1/2 chopped nuts
1/2 cup vegetable oil
1/2 cup water
2 eggs
1-1/2 cups applesauce

- In a large bowl, stir together flour, sugar, baking soda, baking powder, salt, cinnamon, cloves, allspice, raisins and nuts.
- In a separate bowl, whisk together vegetable oil, water, eggs and applesauce.
- Add oil mixture to flour mixture and beat with electric mixer for 3 minutes on medium speed.
- Pour batter into a buttered and floured Bundt or tube pan.
- Bake in a preheated oven at 350 degrees for 45 to 55 minutes. Cool before inverting to remove.

Tester's Comments: This moist cake tastes like fall. It's a winner. Could be baked in loaf pans for a wonderful harvest bread. Dust the top with powdered sugar, if you like.

Makes about 20 servings

from **The Victorian by the Sea**
Sea View Drive
P.O. Box 1385
Camden, ME 04843
207-236-3785
800-382-9817

This is Innkeeper Marie Donner's grandmother's cake, and perhaps something similar would have been served in 1881 when this summer "cottage" was built for a New York family. Located five minutes from Camden, the home was built off Route 1, down a quiet, private road, 300 feet from the shore.

Marie and Ray bought the home in 1992 and opened it as a B&B. "We wanted to open an inn for 10 years" before they bought this inn, said Marie. They moved from New York after falling in love with the Maine coast. Since then, they have doubled the size of the structure to about 10,000 square feet, and added a wrap-around porch for views of Penobscot Bay. Guests have breakfast in the turret, which has views of the Bay and the grounds.

Indian Pudding

Ingredients:

    3 quarts milk
    1/2 cup butter
    3 cups molasses
    1-1/2 cups sugar
    1-1/2 cups yellow cornmeal
    1 teaspoon cinnamon
    1 teaspoon ginger
    1 teaspoon nutmeg
    6 eggs

Also:

    Vanilla ice cream or heavy cream

- In a large saucepan, slowly scald milk and butter. Stir in molasses.

- In a large bowl, stir together sugar, cornmeal, cinnamon, ginger and nutmeg. Slowly whisk into milk mixture.

- In a separate bowl, whisk eggs. Ladle some of hot milk mixture into eggs while whisking.

- Slowly whisk thinned egg mixture into rest of milk mixture.

- Cook over low heat, stirring constantly, until mixture begins to thicken.

- Pour into a buttered oven-proof pan with a cover, like a Dutch Oven. Cover and bake in a preheated oven at 350 degrees for about 2 hours, or until very thick.

- Remove from oven, spoon hot pudding into pretty dessert bowls. Top with ice cream or heavy cream.

Makes 12 very large servings

from **The Ram in the Thicket**
24 Maple Street
Milford, NH 03055
603-654-6440

Innkeeper/Restauranteur Priscilla Tempelman has enhanced a traditional New England recipe for Indian pudding by adding spices, noting the classic "is too bland for my taste." Guests might enjoy this hot dessert for breakfast along with cream and fresh fruit. Breakfast is served in the two dining rooms or on the screened porch in the summer.

The Tempelman family – including husband Andrew, a minister, and three young sons -- relocated in New England after many years in the Midwest, spent dreaming of New England. That was 1977. The Tempelmans are still running this 100-year-old mansion as an inn and restaurant two decades later.
The Ram in the Thicket, named after a Bible passage, is minutes away from antiquing, summer theater, hiking trails and swimming, ski areas and several sugarbushes where guests can watch maple syrup being made in the spring.

♠ Another Ram in the Thicket recipe:
Sausage with Cider Cranberry Glaze, page 147

Mascarpone Stuffed Strawberries

Ingredients:
1/2 cup Mascarpone cheese
3 ounces cream cheese, softened
3 tablespoons sugar
1 tablespoon minced orange zest
24 large strawberries (stems intact, if possible), washed and dried
1/4 cup pistachios, shelled and finely chopped, optional

- With an electric mixer, beat together Mascarpone, cream cheese, sugar and orange zest.
- With a small melon baller, cut a cavity into a strawberry. Repeat with all the berries.
- Place cheese mixture in a piping bag equipped with a small star tube. (If you have none, you can spoon filling into berries with a small spoon, like a baby or jam spoon.)
- Pipe Mascarpone mixture into berries.
- Sprinkle with pistachios, cover and refrigerate until ready to serve.

Tester's Comments: Fabulous. Green pistachios and red berries are particularly festive and could be made at Christmas, if you can find good strawberries then.

Makes 8 servings

from **Stonecrest Farm B&B**
119 Christian Street
P.O. Box 504
Wilder, VT 05088
802-296-2425

These strawberries are a light, yet very tasty, dessert to follow a spectacular breakfast at this country inn. Innkeeper Gail Sanderson may whip up fresh fruit, homemade breads or muffins, and a ricotta-herb omelette with red pepper sauce, followed by these strawberries. For guests staying more than one night, Gail changes the menu daily.

Stonecrest Farm is situated on two acres with the same shade trees and red barns that were part of the working dairy farm founded in 1810. Arthur Stone, a prominent local citizen, hosted President Calvin Coolidge and Amelia Earhart in his large home. The estate remained in the Stone family until 1967.

Gail, who was suddenly widowed while finishing law school, opened the B&B after completing her degree. She thrived on entertaining company and loved the big house, full of family antiques. She made many changes to the house, adding bathrooms, for instance, and a law office over the garage. Her daughter-in-law, Kathleen, has created many wonderful signature dishes for the inn. Kathleen's recipes always win praise and often win awards.

🏠 *Other Stonecrest Farm recipes:*
Lemon Cream with Berries, page 100
Fried Green Tomatoes Au Gratin, page 192

Orange Ambrosia

Ingredients:

2 large oranges, peeled and cut into 1/4-inch slices
1/4 cup flaked coconut
1/4 cup sour cream
1-1/2 teaspoons brown sugar, packed
1/4 teaspoon grated orange rind
Pinch of salt
2 tablespoons pecans, chopped

- Set aside 2/3 of the orange slices.
- Divide remaining orange slices between two small dessert bowls. Top with 1/3 of the coconut.
- Repeat layers of oranges and coconut two additional times.
- Cover bowls and refrigerate at least one hour (or overnight).
- Meanwhile, in a separate bowl, whisk together sour cream and brown sugar, mixing well.
- Stir in orange rind and salt. Cover bowl and refrigerate at least one hour (or overnight).
- Before serving, remove fruit and sour cream mixture from refrigerator. Top fruit with sour cream and sprinkle with pecans.

Makes 2 servings

from **Placidia Farm B&B**
R.D. 1, Box 275
Randolph, VT 05060
802-728-9883

This is an easy dessert, perfect in mid-winter to add a little "sunshine." Innkeeper Viola Frost-Laitinen received the recipe along with a gift box of oranges from one of her first B&B guests.

Viola operates one of the state's smallest B&Bs, with one guest suite, and has done so consistently for what appears to be a record for innkeepers – 15 years. She and her late husband had purchased this hand-hewn log home on 81 quiet acres as a weekend getaway, but she opened the apartment as a B&B after being widowed in 1982.

Now remarried, she and Don enjoy having one guest or family at a time. Guests are treated to a hearty country breakfast on the sunporch, with views of the Green Mountains. They can wander down by the pond or brook or pursue more vigorous outdoor activities in the area. Viola and Don offer hiking, x-c skiing and sleigh rides on the property. They can direct guests to plays, concerts, downhill skiing, maple syruping, swimming, golf or tennis.

Other Placidia Farm recipes:
Blueberry Cinnamon Sauce, page 81
Islands Jam, page 88

Peach Cream Pie

Ingredients:

5-1/2 cups fresh peaches, peeled and sliced
1/2 to 3/4 cup sugar
3 tablespoons quick tapioca or cornstarch
1/4 teaspoon nutmeg
1/4 teaspoon cinnamon
Juice of one lemon
2 tablespoons unsalted butter, cut in cubes

Pie Crust:
1 teaspoon vinegar
1/2 cup milk
2-1/2 cups flour
1/2 teaspoon salt
1 cup lard or shortening

Also:

Fresh strawberries, sliced, and blueberries
Whipped cream
Sugar

- For Pie Crust: Add vinegar to milk and set aside to sour.
- Blend flour, salt and shortening with pastry cutter. Add soured milk to flour mixture and blend.
- Roll out two crusts, placing one in bottom of 9-inch pie pan.
- For Filling: In a large bowl, toss together peaches, sugar, tapioca, nutmeg, cinnamon and lemon juice.
- Pour into pie pan and dot with butter.
- Cover with top crust and crimp edges.
- Bake in an oven preheated to 425 degrees for 10 minutes.
- Reduce heat to 350 degrees and bake 35 to 40 more minutes.
- Meanwhile, whip cream and add sugar to taste.
- After pie cools completely, cover with whipped cream. Place strawberries and blueberries in a decorative pattern on the top.

Makes 8 servings

from **Rooms With a View B&B**
Forbes Road
RR1, Box 215
Colebrook, NH 03576
603-237-5106
800-499-5106

Dessert for breakfast is not unheard of at Sonja Sheldon's inn. This summertime treat took the grand prize for taste and presentation at Old Time Farm Day at the Shelburne Museum in Shelburne, Vermont.

Sonja's cooking skills got lots of practice in Boston, where she cooked church suppers once a month for 125 to 300 people. At the inn that she and her husband, Charles, operate, the number of guests in the seven guestrooms is considerably smaller, but the effort to please continues. Sonja cooks eggs any style, for instance. The Sheldons built this home as a B&B because of the hilltop views. They opened their B&B in 1991.

Other Rooms With a View recipes:
Buttermilk Oatmeal Muffins, page 47
Mimi's Favorite Cookies, page 197

Rhubarb Custard Kuchen

Ingredients:
 1-3/4 cups flour
 1/2 teaspoon baking powder
 Dash of salt
 3/4 cup solid vegetable shortening
 2 eggs
 1 tablespoon milk
 4 cups chopped rhubarb, fresh or frozen "dry pack"
 1-1/4 cups sugar
 2 tablespoons flour
 1 teaspoon cinnamon
 3/4 cup milk
 1 teaspoon vanilla extract

- In a large bowl, sift together flour, baking powder and salt. Cut in shortening with a pastry cutter.
- Beat 1 egg with 1 tablespoon milk. Stir into flour mixture. Pat into a buttered 9 x 13-inch pan.
- Top with rhubarb.
- In a medium bowl, stir together sugar, flour and cinnamon. Sprinkle over rhubarb.
- In a separate bowl, beat second egg, 3/4 cup milk and vanilla. Pour over entire cake.
- Bake in a preheated oven at 425 degrees for 20 minutes, then reduce heat to 375 degrees and bake 15 minutes more. Cut while still warm.

Tester's Comments: Mmmm. And good warm or cold. Like a rich rhubarb bar cookie, if there is such a thing!

Makes 16 to 24 servings

from **Liberty Hill Farm**
RR 1, Box 158
Rochester, VT 05767
802-767-3926

Rhubarb, from the patch on the farm, is one of the homegrown foods that find their way to the breakfast or dinner table here. This is one of Innkeeper Beth Bennet's most frequently-requested recipes.

Guests who come to this 105-acre working dairy farm for their vacation can choose from seven guestrooms in the farmhouse and countless chores on the farm: milk cows, clean stalls, feed the many animals, gather eggs, or maybe experience seasonal work, such as haying or watching calves being born. In addition to farm life, Beth and Bob, her husband, and their sons, Tom and Dave, help guests swim, fish or tube the White River, which borders the farm, having a bonfire, make homemade ice cream, pick berries or find enough other activities so families have been known to not leave the farm for a week.

Another Liberty Hill Farm recipe:
Almond Butter Cake, page 170

Southwestern Fiesta Cheesecake

Ingredients:

- 1-1/2 cups tortilla chips, crushed
- 2 tablespoons butter, melted
- 4 8-ounce packages cream cheese, softened (not low-fat or fat-free)
- 3 eggs
- 2 cups Monterey Jack cheese, grated (may substitute jalapeno cheese)
- 2 garlic cloves, crushed
- 2 4-ounce cans green chilies, drained and chopped
- 1 cup sour cream (low-fat is OK)
- 1/2 cup salsa, drained

Also:

Orange, yellow and/or red bell peppers, scallions, black olives, chopped tomato, cilantro or parsley, jalapeno or chili peppers

- Stir together tortilla chips and melted butter. Spread on bottom of a springform pan.
- In a food processor or with a mixer, beat cream cheese until fluffy.
- Beat the eggs, one at a time, into the cream cheese.
- Stir in grated cheese, garlic and chilies. Blend well. Pour into the prepared crust.
- Bake in a preheated oven at 325 degrees for 50 minutes, or until firm.
- Turn the oven off and let sit for 60 minutes, or place in the refrigerator, uncovered until cool. Let chill for 2 hours.
- Remove from pan. Stir together sour cream and salsa and spread over top of cheesecake. Decorate with garnishes.

Makes 20 servings

from **The Inn at The Round Barn Farm**
East Warren Road
RR 1, Box 247
Waitsfield, VT 05673
802-496-2276
800-326-7038

Innkeeper Anne Marie DeFreest, who combines managing this inn with raising a family and dairy farming, might serve this decorated with onion flowers or tomato rose garnishes. Guests in the 11 guestrooms might enjoy it before taking on the inn's own 30 km of groomed x-c ski trails, or before swimming in the inn's lap pool, built in the lower level of the 1910 round barn.

Anne Marie's parents, Doreen and Jack Simko, first restored the farmhouse and connected buildings on 85 acres into the inn, opening in 1987. Painstaking restoration of the three-level, 12-sided barn took two years; it has space for weddings, meetings, workshops and community events. The Simkos, nearing retirement from their New Jersey floral business, instead sold that and took on innkeeping, with the assistance of Anne Marie.

Another Inn at the Round Barn Farm recipe:
Cranberry Eggnog Tea Bread, page 157

Other Favorites

Cranberry Bars

Ingredients:

3 cups flour
2 teaspoons baking powder
1/2 teaspoon salt
3-3/4 cups rolled oats
1-1/2 cups light brown sugar (not packed)
1 cup butter
1/2 cup margarine

Filling:
1 pound (16 ounces) cranberries
1 cup sugar (more or less to taste)
1 teaspoon grated lemon peel, optional
1/4 to 1/3 cup water

☛ In a large bowl, stir together flour, baking powder, salt, oats and brown sugar.

☛ Cut in butter and margarine until it resembles coarse cornmeal.

☛ Line a 13 x 9-inch pan with parchment paper or butter it well. Press half of oat mixture into pan.

☛ For Filling: In a saucepan, stir together cranberries, sugar, lemon peel and water. Cook over medium heat, stirring often, until most of cranberries pop.

☛ Taste and adjust sugar. Cook, stirring constantly, until sugar is dissolved.

☛ Spread warm cranberry mixture over oat mixture in pan.

☛ Crumble remaining oat mixture on top. Press lightly into cranberries.

☛ Bake in a preheated oven at 325 to 350 degrees for 30 to 40 minutes or until top is golden. Remove and cool for several minutes.

☛ If parchment was used, loosen edges and place up-side-down into another pan, peel off paper, and re-invert. Even if parchment was not used, cut into 24 bars and enjoy (Caution: filling stays hot a long time!).

Tester's Comments: These are a great sweet-tart version of old-fashioned date bars. Be sure to buy a 16-ounce bag (they come in 12-ounce bags, too) of cranberries or you won't have enough filling.

Makes 24 servings

from **Fairhaven Inn**
North Bath Road
Bath, ME 04530
888-443-4391
Fax 207-443-6412

Innkeeper Susie Reed concocted this version of a bar cookie she used to make at her pastry shop out of necessity: she had 10 gallons of wild cranberries picked in a Maine bog to use up! "We usually put out cookies in the evening so guests can have a snack when they come in," Susie said. Even if wild cranberries aren't used, these have become a favorite with guests. They may be returning from a day cruising to lighthouses, touring historic homes and buildings in town, or just birdwatching from the dining room window.

🏠 *Other Fairhaven Inn recipes:*
Gaye's Currant Scones, page 52
David's Gingergread, page 69
Vegetable Hash, page 150

Firehouse Brownies

Ingredients:

4 ounces unsweetened chocolate
1 cup butter or margarine
4 eggs
2 cups sugar
1 teaspoon vanilla extract
1 cup flour
1/2 teaspoon salt
1 cup pecans or walnuts, chopped

Frosting:
2 tablespoons butter, softened
1-1/4 cups powdered sugar
3 tablespoons half-and-half
Decorative Drizzle Icing:
2 ounces semi-sweet chocolate
1 tablespoon butter

🔥 In a microwave-safe bowl, melt together the unsweetened chocolate and butter or margarine by "miking" at 25-second intervals, stirring and miking again.

🔥 In a separate bowl, beat the eggs, sugar and vanilla together.

🔥 In another bowl, stir together the flour, salt and chopped nuts. Add the melted chocolate-butter mixture and the egg-sugar mixture to the rest of the ingredients, and blend well.

🔥 Pour into a buttered 9 x 13-inch pan. Bake in a preheated oven at 325 degrees for 35 minutes.

🔥 While the brownies are baking, make the frosting and the icing. For the Frosting: With an electric mixer, cream the butter. Beat in the sugar. Add the cream and mix until smooth. ("It will not look like much, but it'll be enough" to cover the brownies.)

🔥 For the Icing: Melt together the chocolate and butter in a small pan over low heat, or microwave.

🔥 When brownies are done, cool on a wire rack. Spread frosting over the top of the cooled brownies. With a wire whisk or fork, drizzle the icing over the top of the frosting in quick circles or up, down, and across.

Makes 18 to 24 brownies

from **Watch Hill B&B**
Old Meredith Road
P.O. Box 1605
Center Harbor, NH 03226
603-253-4334

These brownies are named in honor of the Center Harbor Fire Department spaghetti supper at which Innkeeper Barbara Lauterbach served 14 pans of them! "My neighbor was the fire chief, and he helped me out on Christmas Eve when the pipes froze at the B&B. He spent hours in my 1772 basement crawl space, armed with a hair dryer, thawing the frozen pipes." It was minus 10 degrees and she had guests in all four guestrooms. She made brownies as partial payback for his able assistance. Barbara's cooking is appreciated more than just locally. She's taught cooking classes and been a food spokesperson. B&B guests might get to sample these brownies as an afternoon treat.

🏠 Other Watch Hill B&B recipes:
Buttermilk Whole Wheat Bread, page 67
Spiced Tomato Jam, page 92
Mulled Cider Applesauce, page 102
Savory Christmas Bread, page 163

Fried Green Tomatoes Au Gratin

Ingredients:

3 green tomatoes, cut into 5 slices each
Salt and freshly-cracked pepper
Flour
2 eggs, beaten with 1 to 2 tablespoons water
1-1/2 cups fine yellow cornmeal
Oil as needed
4 ounces Gorgonzola cheese
4 ounces Mascarpone cheese
1/4 cup grated Parmesan cheese
3 tablespoons parsley, chopped
2 tablespoons chives, chopped

🍢 Season tomatoes slices with salt and pepper. Coat slices with flour, then egg.

🍢 Dredge tomatoes in corn meal and let rest on a rack for at least 5 minutes (may rest up to 2 hours).

🍢 In a 12-inch skillet, heat oil. Pan fry coated tomatoes, turning once, for 3 to 4 minutes, or until golden on both sides. Let cool on wire rack.

🍢 In a medium bowl, mix Gorgonzola, Mascarpone, Parmesan, parsley and chives with a fork. Mixture will be stiff.

🍢 Top each tomato slice with 1 tablespoon of cheese mixture. Place on a jelly-roll pan or baking pan with sides. Broil until cheese turns golden.

🍢 Serve tomatoes immediately.

Tester's Comments: An upscale version of fried green tomatoes that brought requests for seconds at a barbeque.

Makes 6 servings

from **Stonecrest Farm B&B**
119 Christian Street
P.O. Box 504
Wilder, VT 05088
802-296-2425

Innkeeper Gail Sanderson serves these tomatoes alone or with a mixed green salad. The recipe was developed by Kathleen Sanderson, a food consultant who has worked as a food editor, and who happens to be Gail's daughter-in-law. Kathleen has created extra-special recipes for the inn.

Gail, who practices law, opened the inn in 1987 after finishing her law degree. Many of the inn's guests come to visit Dartmouth, only 3.5 miles up the road. Guests in the six guestrooms also enjoy the living room, with beamed ceiling and curved staircase, the stone terrace and the two acres of lawn and gardens. Stonecrest summer guests can participate in an "inn to inn" program with two days of canoeing on the Connecticut River.

🏠 *Other Stonecrest Farm recipes:*
Lemon Cream with Berries, page 100
Mascarpone Stuffed Strawberries, page 184

Granola Trail Mix Cookies

Ingredients:

1/4 cup unsalted butter, softened
1/4 cup shortening
1/4 cup sugar
1/2 cup light brown sugar, packed
1 large egg
1/2 teaspoon vanilla extract
1/2 teaspoon baking soda, dissolved in 1 tablespoon warm water
1/2 cup plus 2 tablespoons flour
1/2 teaspoon salt
1-1/2 cups granola cereal with almonds
1/2 cup flaked coconut
1 6-ounce package semi-sweet chocolate chips
1/2 cup raisins, optional
1/3 cup peanuts, optional

- With an electric mixer, cream butter, shortening, sugar and brown sugar.
- Beat in egg, vanilla, baking soda mixture, flour and salt.
- By hand, stir in granola, coconut, chocolate chips, and optional raisins and peanuts.
- On ungreased cookie sheets, drop rounded teaspoonfuls of dough about 4 inches apart.
- With a fork, flatten each mound.
- Bake in a preheated oven at 350 degrees for 8 to 10 minutes, or until golden.
- Remove from oven and with a metal spatula, transfer cookies to racks to cool.

Makes about 30 cookies

from **Molly Stark Inn**
1067 Main Street
Bennington, VT 05201
802-442-9631
800-356-3076

Many of the guests at this B&B come to hike, ski or pursue some other type of outdoor sport, so it's appropriate that Innkeeper Reed Fendler have some hearty cookies on hand when they hit the trail. Or guests might gather in the sunroom in the afternoon to enjoy them with a cup of coffee, tea or cider.

Bennington, located 30 minutes south of Manchester and Arlington, is home to many distinctive shops and restaurants, several of which are within walking distance of the inn. The Appalachian Trail and Green Mountain trail systems are four miles away. Those who prefer can spend time in the acre of gardens near Barney Brook or in a rocker on the wrap-around porch. Reed bought this operating inn in 1988 and now has seven guestrooms in the main house, an 1890 Queen Anne Victorian, and a guest cottage by the brook.

Other Molly Stark Inn recipes:
Almond and Dried Cherry Muffins, page 44
Smoked Salmon Quesadilla, page 148

Low-Fat Granola

Ingredients:

6 cups old-fashioned rolled oats (not quick-cooking)
1/2 cup sliced almonds
1/4 cup canola oil
1/2 cup honey
1/2 cup molasses
1 cup water
1/4 cup brown sugar, packed
3/4 cup raisins

☛ In a large bowl, mix oats and almonds.

☛ In a large saucepan, heat canola oil, honey, molasses, water and brown sugar, stirring constantly until the mixture comes to a low boil.

☛ Pour the hot honey mixture over the oats and almonds, mixing with a long-handled spoon.

☛ Spread the granola on a baking sheet. Bake in a preheated oven at 350 degrees for 35 minutes, stirring every 5 to 10 minutes.

☛ Remove from oven and cool thoroughly, then stir in raisins.

☛ Store in an airtight container. Serve as a cereal, with milk, or sprinkle over fruit dishes or on top of baked dishes, such as muffins or apple crisp.

Makes 12 servings

from **The Weare-House B&B**
76 Quaker Street
Weare, NH 03281
603-529-2660

Innkeeper Ellen Goldsberry looks for lower-fat recipes that taste delicious, and finding a granola that met those standards was so difficult that she went through several recipes before adapting this one. "This is generally served as an alternative entree at breakfast, but many guests find it so tempting they have it in addition to the main entree -- which we take as a great compliment!" Ellen said. A hearty, healthy country breakfast is served on a long harvest table from 8 to 9:30 a.m. daily.

The eggs for the egg dishes featured at breakfast may come from the Goldsberry's flock of hens, whom guests may visit in the impressive barn. It is also home to miniature donkeys and horses. The barn was part of the reason the Goldsberrys purchased this colonial farmhouse and opened it as a four-guestroom B&B. They have two young sons and enjoy hosting children, as well as adults. The two family dogs also help welcome guests. The Weare area has a lake for swimming, trails for hiking or cross-country skiing, as well as downhill skiing, antiquing and golf.

🔺*Other Weare-House recipes:*
Hot Cocoa Mix, page 22
Applesauce Muffins, page 45

Maplewood Farm Granola

Ingredients:

1 cup wheat germ
5 cups rolled oats
1 cup sesame seeds
1 cup coconut
1 cup walnuts, chopped
1 cup sliced almonds
1 cup sunflower seeds
1/2 cup bran (100% bran cereal or wheat bran)
3/4 cup safflower or sunflower oil
1/2 cup honey
1 cup maple syrup

Also:

1 cup raisins, currants or other dried fruit

- Toast wheat germ in an oven preheated to 350 degrees for 5 minutes.
- In a very large bowl, stir together wheat germ, oats, sesame seeds, coconut, walnuts, almonds, sunflower seeds and bran.
- In a small saucepan, heat oil, honey and maple syrup just until warm.
- Pour maple syrup mixture over dry ingredients and stir. Spread out onto several baking pans.
- Bake in an oven preheated to 300 degrees for 40 minutes or until lightly browned.
- Remove from oven. When cooled, add cup of dried fruit, if desired. Store tightly covered.
- Serve with milk or yogurt. Remaining granola can be stored in an airtight container for up to 4 weeks.

Makes 10 cups (20 1/2-cup servings)

from **The Inn at Maplewood Farm**
447 Center Road
P.O. Box 1478
Hillsborough, NH 03244
603-464-4242
800-644-6695

"Especially great when topped with Stonyfield Farm Vanilla Yogurt, another great New Hampshire product," says Innkeeper Laura Simoes. She makes it a priority to use fresh, local products, right down to free-range eggs from "townie" chickens, in her award-winning breakfasts. Guests who can tear themselves away from coffee on the front porch are off for a day of hiking, antiquing, biking, or exploring. Jayme Simoes can provide directions to stone-arched bridges, swimming holes, or hot air balloon rides. At night, guests in the four guestrooms return to find homemade cookies at bedside and old-time radio shows broadcast to guestrooms on Jayme's collection of vintage radios.

Other Inn at Maplewood Farm recipes:
Decadent Praline Sauce, page 83
Fresh Salsa, page 84
Spiced Peach Soup, page 103
Valentine Cranberry Buttermilk Scones, page 166

The Megunticookie

Ingredients:

    1-1/4 cups brown sugar, packed
    1/4 cup margarine or butter, softened
    2 tablespoons honey
    1 egg white
    1 cup flour
    1 teaspoon cinnamon
    1/2 teaspoon baking powder
    1 cup quick-cooking rolled oats
    1 cup raisins
    1/2 cup peanuts
    1/2 cup semi-sweet chocolate chips or mini-chips
    1/2 cup shelled sunflower seeds

🍂 With an electric mixer, beat together brown sugar, margarine, honey and egg white.

🍂 Beat in flour, cinnamon and baking powder, mixing well.

🍂 Stir in oats, raisins, peanuts, chocolate chips and sunflower seeds by hand.

🍂 Spray a 9 x 13-inch pan with nonstick cooking spray. Press mixture firmly in bottom of pan.

🍂 Bake in a preheated oven at 350 degrees for 14 to 18 minutes, or until edges are light golden brown and center appears set.

🍂 Cool completely and cut into bars. Store in a tightly covered container.

Makes 36 bars

from **The Elms B&B**
84 Elm Street
Camden, ME 04843
207-236-6250
800-755-ELMS

This was a recipe waiting to happen -- the name came before the recipe, said Innkeeper Ted Panayotoff. "We always encourage our guests to take some of the breakfast coffeecake or muffins with them for extra energy as they hike up Mt. Megunticook or canoe or kayak in Megunticook Lake. One guest joked that we should make a coffeecake called 'Megunticake.'" That gave Ted and Jo, his wife, incentive to come up with a energy-packed breakfast cookie.

Jo and Ted bought this 1806 Federal-style home, an operating B&B, after coming to Camden to satisfy their interests in maritime history. They had intended only to relax aboard a windjammer cruise, but three months later, they had quit their jobs, sold their house and become innkeepers. They can recommend cruises from Camden harbor, only four blocks away, to guests who dare take the chance the same thing may happen to them! They'll also provide directions to Camden Hills State Park, Megunticook Lake, Mt. Battie and other recreational destinations in the Camden area.

🏠*Another Elms recipe:*
Blueberry Cornmeal Pancakes, page 128

Mimi's Favorite Cookies

Ingredients:

  1/2 cup butter
  1 cup sugar
  2 eggs, beaten
  2 cups flour
  2 tablespoons milk
  1 teaspoon vanilla extract
  2 teaspoons baking powder

- With an electric mixer, cream butter and sugar. Beat in eggs and scrape bowl.
- Sift flour twice. Beat 1 cup into butter mixture.
- Beat in milk and vanilla.
- Mix in remaining flour and baking powder.
- Drop cookies by the teaspoonfuls onto buttered cookie sheets.
- Bake in an oven preheated to 375 degrees for 8 to 10 minutes or until cookies appear dry and little holes appear on the top. Remove and cool on a wire rack before removing cookies.

Tester's Comments: These are homemade butter cookies that taste just as good cold as warm from the oven.

Makes 3 dozen cookies

from **Rooms With a View B&B**
Forbes Road
RR1, Box 215
Colebrook, NH 03576
603-237-5106
800-499-5106

"This was my husband's grandmother's recipe, and it's very, very good," said Innkeeper Sonja Sheldon. She keeps a cookie jar available for guest use, and guests often gather around the 3-ton soapstone stove while she's baking.

Sonja's homemade bread and cookies are just a part of the generous food offerings guests find here. In addition to a large breakfast, guests can help themselves to the board games, Adirondack chairs or the hot tub out back after a day of exploring this neck of the New Hampshire woods.

The Sheldons moved from Massachusetts and built this home as a B&B, opening in 1991. They designed it specifically to capture the views in all directions from the guestrooms, porch and dining room. Snowmobilers can leave from the property, and skiers drive 10 miles to The Balsams at Dixville Notch. In the summer, the wildflower garden and wrap-around porch beckon guests. Shopping and dining in Colebrook is a six-mile drive. Fishing, hiking and canoeing are nearby.

⌂Other Rooms With a View recipes:
Buttermilk Oatmeal Muffins, page 47
Peach Cream Pie, page 186

Mom's Shortbread

Ingredients:

1 cup butter
1 cup powdered sugar
3 cups flour

- With an electric mixer, beat butter until creamed. Cream again with sugar. Scrape bowl.
- Beat in flour gradually, continuing to beat until mixture is crumbly.
- Press mixture into an ungreased 9 x 13-inch cookie sheet with sides or baking pan.
- Prick with tines of fork all the way through the dough.
- Bake in a preheated oven at 325 degrees for 25 minutes or until golden.
- Cut in squares while warm. Devour immediately.

Tester's Comments: This makes a lot but they disappear fast. Especially good right out of the oven.

Makes 24 servings

from **Maine Stay Inn**
22 High Street
Camden, ME 04843
207-236-9636
Fax 207-236-0621

This really *is* Mom's Shortbread recipe, the one twin sisters Donny Smith and Diana Robson remember from their childhood. Today, they are serving it in the afternoons to B&B guests at their inn, who may want to munch it outside in the two acres of gardens and forested paths (it's hard to tell where the garden stops and the forest begins).

These interconnected farm buildings -- the main inn, a carriage house and a barn -- now have eight guestrooms and plenty of public space for guests. Built in 1802, the home is part of the historic district in which it resides. Diana, Donny and her husband, Peter, didn't come on the scene here until 1988, when Peter retired from the Navy and the three decided to throw in their lot together with a new career as innkeepers.

Expect the unexpected at this B&B inn. Guests may be summoned to breakfast on Peter's bosun's pipe or serenaded afterward by all three, who have a barbershop "trio"-like harmony. Those who wish travel or sightseeing info can have any of 30 detailed itineraries printed from the inn's computer. And those who arrive car-less will be cheerfully shuttled from the airport or harbor.

Camden Hills State Park offers hiking. The downtown and harbor, which Peter believes is the most scenic in the country, is just a couple block's walk. Mt. Battie and Lake Megunticook are nearby, as are many other attractions.

Another Maine Stay Inn recipe:
Savory Eggs, page 117

Mrs. Milld's Oatmeal Cookies

Ingredients:

1 cup butter, softened
1 cup sugar
1 cup flour
2 cups rolled oats
1 teaspoon baking soda

Also:

Additional sugar

- With an electric mixer, cream butter and beat in sugar.
- Add flour, oats and baking soda and mix well.
- Form dough into 1-inch balls.
- Place balls on a buttered cookie sheet (cookies spread when baking) and flatten each cookie to about 1/3-inch thick with the bottom of a glass dipped in sugar.
- Bake in a preheated oven at 350 degrees for 10 minutes.
- Remove from oven and cool on wire racks.

Tester's Comments: Rich and buttery, these are melt-in-your-mouth shortbread cookies with oatmeal.

Makes about 30 cookies

from **Maine Stay Inn & Cottages**
34 Maine Street
P.O. Box 500-A
Kennebunkport, ME 04046
207-967-2117
800-950-2117

These light cookies are perfect with afternoon tea, said Innkeeper Carol Copeland, who inherited the much-requested recipe from the inn's previous owners. Guests might gather in the parlor for tea, lemonade or cider, or enjoy their sweets in the rockers on the wrap-around porch or out on the yard lawn.

At tea-time, they get a chance to talk with Carol and Lindsay, who moved from Seattle and left careers in banking in order to become self-employed. They chose Kennebunkport, where they had vacationed, to work and raise their daughters. Now they help guests enjoy the things that drew them to the area -- beachcombing at Goose Rocks Beach, picnicking and seeing deer at Russell Acres, or walking across the mud flats at low tide to a lighthouse. Because they offer accommodations in private cottages, as well as in the main inn, they often find their guests include families looking for child-friendly activities.

Other Maine Stay Inn & Cottages recipes:
Apricot Scones, page 46
Pumpkin Ginger Muffins, page 56
Applesauce Spice Pancakes, page 126
Christmas Prelude Gingersnaps, page 156

Old-Fashioned Hermits

Ingredients:

1/2 cup butter or margarine, softened
3/4 cup brown sugar, packed
1 egg
1/2 cup molasses
1-1/2 cups flour
1/2 teaspoon cinnamon
1/2 teaspoon nutmeg
1/2 teaspoon cloves
1/2 teaspoon baking soda
1/4 teaspoon salt
1-1/2 cups raisins
3/4 cup chopped walnuts, optional

☛ With an electric mixer, cream butter and sugar until fluffy. Beat in egg, then molasses.

☛ Sift together flour, cinnamon, nutmeg, cloves, baking soda and salt. Stir into creamed mixture.

☛ Stir in raisins and optional walnuts by hand.

☛ Drop dough by rounded teaspoonfuls onto buttered cookie sheets. Bake in a preheated oven at 400 degrees for 8 to 10 minutes. Or, for the "new-fashioned" version of bar cookies, spread batter into a buttered 9 x 13-inch baking pan. Bake in a preheated oven at 350 degrees for 20 to 25 minutes. "Center should be soft but springy when touched." Cool on a wire rack.

Makes about 3 dozen cookies or 24 bars

from **The Whispering Pines B&B**
Route 113 A and Hemenway Road
Tamworth, NH 03886
603-323-7337

Guests might enjoy these cookies after a day of x-c skiing on the inn's trails, or after a day at nearby lakes. They are often munched in the guest sitting room by the antique soapstone stove or on the screened porch.

This large farmhouse once welcomed guests as "The Pines," back in the early 1900s. Karen and Kim Erickson spent three years winterizing, restoring and improving the house, in Karen's family since the 1940s, before opening four guestrooms in 1992. Karen, an analyst, and Kim, an engineer and estimator, quit their jobs in Sacramento to come here and open the B&B.

The inn is only 20 minutes to North Conway and the White Mountains. Guests can hike Mt. Chocorua, bike back country roads, enjoy White Lake State Park and beach, and attend square dances and fairs. In addition to moose watching and x-c skiing from the inn, there is berry picking, auctions, country stores, sleigh rides, ice skating, sled dog racing and other attractions nearby.

🏠*Another Whispering Pines recipes:*
Pumpkin Spice Bread, page 161

Peanut Crunch Cookies

Ingredients:

- 1/2 cup vegetable shortening, such as butter-flavored Crisco®
- 1/2 cup creamy or crunchy peanut butter
- 1/2 cup sugar
- 1/2 cup brown sugar, packed
- 1 egg, well beaten
- 1-1/2 cups flour
- 3/4 teaspoon baking soda
- 1/2 teaspoon baking powder
- 1/2 teaspoon salt

- With an electric mixer, cream together shortening and peanut butter.
- Gradually add sugar and brown sugar and cream thoroughly.
- Add egg to creamed mixture.
- In a separate bowl or on a piece of waxed paper, sift together flour, soda, baking powder and salt.
- Beat flour mixture into creamed mixture.
- Cover and chill dough well (at least 1 hour, overnight if you wish).
- Roll dough into 1-inch balls.
- Place dough on a lightly-buttered baking sheet. Flatten with fork, making a criss-cross pattern.
- Bake in a preheated oven at 375 degrees for 10 to 12 minutes, or until golden. Remove, let pan sit for a few minutes before removing cookies to cool completely.

Tester's Comments: These are the old-fashioned peanut butter cookies on which there's no improving - yum!

Makes 30 2-inch cookies

from **The Buttonwood Inn**
Mt. Surprise Road
P.O. Box 1817
North Conway, NH 03860
603-356-2625
800-258-2625

"This recipe is an old family recipe that Mother made when she was a little girl," said Innkeeper Claudia Needham. The key is to use shortening instead of butter, she explained. "Our guests love them with afternoon tea."

In the summer, they might enjoy their tea and cookies by the pool or before hiking the trails that leave from the property. In the winter, those same trails connect to 65 kilometers of groomed cross-country ski trails, and the Mt. Washington Valley boasts more kilometers of x-c ski trails than anywhere else in the U.S. Sleigh rides and downhill skiing also are available nearby.

Other Buttonwood Inn recipes:
Chocolate Chip Sour Cream Coffeecake, page 34
Overnight Cranberry Scones, page 55

Rugalach

Ingredients:

1/2 cup butter
1 8-ounce package cream cheese (not low-fat, sorry!)
1 egg, separated
3 tablespoons sugar
2 cups flour
Cinnamon-sugar mixture

Walnut Filling:
1 teaspoon cinnamon
1/4 cup sugar
1/4 cup raisins
1/4 cup walnuts, chopped

- For Filling: In a shallow bowl, stir together cinnamon, sugar, raisins and walnuts. Set aside.
- For Pastry: With an electric mixer, beat together butter, cream cheese, egg yolk and sugar. Then beat in flour, making a soft dough. Cover and refrigerate for 1 hour.
- Divide dough into 4 parts. Roll out each part into a circle about 1/4-inch thick. Sprinkle with Filling.
- Cut each circle into 8 wedges. Roll each wedge from the wide edge to the point to create a crescent.
- In a small bowl, slightly beat egg white. Dip each crescent first into egg white, then sprinkle with cinnamon and sugar. Place each crescent on a lightly-buttered cookie sheet.
- Bake in a preheated oven at 350 degrees until golden brown, 20 to 30 minutes.

Tester's Comments: I rolled dough out on waxed paper, cut in eighths first, then sprinkled with Filling. Note that baking times vary depending on thickness of dough, ovens and types of fillings - try raspberry or apricot jam, too!

Makes 32 rugalach

from **The Quail's Nest B&B**
Main Street
P.O. Box 221
Danby, VT 05739
802-293-5099
800-599-6444

This is one of Nancy Diaz' old family recipes, dating back to the 1800s. Her pastries are part of a large breakfast, which she serves wearing an innkeeper's costume from an earlier era which she sewed herself.

This unpretentious B&B has Nancy's handmade work all over it, from the curtains to the quilts. She and Greg, her spouse, are do-it-yourselfers whose blue-and-white inn, circa 1835, used to serve as the post office. Danby is only 13 miles from Manchester, less than 3 miles to the Appalachian Trail, 30 minutes to five ski areas. Greg and Nancy quit corporate jobs, managed an inn together and then looked for a B&B of their own. They have since opened a gift shop in one of the back buildings, which features Nancy's window quilts and other sewing, homemade jams and jellies, and the works of other local artists. They offer six guestrooms, a fire in the parlor fireplace, a hammock and lemonade, travel advice and dinner recommendations, as well as an occasional piano sing-a-long. Porch rockers welcome the weary traveler.

Other Quail's Nest recipes:
Vermont Challah, page 167
Apple-Blueberry Breakfast Pie, page 171

Scottish Shortbread

Ingredients:

2-1/2 cups flour
1/2 cup sugar
1 cup butter

🥄 With a pastry blender and then your clean hands, mix flour, sugar and butter until all ingredients are combined.

🥄 Divide the dough in half and form into two balls. Press each ball into a 7-inch circle on a lightly-buttered cookie sheet or pie pan.

🥄 With a fork, prick through to the bottom of the dough.

🥄 Bake in a preheated oven at 325 degrees for 30 minutes. Remove and cut each circle into 16 wedges while still hot or very warm.

Tester's Comments: I used an electric mixer and added 1/2 teaspoon vanilla extract and almost 2 tablespoons, a teaspoon at a time, of cold water to get dough to form a ball. These are very rich and satisfying! Kids can help with kneading and patting, too. (Celia suggests adding almond extract instead of vanilla.)

Makes 2 7-inch circles, making 32 wedges

from **Maple Grove House**
Maple Grove Road
P.O. Box 340
Madison, NH 03849
603-367-8208

"The shortbread is from my husband's grandmother, who was from Edinborough, Scotland," said Innkeeper Celia Pray. "Being English, I love a 'cuppa' tea in the afternoon, and the shortbread is a great complement. I love my guests to join me!" Celia has an interesting collection of recipes. Raised in Barbados and Jamaica, she spent several years living at sea while working as a charter boat cook. She met her husband, Donald, in the islands, and they eventually ended up in Massachusetts, where he worked as marine surveyor.

After frequent visits to a relative in nearby Eaton, they decided to move to the area with their two children. They found the Maple Grove House in need of much repair and renovation, having sat vacant for six years and with outdoor plumbing still in use. But the large house with the wrap-around porch and the 216 acres on which it sits were very appealing. "We are in a nice quiet spot, but really close to everything," Celia notes. "We just *love* it here in Madison."

The home originally was a guest house that burned down in 1911 and was quickly rebuilt. The Prays have tried to be faithful to the original home while adding four guestrooms and a large family suite. Guests can explore the property during all seasons as well as the attractions of nearby North Conway.

🏠 *Another Maple Grove House recipe:*
Raspberry Streusel Coffeecake, page 39

Swiss Apple Müesli

Ingredients:

- 1 cup rolled oats
- 1 cup high-protein cereal, such as Grape Nuts®
- 1 cup milk
- 8 to 10 assorted apples (hard, crunchy variety that retain whiteness such as Granny Smith, Macouns, and Red/Yellow Delicious), quartered, with stem removed
- Juice of 1 lemon
- 1 cup honey
- 1 cup vanilla yogurt

Also:

- Raisins, dried cranberries and nuts, optional

- In a large bowl, soak oats and cereal with milk.
- In a food processor, chop apples (chunks can be large; seeds can be included). Add to cereal mixture.
- Add lemon juice and mix well.
- Add honey, then yogurt, mixing well with each addition.
- Cover mixture and refrigerate (keeps for 3 to 4 days).
- To serve, remove from refrigerater, spoon into serving bowls, and sprinkle with raisins, dried cranberries and nuts, if you wish.

Makes 10 servings

from **The Bagley House**
1290 Royalsborough Road
Durham, ME 04222
207-865-6566
800-765-1772

This is a favorite of Innkeeper Susan Backhouse, British by birth, and she may serve it as an optional breakfast dish. "It's very refreshing ona hot day," she notes. British guests and those who have traveled in Europe appreciate her "real" scones, tea or other dishes such as this. Guests join her and co-innkeeper Suzanne O'Connor, "the two Sues," in the large kitchen for conversation and breakfast. The breakfast table may be laden with sourdough waffles or pancakes, bacon or sausage, fresh fruit, and scones or other homemade treats.

Guests are invited to enjoy the parlor of this 1772 home, which was originally built as an inn and is believed to be the oldest in the area. Five guestrooms are original to the Colonial-style inn. The six acres of woods, fields and blueberry bushes welcome explorers. Set on a country road, the inn is only a 10-minute drive to bustling downtown Freeport and its outlet shops, including L.L. Bean's headquarters. The Sues direct guests to the best restaurants, coastal views, x-c skiing and biking, as well as antiquing, theater, fairs and concerts.

🏠*Another Bagley House recipe:*
Scones for Aspiring Anglophiles, page 58

Contents by Inn

MAINE

NEW HAMPSHIRE

Bradford
 The Candlelite Inn
  Marilyn's Fruit Pancake (Entrees - Pancakes), 139
  Bread Pudding with Custard (Dessert for Breakfast), 178
 Rosewood Country Inn
  Grandma's Peach Chutney (Preserves), 86
  Spiced Apple Brandy (Holiday Fare), 164

Center Harbor - Watch Hill B&B
  Buttermilk Whole Wheat Breads (Breads), 67
  Spiced Tomato Jam (Preserves), 92
  Mulled Cider Applesauce (Fruit), 102
  Savory Christmas Bread (Holiday Fare), 163
  Firehouse Brownies (Other Favorites), 191

Charlestown - MapleHedge B&B Inn
  Banana Froth (Beverages), 21
  Cheese Cream-Filled Baked Pears (Fruit), 96
  Grandma's Fruit Bread (Holiday Fare), 158

Colebrook - Rooms With a View B&B
  Buttermilk Oatmeal Muffins (Muffins), 47
  Peach Cream Pie (Dessert for Breakfast), 186
  Mimi's Favorite Cookies (Other Favorites), 197

Durham - University Guest House
  Good Morning Fruit Crepes (Entrees - Pancakes), 133

Fitzwilliam - Hannah Davis House
  Hannah's Baked Apple Puff (Entrees - Pancakes), 134
  Spanikopita (Entrees - Other), 149

Glen - The Bernerhof Inn
  Summer Cantaloupe Cooler (Beverages), 27
  Cider Molasses Doughnuts (Breads), 68
  Eggs Bernerhof (Entrees - Eggs), 109

Greenfield - The Greenfield Inn B&B
  Miracle Muffins (Muffins), 54
  Barb's Cranberry Nut Bread (Breads), 65

Hart's Location - The Notchland Inn
  Notchland "Muddled" Cider (Beverages), 24
  Favorite Popovers (Muffins), 51
  Boiled Fruit Cake (Holiday Fare), 154
  Cranberry Bread Pudding (Dessert for Breakfast), 181

Hillsborough - The Inn at Maplewood Farm
  Decadent Praline Sauce (Preserves), 83
  Fresh Salsa (Preserves), 84
  Spiced Peach Soup (Fruit), 103
  Valentine Cranberry Buttermilk Scones (Holiday Fare), 166
  Maplewood Farm Granola (Other Favorites), 195

Holderness - The Inn on Golden Pond
  Rhubarb Jam (Preserves), 91

Index

Ordering Information

Order additional copies of any of our popular B&B cookbook editions from your bookstore, gift shop or by mail. (FYI, bookstores can get these books in a matter of days and won't charge you shipping!)

Innkeepers' Best Muffins and *Innkeepers' Best Low-Fat Breakfast Recipes* are the first in a series of practical one-topic cookbooks showcasing Bed & Breakfast innkeepers' outstanding recipes. Each 6 x 9 inch paperback has Down to Earth's usual information on the inn: $9.95 each
Next in this series: *Innkeepers' Best Cookies* and *Innkeepers' Best Quick Breads*.

Chocolate for Breakfast and Tea is our beautiful four-color, hardcover book, 7 x 7 inches, featuring 67 mouthwatering chocolate recipes from inns across the country. The Entrées, Breads, Coffeecakes, Muffins & Scones, and Desserts, Snacks and Tea-Time Favorites are scrumptious and easy to prepare. As always, information on the inn and innkeepers is included, with color photos! A fabulous gift - everyone knows someone who loves chocolate! $21.95

WAKE UP & SMELL THE COFFEE is a series of hefty 8-1/2 x 11 inch softcover cookbooks that feature travel information, maps and an index, as well as more than 10 chapters of breakfast, brunch and other favorite fare from B&Bs in a particular region.
If you need extra copies of this *Northern New England Edition*, they are $14.95 each
Lake States Edition has 203 recipes from 125 B&Bs in Michigan, Wisconsin and Michigan, $15.95
Southwest Edition boasts more than 170 recipes from 65 B&Bs in Texas, Arizona and New Mexico, $14.95
Pacific Northwest Edition features more than 130 of innkeepers' best recipes from 58 B&Bs in Washington and Oregon, $11.95

TO ORDER BY MAIL, send a check to Down to Earth Publications, 1032 W. Montana, St. Paul, MN 55117. Make checks payable to Down to Earth Publications. MN residents please add 7% sales tax. **TO ORDER WITH VISA or MasterCard,** call us at 800-585-6211, or fax 612-488-7862.

Mail to: Down to Earth Publications, 1032 W. Montana, St. Paul, MN 55117

Please send me:
_____ "Innkeepers' Best Muffins" @ $9.95
_____ "Innkeepers' Best Low-Fat Breakfasts" @ $9.95
_____ "Innkeepers' Best Cookies" @ $9.95 (due out in January 1999)
_____ "Innkeepers' Best Quick Breads" @ $9.95 (due out in January 1999)
_____ "Chocolate for Breakfast and Tea" @ $21.95
_____ "WAKE UP & SMELL THE COFFEE - *Northern New England* Edition" @ $14.95
_____ "WAKE UP & SMELL THE COFFEE - *Pacific Northwest* Edition" @ $11.95
_____ "WAKE UP & SMELL THE COFFEE - *Lake States* Edition" @ $15.95
_____ "WAKE UP & SMELL THE COFFEE - *Southwest* Edition" @ $14.95

S&H: _____ please add $3/book for 4th Class Mail (book rate) or $4.95/book UPS ground service

I have enclosed $_____ for _____ book(s). Send it/them to (no P.O. boxes for UPS):
(If sending a gift, we can enclose a gift card - please tell us what to say and include your address, too)

Name: _____

Street: _____ Apt. No. _____ (No P.O. boxes for UPS)

City: _____ State: _____ Zip: _____ Phone: _____

About the author

Laura Zahn discovered the wonderful "Breakfast" part of "Bed & Breakfast" while traveling the backroads of Minnesota, Wisconsin and Illinois to write her series of "Room at the Inn" guidebooks to historic B&Bs and country inns. During that time, she did "wake up & smell the coffee," and all the other scrumptuous things innkeepers were cooking, and came up with the idea of regional cookbooks by that name.

In St. Paul, Minn., she is president of Down to Earth Publications, a writing, publishing and public relations firm specializing in travel. Her travelwriting has appeared in many U.S. newspapers and magazines. Zahn has worked in public relations in Minnesota and as a reporter and editor.

"Wake Up and Smell the Coffee - Northern New England Edition" is fifth in the series, following the Upper Midwest (now out-of-print), Pacific Northwest, Southwest Editions and Lake States Editions.

"Chocolate for Breakfast and Tea," her first all-color hardcover, indulged two of her passions in life, B&B travel and chocolate. It features chocolate recipes from B&Bs around the country.

A new series, "Innkeepers' Best," was started in 1997. Two cookbooks, "Innkeepers' Best Muffins" and "Innkeepers' Best Low-Fat Breakfasts," share great recipes and information about inns serving wonderful breakfasts nationwide. "Innkeepers' Best Cookies" and "Innkeepers' Best Quick Breads" are next in this series.

Zahn is also the author of the award-winning "Bringing Baby Home: An Owner's Manual for First-Time Parents." She is the proud mother of two young boys who don't yet appreciate her recipe testing.